The stunning correspondence between Rita Smilkstein's research results and Piaget's six stages validates this book. Smilkstein's work grounds in brain research theories and assumptions that educators have worked with for years. It is as if a missing link has now been unearthed to connect all that we have observed in our teaching.

Jonathan Baylis
Pacific Rim Educational Services,
New Westminster, British Columbia

Being a community college English instructor who has used the Natural Human Learning Process approach for several years, I have had the opportunity to see the results it produces. There is no better way to experience the joy of teaching than to see students' joy of learning blossom. There is no greater motivator than success, and that's what all of us—students and teachers alike—experience in an NHLP learning environment.

Julie Noble
Olympic College, Bremerton, WA

Gives students the opportunity to learn from one another and more chances to be successful than on just one try. Thank you for this gift of a learning lifetime.

Deborah Cuevas, Student Teacher

The application of existing theories of learning and instruction has not improved the academic performance of presently under-served populations, most especially African American learners. Yet, a funda- mental tenet of the learning paradigm is that community colleges must do more for under-represented groups, such as African Americans, than open doors to higher education; community colleges must take responsibility for producing student success. A new theory more directly linking culture, information processing, instruction, and how the brain learns is needed to transform classroom practice for culturally diverse learners.

Rita Smilkstein, the ranking scholar-practitioner-activist in the brain-based, natural learning movement, offers concrete, research- based classroom strategies for achieving this vision. Until and unless we find ways to make classroom and institutional practices in the community college multicultural, multicognitive, and brain-based, the promise of the learning-centered community college shall remain ephemeral for African American and other learners of color.

Dr. Irving Pressley McPhail, Chancellor
The Community College of Baltimore County, Baltimore, Maryland
and
Dr. Christine Johnson McPhail
Professor and Graduate Program Coordinator
Doctor of Education Program in Community College Leadership
Morgan State University, Baltimore, Maryland

This is dedicated to the memory of my dearest Uncle Harry, who taught me that thinking, learning, discovering, and creating are sublime things to do. This is also for my children, Jessica, Susanna, Diana, and Georgia, and for my grandchildren, Laurel, Rome, Jesse, and other grandchildren to come.

We're Born to Learn

Using the Brain's Natural Learning
Process to Create Today's Curriculum

Rita Smilkstein

CORWIN PRESS, INC.
A Sage Publications Company
Thousand Oaks, California

Anatomy illustrations by Jessica Dodge, Seattle, WA. www.jessicadodge.net / Digital production by Steven Miller, Seattle Miller, Seattle, WA. Steven@smiller555.com

For information:

Corwin Press, Inc.
A Sage Publications Company
2455 Teller Road
Thousand Oaks, California 91320
www.@corwinpress.com

Sage Publications Ltd.
6 Bonhill Street
London EC2A 4PU
United Kingdom

Sage Publications India Pvt. Ltd.
B-42 Panchsheel Enclave
Post Box 4109
New Delhi 110 017 India

Printed in the United States of America

Library of Congress Cataloging-in-Publication Data

Smilkstein, Rita.
We're born to learn: Using the brain's natural learning process to create today's curriculum / Rita Smilkstein.
    p. cm
Includes bibliographical references and index.
ISBN 0-7619-4641-1 (cloth)
ISBN 0-7619-4642-X (paper)
 1. Learning. 2. Curriculum planning. 3. Brain—Research. I. Title.
LB1060 .S544 2003
370.15′23—dc21

                            2002152679

This book is printed on acid-free paper.

03 04 05 06 10 9 8 7 6 5 4 3 2 1

Acquisitions Editor:	Faye Zucker
Editorial Assistant:	Julia Parnell
Copy Editor:	Elizabeth Budd
Production Editor:	Denise Santoyo
Typesetter:	C&M Digitals (P) Ltd.
Indexer:	Pamela VanHuss
Cover Designer:	Michael Dubowe
Production Artist:	Janet Foulger

Contents

Foreword

I have taught, facilitated and studied learning and education in public institutions for more than 30 years. I have known Rita Smilkstein for nearly 8 years. In my experience, I have not encountered a single concept or paradigm that has the potential to transform learning more than Dr. Rita Smilkstein's work on the natural human learning process. Whether it be as a teacher in training, a teacher in the "field," or a person interested in brain approaches to learning, this work, *We're Born to Learn: Using the Brain's Natural Learning Process to Create Today's Curriculum* is a winner, a must read!

Rita has taken the very essence of what is important for you to know about brain research and classroom research and provided an easy-to-use template for helping your students learn. I say helping, because they do the learning. "We can't give them our dendrites!"

We're Born to Learn will entice you to shift your paradigm. Yes, it will provide the necessary tools to do what you know intuitively to be more appropriate. From my early days in Cleveland Public Schools to teaching in prisons and juvenile detention facilities to teaching at a college level at the University of Michigan-Flint to the present day at St. Clair County Community College, I have never found a theoretical construct that could be applied as easily and as simply as the natural human learning process. Many teachers, if not most, struggle continuously with several key questions: How do I help my students learn? When they are learning, can I accurately assess them? Will my job of teaching ever get easier?

If you are like me, and I consider myself to be fairly normal, you not only ask yourself these kinds of questions, you struggle with their answers. In attempting to use Rita's work in elementary classrooms, high schools, and now college, I can attest to the fact that the foundation of these ideas are solid, their use easily adaptable to any grade level, and the results absolutely amazing. You will see the results.

Consider Joy Middle School in Detroit, Michigan, which made some recent gigantic jumps in state standardized testing due in part to the natural human learning process (Contact: Mr. Larry Till). I currently teach "wanna-bes," teachers in training, as I like to call them affectionately. Many are now doing their student teaching, and many have completed their degrees and certificates. A semester doesn't go by that I don't get a phone call from a former student thanking me for teaching them about the natural human learning process and its application to education.

We're Born to Learn is so reader-easy. Rita cross-references her own work, pointing out which chapter you can resource as you move your way through the informative pages, charts, and graphs. I am honored to write this foreword for Dr. Smilkstein, as her work will undoubtedly gain continued support and accolades around the country and perhaps the world. Thank you, Rita, for bringing to the world the Natural Human Learning Process and for allowing those of us who work in education to facilitate our students' learning. Indeed, we can't give them our dendrites, but we can facilitate theirs!

James H. Berry
St. Clair County Community College, Michigan

Acknowledgments

There is no way I could have written this book without the help of many wonderful people. First and foremost, my students, over the 30 and more years I have been teaching, have taught me invaluable lessons about how to teach. I also want to thank my students in Cycles 11 and 12, Woodring College of Education, Western Washington University, for their invaluable feedback while I was writing this book.

I also want to thank those excellent colleagues who also taught me many valuable lessons about teaching. This includes faculty and friends at The Evergreen Stage College, Thad Curtz, Peta Henderson, and Sherry Walton; at Seattle Central Community College, Valerie Bystrom, Wadiyah Nelson, Bobby Righi, and Larry Silverman; and at my home base, North Seattle Community College, Steve Anderson, Marcia Barton, Val Donato, Tom Drummond, Pesha Gertler, Larry Hall, Carol Hamilton, James Harnish, David Harris, Dennis Hibbert, Diane Hostetler, Tom Kerns, Michael Kischner, Carolyn Lord, Steve Quig, Dave Rigby, Lynn Sharpe, Fran Schmitt, Gerald Schneider, Marilyn Smith, Karen Stuhldreher, and Edith Wollin; at St. Petersburg Junior College, Florida, Iris Yetter; at Spokane Falls Community College, Washington, Jan Swinton. I also want to thank my friend Dale Chase, the librarian, who is always generous with good advice about research materials and who always tells the truth.

Another group I want to thank are those dedicated teachers who attended the Advanced Kellogg Institute I taught at the National Center for Developmental Education. Some of the Natural Human Learning Process learning activities they developed are posted on the Born to Learn Web site (www.borntolearn.net).

I especially learned from the colleagues with whom I taught coordinated studies courses (Chapter 9). I cannot think of a better way to teach. Endless appreciation to Barbara Leigh Smith who, with Jean MacGregor, created the Washington Center for the Improvement of Undergraduate

Education, which has been the foremost promoter and disseminator of learning communities in this country. Also, I want to acknowledge the exceptional leadership in the developmental education movement of Hunter Boylan, Professor and Director of the National Center for Developmental Education, Reich College of Education, Appalachian State University.

Other teachers have been my children, Jessica Dodge, Susanna Burney, Diana Phipps, and Georgia Franklin, and my grandchildren, Laurel, Rome, and Jesse. I have learned a great deal about learning from all of them. As part of my extended family, Ralph Blum (author of *The Book of Runes*) was with me every step of the way. Words cannot express my gratitude to him.

Moreover, how can I ever thank enough the educators who read my manuscript and gave me absolutely essential feedback? Special thanks to Julie Noble (Olympic Community College, Washington), who read and read and was unstinting in her comments, which were always clear, specific, and helpful. Others who also gave helpful feedback are the members of the Douglas College (British Columbia, Canada) English As a Second Language faculty's Mindful Learning Group, Jan Bromley, Judith Dale, Cyndy Reimer, Debbie Smith, and, most especially, Jonathan Baylis (also Consultant, Pacific Rim Educational Services). Others are Amauri Bartoszeck (Associate Professor of Neurophysiology, University of Parana, Brazil), James H. Berry (St. Clair County Community College, Michigan), Julia H. Bronkowski (Ferris State University, Michigan), Jane Harradine (North Seattle Community College), Judith A. Hooper (Ferris State University), Sherry Kam (Portland Community College, Oregon), Jean MacGregor (National Learning Communities Project, The Evergreen State College, Washington), and Kenneth Wesson (Office of the Chancellor, San Jose Community College District, California; Consultant in neuroscience).

I am also forever grateful, for their being such true comrades, to Dr. Irving Pressley MacPhail, Chancellor, The Community Colleges of Baltimore County, Baltimore, MD, and Dr. Christine McPhail, Professor, Graduate Program Coordinator, and Director of the Educational Program in Community College Leadership, Morgan State University, Baltimore, MD.

And to my friends, who have enthusiastically rallied around, I can only say how much I appreciate their confidence and support, especially Liz Burbank and Edith Clarke. Also thanks to Joan and Louis Fiset for our writing circle and longtime friendship.

My daughter Susanna gave me good advice about the Introduction, and all of my beloved family and extended family, parents, grandparents, aunts, uncles, cousins, and sons-in-law, especially my daughters, were always there 1,000% and more to encourage and support me. This includes my extended-family daughters Starlyn and Lisa. Also, a word of thanks to Dan Bockman, who asks important questions and is always ready to help in whatever way I might need. Special thanks are due to Michael Rosenberg who, as my agent, connected me with Corwin Press and to my agent Barbara Collins-Rosenberg for taking care of the details.

Most especially, great appreciation and thanks go to my editor Faye Zucker and to Julia Parnell for their unfailing support and help from beginning to end—always given with kindness and understanding. Also, endless thanks to Elizabeth S. Budd, my copyeditor, for her close reading and excellent suggestions, and to Denise Santoyo, Production Editor, for seeing the book through to the end. And thanks as well to Michael Dubowe for the cover. In addition, the contributions of the following reviewers are gratefully acknowledged:

Margaret Laughlin
Professor, Education Department
University of Wisconsin at Green Bay

Dianne Koontz-Lowman
Assistant Professor, Department of Occupational Therapy
Virginia Commonwealth University, Richmond

Finally, if I have left anyone out, please forgive me—and let me thank you, too.

About the Author

Rita Smilkstein is Professor Emerita (English), North Seattle Community College, and, as an invited lecturer, teaches educational psychology at Western Washington University's Woodring College of Education. Her area of expertise is teaching learning theory based on brain research and how to teach according to the brain's natural learning process. A frequent speaker throughout the United States and Canada, her publications include textbooks for teaching study skills and grammar as well as articles on how to apply the brain's natural learning process to curriculum development and instructional methods across the disciplines.

Smilkstein has a bachelor's degree in English from the University of Iowa, a master's in speech from Michigan State University, and a doctorate in educational psychology from the University of Washington. She has taught in middle school through graduate school, including 28 years at North Seattle Community College. She has received a number of teaching awards, including the Excellence Award from the National Institute for Staff and Organizational Development in 1991, 1995; Outstanding Teacher Award, Washington Association of Developmental Education, 1994; Award of Recognition for Outstanding Contribution to Education Excellence, Washington Community Colleges/Vocational Technical Institutes Councils, 1991; Burlington Northern Award for Significant and Meritorious Teaching, 1990.

Her professional affiliations include the Association of Supervision and Curriculum Development, College Reading and Learning Association, National Association of Developmental Education, and National Council of Teachers of English.

Introduction

*W*e're Born to Learn: Using the Brain's Natural Learning Process to Create Today's Curriculum is intended to make it possible for all students to realize their potential as natural learners. The brain is born to learn, and when educators make it possible for students, young and old, to learn the way the brain naturally learns, they will be the eager, motivated, successful learners they were born to be.

This book is for educators, from K–12 through higher education. It is also for those who one day will be teachers—education majors and students in colleges of education. In addition, it is for parents, students in general, and everyone else who wants to know how the brain learns.

WHY STUDY THE BRAIN?

Why do educators, parents, students, or others need to know how the brain learns? Why did an English teacher, as I was, begin studying how the brain learns?

One September day many years ago, I was walking through our college campus on my way to class for the first day of the term. I had a new textbook for my English composition class, along with a new set of strategies suggested in another article in yet another journal for English teachers. But something was troubling me—the thought that I could not go on this way, new book after new book, new strategy after new strategy, year after year when nothing worked well enough. There was even an article I had just read about teaching composition, "Why Nothing Works" (Forrester, 1983).

I stopped walking and just stood there on the pathway in the middle of campus, my briefcase hanging heavily from my hand.

Then another thought came to me: "If only there were a way to teach based on . . . something tangible. . . . Maybe if we knew how people learn we could teach the way they learn."

1

Then, suddenly, the answer was there: the brain. The brain does the learning. If we could find out how the brain learns, we would have a basis for knowing how to teach so that students' brains could learn.

My incipient depression went away and, instead, I was filled with hope and excitement at the prospect of learning about the brain and, perhaps, from that, learning what the science of teaching might be. Within the year, I was taking courses at the University of Washington and, by the next year, I had entered the doctoral program in educational psychology. Over the next 10 years of graduate school, I learned, and am still learning as research progresses, how the brain learns (Chapter 3).

THE RESEARCH

Chapters 2 and 3 report on two areas of research related to learning: classroom/field research and neuroscience research. The classroom/field research has been done with students from second grade to graduate school and with educators, both faculty and administrators. This research shows that human beings, young and old, have an innate, natural learning process. The neuroscience research explains the brain's physiological learning process.

These two areas of research converge (Chapter 6), leading to principles for developing brain-compatible, natural-learning curriculum for any subject at any level so that students can be the successful learners they were born to be.

EXPERIENCED EDUCATORS AND THE RESEARCH

For educators who have seen from their own experience in the classroom what helps their students learn and who are already teaching in a brain-compatible, natural learning way—although they might not identify it as such—this book explains why what they do works. And if there is a lesson or unit that does not work as well as others, educators who know about this research-based method for developing curriculum will be able to see what the problem is and how to solve it so that this lesson or unit will be as successful as their other ones.

THE THEORY AND THE APPLICATION

Chapters 6 and 7 translate the research into a theory of learning and teaching. Chapters 8 and 9, using guidelines and models, show how this research-based theory can be applied to the development of curriculum for any classroom. These chapters provide examples of classroom-proven applications of the theory. They also focus on how to develop lesson plans and curricula for a unit, a course, and a program. These examples might be useful for teachers who are developing their own lesson plans and curricula.

BRAIN-COMPATIBLE CURRICULUM

This book describes a classroom-proven, research-based method for creating coherent, complete curricula that can motivate all students and help them learn successfully. It shows educators how to make this possible—not with attention-getting activities that are more or less peripheral to a curriculum but with the curriculum itself.

This might seem like an exaggerated claim, but *We're Born to Learn* helps students learn the curriculum by resolving the dilemma that can arise about whether to focus on teaching the student or on teaching the curriculum. This book does that because its approach is curriculum-centered and, at the same time, the curriculum itself is student-centered.

We're Born to Learn focuses on student-centered curricula to teach not only one unit, one skill, or one concept (Chapter 8) but also on curricula to teach multiunit courses as well as multicourse programs (Chapter 9).

The Learning Paradigm

In 1995, R. B. Barr and J. Tagg proposed that the focus of education change from teaching to learning. Their article "From Teaching to Learning: A New Paradigm for Undergraduate Education" was a landmark work. The learning paradigm, however, is just as applicable to and valuable for K–12 teachers and students as it is for those in higher education. This book's active-learning, student-centered approach is an example of the learning paradigm.

ASSUMPTIONS

Nonnatural Learning Assumptions

Teaching based on some of the following accepted assumptions about learning might help students memorize material and pass tests on what they have been told or shown. However, they will not help students be the critical and creative thinkers they were born to be; instead, teaching based on these assumptions can be counterproductive.

1. The brain is a container into which knowledge is to be put.

2. Real teaching is done when teachers impart knowledge to students.

3. If the teacher does this and the students still cannot understand and apply the material, then the students do not have the ability to think at high levels.

4. The proper sequence for teaching is that the teacher should first give an overview in a lecture and then, in subsequent lectures or demonstrations, give definitions, background, technical terms, explanations, examples, and so forth. As a result of these activities, the students should be able to prove on a test that they understand what they have been told and shown.

5. Learning is pleasant for students only when the teacher, the materials, or the assignments are entertaining.

Changing Nonnatural Learning Assumptions to Natural Learning Assumptions

On the other hand, we could change these assumptions into ones that see students as wanting and able to learn when they have the opportunity to learn by the brain's natural learning process.

1. The brain actively constructs its own knowledge.

2. Real teaching is done when teachers give students the opportunity to be active learners.

3. If the teacher does this and a student still cannot understand and apply the material, then perhaps that student needs more background and preparation (Chapter 3, Figure 3.14) or special help (Chapters 2 and 4).

4. The proper sequence for teaching is that the teacher should first give students opportunities to be active learners; then the teacher, if necessary, can add to what the students have discovered on their own by giving a lecture, definitions, background, technical terms, explanations, examples, demonstrations, and so forth. As a result of their own activities, plus any further information and insights the teacher contributes, the students should be able to prove on a test that they understand and are able to apply the material.

5. Learning is pleasant for students only when the teacher, the materials, or the assignments give them the opportunity to be active learners and use the brain's natural learning process.

See Chapter 7 for a discussion of how teachers of education or faculty development leaders might include this book in their programs.

WHERE WE HAVE BEEN

This introduction ends with a brief history of education in the United States, where we have been and where we can go from here. Our history has been that we have successfully educated only some students, not all students. Where we can go from here is to make it possible for all students to be the critical thinking, creative, motivated, and successful learners they were born to be.

The Pseudo-Aristocracy

In 1813, Thomas Jefferson wrote to John Adams about his idea of "a general diffusion of learning," which would make education available to all boys so that the boys who have the ability to become the worthy future leaders of this democratic country would be discovered and educated:

> [D]ivide every county into wards . . . to establish in each ward a few schools for reading, writing, and common arithmetic; to provide for the annual selection of the best [students] from these schools, who might receive at the public expense a higher degree of education at a district school; and from these district schools to select a certain number of the most promising [students] to be completed at a University, where all the useful sciences should be taught. Worth and genius would thus have been sought out from every condition of life and completely prepared by education for defeating the competition of wealth and birth for public trusts. (Dumbauld, 1955, p. 100)

When Jefferson had submitted this proposal to the legislature after the Declaration of Independence in 1776, it had not been adopted. In his 1813 letter to Adams, Jefferson wrote that he had written laws that "laid the axe to the foot of pseudo-aristocracy." Then, referring to his "general diffusion of learning" plan, continued, "And had another [law] which I prepared been adopted by the legislature, our work would have been complete" (Dumbauld, p. 100). The United States, he believed, would thus have been saved from the pseudo-aristocracy of the rich and wellborn. One problem with his plan, though, was that the promising students would have been those who were obedient, diligent, and good memorizers. As Rousseau had said and as Jefferson repeated, children's minds are not capable of complex thinking; therefore, we should not tax them beyond their limited capacity (with what we now call critical thinking activities) but should only impart knowledge to them. A related and familiar dictum is that children should be seen and not heard.

Moreover, schooling beyond readin', 'ritin', and 'rithmetic at that time was typically for rich boys who would grow up to be the pseudo-aristocracy that Jefferson deplored. In Puritan towns in New England, it also did not mean more than teaching just the three R's; for example, reading the Bible, writing personal communications, and using arithmetic to buy and sell.

The Test Scores Aristocracy

Another sort of aristocracy, however, entered schools in the United States: intelligence measured by tests. The first tests of mental ability (later called "intelligence") were in the 1890s and measured such abilities as digit-span memory. In 1933, the *Mental Measurements Yearbook* was first published. It documented all available standardized tests and was 19 pages long. By 1944, it had grown to 1,000 pages. After World War II, tests were used in the United States to discriminate between who should and who should not go to college.

When, after Sputnik in 1957, the United States was seen as not keeping up in the Cold War, the National Defense Act gave money to educators to improve science and math education. The federal government also provided money for testing, which resulted in national norms and standards. As before, however, the definition of intelligence was tied to what could be measured.

The Swinging Pendulum

In the 1960s, Title I gave federal money to remediate social inequities—and standardized tests to measure abilities were used in a different way. They were used at that time to reveal the problems caused by inequity and to measure the results of remediation efforts.

Throughout the history of education in this country, the pendulum has swung back and forth between education to help every student fulfill his or her own unique potential (e.g., Dewey, Montessori, and Title I) and education to prepare all students to be measured by the same standard as if everything else were equal.

WHERE WE ARE TODAY

Today the pendulum has again swung far to the side of standardized testing (Chapter 4). The belief now seems to be that if all schools and teachers do an equally good job, students will have an equal chance to do well—unless they do not have what it takes to do well. Although, of course, all else not being equal, they do not have an equal chance.

Will the best students be, as thought in Jefferson's time, those who are the most obedient, the most diligent, and the best memorizers? Will they also be those who begin school adequately prepared from previous experience and upbringing?

How much can schooling equalize the life experiences of all students so that every student will be on the same playing field?

Also, what about all the diverse, nonmeasurable potentials, talents, interests, and abilities that make each student a richly unique human being? If these different elements are not what standardized tests measure, these elements will not be invited to the party.

Assessment is invaluable, of course (Chapter 7), but taking it to the extreme of standardized tests might be counterproductive.

THIS BOOK

This book is about the richly unique human beings who are our students. It is about helping them fulfill their potential to be the natural, motivated, and successful learners they were born to be.

And if they also have to pass standardized tests—well, they can do that, too.

Part I

Research in
the Classroom
and in the Brain Lab

Learning and Teaching

1

EYE-OPENING EXPERIENCES IN THE CLASSROOM

Having been well prepared for school, in a literate family with expectations, support, and encouragement for my academic success, I did well in school. When I began teaching, I was eager to impart my knowledge and insights to my students. I wanted to do this despite the fact that I had not enjoyed or been excited by my teachers imparting their knowledge to me. I wanted to do this despite the fact that my single most enjoyable class session in college was when a literature professor asked us one day what *we* thought a phrase in a poem meant. I wanted to do this despite the fact that most of my insights had come from my own reading and thinking and from talking with classmates outside of class. However, I was a college teacher; and, in my college experience, teaching was largely imparting knowledge to students in well-researched, well-developed lectures.

Starting Where They Are

I had an understanding of and love for literature, my area of specialization, and greatly enjoyed preparing to teach my first course, an introduction to the humanities, at Michigan State University. The challenge was to place literature in context, to relate it to the other arts and to philosophy. I spent all summer working on the course, reading new material, seeing patterns and relationships, getting excited about the lectures I was preparing. When the fall term began, I was well organized and well prepared. My lectures were so good, so clear, logical, informative, insightful, even entertaining—and I worked so hard and enjoyed the work and the teaching so much—that I knew I was a good teacher. Nevertheless, I see now that I was not a good teacher. In fact, I see now that I was a bad teacher.

For example, I thought a student was laughable when he wanted me to give him a date that I had just said was unknown. He sat with his pen poised over his notes, looking up at me anxiously. "Just so you can fill in the blank in your notes?" I asked. "Yes," he said, not seeming to hear—or passively enduring—my sarcasm. "Oh, well," I said, "then write in 1676. It's not the real date, but you just go ahead and write it in so you can fill up that blank." He did. I thought he was a poor student because he had not paid attention to what I had just said about the date. As a result, I felt justified in disrespecting him. I laughed with my colleagues about this incident and student—and continued on my way as a self-respecting lecturer.

The First Experience

The next year, because of my husband's increasing illness, our family, which included four children, had to leave Michigan and move to New York near the hospital that had previously treated him. The only teaching position I could find on short notice was a 1- year position as a replacement English teacher at a public high school. At this school I learned the first of a series of life-changing lessons that helped me see a way to be a better teacher. This lesson gave me not only my first insight into what teaching really is, but it also broke my heart because, not knowing how to carry what I was learning through to the end, it broke some students' hearts.

One of my classes in this high school was a ninth-grade English class for students the school had identified as "losers." They were 18 boys, all working class. Thirteen of them were sons of Italian immigrants who had come 30 years before to build the county dam and reservoir. Five students were African Americans. Only two were freshmen; the others were older than freshmen and could not be said to be in any grade. They were in their classes as in holding tanks until they were 18 and could be called seniors and would be allowed to graduate.

After two weeks with them, I felt I would not be able to go on. They would not be quiet, they would not listen, they would not stay in their seats, they would not work, they would not stop being disrespectful to me or to each other. The 50 minutes a day I spent with them was so agonizing that I wanted to quit my job. But I could not quit; my husband was in the hospital and I had to support our family.

Quietness in the classroom was important because the principal patrolled the halls looking for students on the loose and listening for noisy—that is, uncontrolled—classrooms. He had already burst into my room once and, later, in his office, had warned me to keep the noise down and to, as he put it, "control your students."

In the teachers' lounge, I discussed the problem with my colleagues. They commiserated—and told me that what teachers had to do with rowdy or disobedient students was to assert their authority so these students would know who the boss was. They advised me to be tougher, stricter. They said that these students would not behave and sit quietly and do their work unless they had to, unless I made them. They said I had to be a disciplinarian, accept no disrespect or talking back, and send students to the principal's office the instant they misbehaved. Since I had no interest in being a behavior cop—and probably could not be if I tried—this advice was not going to work for me. Moreover, if I were to do that, I'd have to send most of the class to the office 1 minute after class started.

At Michigan State University and in my other classes at the high school, students generally behaved well. Grades were clearly important to them; the only authority I needed to ensure their cooperation was the authority to give them grades. The students in this class, however, seemed to have no interest in grades. I had already failed most of them on their first assignments, but they did not seem to care.

Desperate to find a way to survive with this class, I thought if I could identify the major source of the conflict between these students and me, perhaps I could resolve it. I came to the conclusion that I wanted to teach and they did not want to learn. This conflict could be resolved if I stopped wanting and trying to make them learn.

The next day I came to class with a pile of automotive and sports magazines and said to them, "I figured out that the problem is that I want to teach but you don't want to learn. So you don't have to learn. You can just sit quietly in the back of the room and read these magazines, and I won't bother you. And if anyone wants to learn anything about anything, then come up front and I'll teach you whatever you want to learn."

I waited for them to move to the back or front of the room. But they just sat there, silently, 18 guys in little tab-arm chairs, staring at me. "Just move your chairs," I said. "It's really okay. If you don't want to learn, you can sit quietly in the back and read. You can even talk to each other if you're quiet. And I'll teach anyone who wants to learn anything up here in the front." They still did not move. They did not speak. They did not look at each other. I felt they might be embarrassed to move while I was looking at them. So I said, "Okay, I'll turn around and you can talk to each other about it. And then you can move to the back or the front. Whichever you decide to do is fine."

I turned around and, instantly, without their saying a word to each other, there was a loud noise as the chairs moved. Then silence. I thought, "Oh, no. They've all moved to the back. It's over for me."

But when I turned to them, I saw they had all pushed their chairs up to my desk, as close and as jammed together as possible. We looked at each other, into each other's eyes. Time stopped. Something happened to us. I started crying. After wiping away my tears with my fingers, I asked them what they wanted to learn. They said they wanted to learn how to read and write.

"If you don't know how to read and write, how did you get to the ninth grade?" I asked.

"They always just passed us on. They don't care about us." They knew the truth, and they had been living with it.

When we began our work, I discovered that they were almost illiterate, not knowing how to write a sentence and reading at the elementary school level.

Unfortunately, I did not know how to teach them. Lectures, no matter how clear and well organized, did not work. These boys had no background to know what I was talking about, and they did not know how to take notes; they did not even know how to ask questions about what they did not know. Reading assignments did not work because of their low reading levels.

Not one student had ever had anyone read to him. So, thinking to start where they were, as one starts with children, I began to read books to them that they might find appealing, like Steinbeck's *The Pearl*. They sat quietly, intense and attentive. One day the principal poked his head in to see what was going on. Later he told me the class was so unusually quiet, he was curious about what we were doing.

I searched in the school's resource room for teaching materials and found grammar worksheets, which I had them do. They did a sheet, and then I gave them the correct answers. Then they did another sheet, using the correct answers from the previous sheet on the new one. One student was peeking at another student's work and was embarrassed when he saw me observing him cheating. I said, "It's okay. You can help each other or get help from each other." This seemed reasonable and humane. And because I did not know how to teach these students, I was grateful for anything that seemed helpful.

Over the rest of the semester, I read to them; and we had discussions about the readings, including topics such as the influence on children of mothers versus fathers, cheating, and the meaning of democracy. We even talked about homosexuality in ancient Greece when two of the boys who were best friends were derisively called fags by their classmates. I also tried to teach them some grammar and writing skills. They worked hard, were angels, and learned. What had changed? What had happened? I had discovered that by putting myself in the service of their desire to learn, a community was born in which teaching and learning could occur.

I also discovered some students worked quickly and broadly and kept wanting more challenges, while others worked slowly and deeply and kept wanting more time for reflection. I felt if they were separated into two classes, one in which some could speed along from challenge to challenge and one in which others could stop and reflect along the way, it would be better for all of them. So, without discussing it with the students, I talked to the teacher who had the other "loser" class and asked her whether in the second semester one of us could have all the slow students and the other all the fast students. She agreed, if she could have the fast students. She apparently believed fast students were smarter or more well behaved than slow students. And so the students were divided.

Her slow students—actually her troublemakers—came into our community like barbarians, and my civilized fast students went into her class as into exile. After the semester started, Danny Severino, one of the fast students, came to me and asked, "Why did you give us away? Did we do something wrong?" I tried to reorganize the class, but the principal would not let me rectify the situation. I mention Danny's name as a memorial; he soon dropped out of school and a few years later died of a drug overdose. Was it my fault? Even partly my fault? It is important for me to think so, because it keeps me aware of how sensitive and precious every student is (also see McPhail & McPhail, 1999; McPhail & Morris, 1986).

The Second Experience

I learned my second lesson at the school I went to as a literature and history teacher after my temporary job at the public school ended. It was a private school for rich, high-IQ high school dropouts. Their parents paid a lot of money to keep their children in this school of last resort. And the owners of the school made sure they stayed there—by having classes no larger than 10 students, by letting students walk out of class any time they felt like it, and by paying the teachers according to how many students were in each class each day.

Here I learned that when students have the freedom to accept or reject how their teachers are teaching, they are not disruptive troublemakers; instead, they simply get up and walk out. It was a chilling experience when students looked into my eyes as I was lecturing and I could see they were thinking, "This means nothing to me," after which, quietly and politely, they picked up their books and left the room. Through trial and error, I eventually learned that, when I told them what I really thought and felt about a topic or idea, asked them what they thought and felt, told them when I was unsure, and invited them to help seek the truth, they stayed and talked, worked hard, were angels—and a community was born in which teaching and learning could happen.

In this school, for example, I learned, with and from the students, more about American history than I had ever learned from the textbooks I had studied unquestioningly in school. But the students refused to use those books: "One reason I dropped out of my old high school was because of those stupid books. They're so completely superficial." The students wanted to study "the real story." So we used primary sources (e.g., biographies, memoirs, scholarly books), and they struggled with them, made discoveries, and were eager to learn more.

Rich students, working-class students, white students, minority students—they were all the same: They all wanted to learn. But they all needed a teacher who would come, with respect, to where they were. In fact, in 1995 Mike Rose published his 4-year study of K–12 "good teaching" and reported that one major aspect of good teaching is that teachers respect their students.

The Third Experience

The next lesson was in a community college literature course. Once again, after 3 years away, I was back in a classroom in which lecturing was expected. I had never taught this course before, but everything was proceeding well. Students read the assigned short stories and could understand and learn from what I told them and explained to them in my lectures, which they seemed to enjoy. The trouble started with the poetry unit. I presented insightful interpretations of the poems, explaining each poem's meaning clearly and with enthusiasm. But every day, fewer students showed up. On the last days of the unit, almost a quarter of the class was absent. They did not return until the poetry unit was over and we started the drama unit.

When I asked them why they had not attended, they said they had never liked poetry, did not understand it, and could not even understand what I had been talking about. When I taught this course again, I taught it very differently.

My new plan was to use an activity created by my friend and colleague, the poet Joan Fiset. It started where the students were—with a task every student could understand and do, a no-fail task: After we read the first poem together, I asked each student to write down just one thing that she or he liked about the poem. Then they talked together in small groups about what they had written. After that, I asked the class what they liked and then wrote what they said, verbatim, on the chalkboard. Now everyone could see and talk about everyone's ideas and I could see where the class was.

The first time I did this, I was so surprised by their clear, rich insights that I said to myself, "They've gone deeper and further than I would have gone in my lecture and in the reading I was going to assign. Thank goodness I didn't start with them!" (See Chapter 8, Figures 8.3-8.5, for the complete Introduction to Poetry lesson plan.)

Moreover, when they proceeded to the second poem, the students increased both their concentration on their individual writing and the vivaciousness of their small-group sharing of what they had written. Then, when we reconvened for the whole-class debriefing and discussion, they leaned toward me with such intense expectation that I involuntarily took a few steps back, startled by the level of energy emanating from them. Then, again, I wrote on the board verbatim what they had to say about the second poem. It was now clear that they had taught themselves and each other more about poetry in these two active and interactive independent-thinking tasks than I had thought they would be capable of learning in a week or more of lectures and textbook readings.

Here seemed proof positive that students are natural learners, are energized by learning, and, apparently, love to learn—when they can start learning something new from where they are, using what they already know, and can do their own exploring, thinking, and discovering.

From there, task by task, with each task connecting to and building on what had gone before, the students increased their understanding of poetry with eager interest.

The Fourth Experience

Another eye-opening experience occurred soon afterward in my first community college developmental reading class, in which students were placed because their reading test scores showed they were reading at the fourth- to-sixth-grade level. The students were reading aloud our first text, *Treasure Island.* Their ability to pronounce the words—to phonetically decode or visually recognize the words—was adequate, but they were not comprehending the meaning of the words and sentences they were correctly pronouncing. How could they not understand what they were reading? I asked them to use their own words to describe a scene they had just read. They could not do it. I asked them to draw pictures of what the words in the story were describing. They could not do it. At last, I went to the board and read the words and drew pictures of what the words were about. After a few sentences, there was a stirring and murmuring. They were getting it. They were having an "aha" experience. To my amazement, it turned out that these students had never realized that words on a page relate to reality and to seeing images in their minds. But all of a sudden, with this help they saw it. And immediately, miraculously, they became better readers.

The lesson? I had not known where they were. I had been assuming they knew about the relationship between reading and reality, about having pictures in their minds as they read, and that they simply did not have the ability to be good readers. But when I started where they actually were, they were able to see and understand.

I used what I had learned from this experience when my cousin Debbie asked me to help her 7-year-old daughter with her reading. Dani was having trouble understanding her reading assignments, and my cousin did not understand what the problem was because Dani was able to read all the words in her assignments. The teacher had told my cousin that her daughter had no understanding of the lessons because she had a reading problem or perhaps even a learning problem. In a minute, though, it was clear to me that Dani was decoding the words but without comprehension, just like the college students. So I did the same thing with her that had helped the adult students. And in just a few paragraphs, the child had her own aha experience and understood what reading really is. Once again, I had seen the same thing happen: When the teacher starts where students are and relies on their innate ability to learn, they can be successful learners.

Adults or children—apparently they learn the same way. But I did not know why. And I would not know until I began to study the brain. Chapter 3 presents research that seems to show the human brain learns by the same innate, natural learning process throughout life. As Chapter 2 notes, however, some students diagnosed with learning problems might need special help.

The Fifth Experience

The next lesson took several years and many eye-opening experiences to learn. It started one day in my community college basic grammar course. I was standing in front of my students not understanding why these adults who desired to learn could not transfer grammar concepts from their successfully completed grammar worksheets and workbooks to their own writing. I had tried to start where they were in their knowledge of grammar, using different workbooks, worksheets, and activities, but nothing worked, the knowledge was not being transferred. I respected them, and we had a community—but because learning was not happening, I had to conclude that teaching was not happening either.

In light of our mutual frustration, I finally stopped the grammar lesson one day and said to them, "I know you're intelligent. I know you know how to learn because you know how to do a lot of things. How did you learn those things? How *do* you learn? Can you think of one thing you learned to do well outside school and tell me how you learned it?" Yes, they could. "Okay, I said, "write down how you learned to be good at that thing. Just write down what you did from when you first started learning it and did not know how to do it to when you got to be good at it."

When they finished writing, I asked them how they had learned their thing and wrote everything they said on the board. They called out a number of different items, including "start basic," "know you want to do it," "necessity," "observed someone." The flurry of responses died down (Stage 1). "And then?" I asked, thinking this could not possibly describe their whole learning process. There was a second flurry of answers including "practice, practice, practice" and "learn from your mistakes." Once again, after a number of responses, they stopped (Stage 2). "Was that it?" No, they began a third flurry, including "more practice" and "felt more comfortable and confident" (Stage 3).

"Is that it or is there more?" I asked again. There was a fourth flurry including "keep it going," "knowing what the results will be," "creative" (Stage 4). Then they stopped. I asked whether there was anything else and there was a fifth flurry, including "becomes second nature" and "improvement" (Stage 5). When that flurry died down, I asked, "Is there more?" A sixth—and final—response began. There were only two items to write on the board: "mastering it," "teaching it" (Stage 6).

When I stepped back from the board to look at their six stages, my scalp prickled. These six stages of learning were almost identical to the six substages of learning that Jean Piaget (Piaget & Inhelder, 1969), one of the past century's most famous biologists and child psychologists, had said were the substages of the first major developmental stage of learning (from birth to about 2 years). He saw these six substages as the way infants learn every new concept and skill. I asked myself, "Can there be a natural, innate human learning process that starts at birth and continues through life?"

THE NATURAL HUMAN LEARNING
PROCESS AND BRAIN RESEARCH

I began to ask students in all my courses, both the developmental skills and the college-transfer courses, to write down how, outside school, they had learned to be good at something. They all reported similar stages in a similar sequence. Then I began to ask teachers at conferences, graduate students, and K–12 students. By now I have asked more than 5,000 people—always with similar results. Chapter 2 describes the research protocol and provides some of the research results.

Everyone can do this research. Teachers can do it with students, parents with their children, and students with themselves and each other. Chapter 2 explains in detail how to do the research.

- Doing this research shows what the natural human learning process is.
- Knowing about this natural process will help educators understand how their students learn, parents understand how they themselves and their children learn, and students understand how they learn.
- Chapters 6 and 7 focus on how to help anyone be a successful learner.

Key to what seems to be the natural human learning process (NHLP) are such elements as making one's own discoveries, making and then learning from one's own mistakes, being active, and being creative, as opposed to doing drills, filling out worksheets, or studying one-right-answer problems. Chapter 2 focuses on this research, and Chapter 3 compares its stages with Jean Piaget's six substages of infant learning (Figure 3.15, Chapter 3).

After doing this research with the first few hundred people, I became convinced that this is a true phenomenon and began experimenting with the NHLP stages in the developmental grammar course, which I taught every term. Term after term, I tried to see how to create a curriculum that comprises these stages. For example, students were now doing their own writing rather than using workbooks and had opportunities to practice, practice, practice. But I could not put it together sufficiently to make a major difference for these students.

Then, as noted in the Introduction, one morning on my way to the first class of a new term, I thought I could not go on if nothing worked well enough. I wondered whether there was any scientific basis for teaching. Does the brain learn in any particular way? If it does, and if we could know how the brain learns, maybe we would have a scientific basis for knowing how to teach.

Over the next 10 years, as a doctoral student in educational psychology, I found out how the brain learns (Chapter 3). When I looked at this neuroscience knowledge side by side with the classroom/field research (Chapter 2), it seemed possible that the brain is learning as—and because—students are going through the stages of the natural human learning process. Or, put another way, students progress through the stages of the natural learning process as—and because—the brain is learning. In short, these two areas of research seemed to converge as a brain-based, natural-learning process.

With this hypothesis in mind, I tried to fuse these areas of research into a brain-based, natural-learning approach to curriculum development and pedagogy (Chapters 6–9). After much trial and error in my grammar classes, I finally was able to develop a convergent brain-based, natural-learning basic grammar course (Chapter 9) in which students are eager and successful learners (Smilkstein, 1998).

In this course, students learn grammar concepts, improve their writing, and are intellectually energized. Figures 5.4 and 5.5 (Chapter 5) and Figures 9.7 through 9.13 (Chapter 9) are examples of one student's progress through this course. Chapter 9 describes the basic grammar curriculum, with details of one of its lesson plans.

Chapter 8 presents brain-based, natural-learning lesson plans for teaching concepts and skills in different subjects at different levels, including this basic grammar course.

EDUCATORS AND THE BRAIN

It seems that some colleges of education do not, as a rule, teach their students how the brain learns and how to teach the way the brain naturally learns. When their students start teaching in the K–12 system, or when new faculty start teaching at the college level without knowing how the brain learns and how to do brain-compatible teaching—is that like a cardiologist who studies veins, arteries, and blood chemistry but never learns how the heart works? To be of most help to their patients, cardiologists need to know as much as possible about how the heart and cardiovascular system work. They also must know how to apply this knowledge in their practice.

Similarly, educators, to be of most help to students, need to know as much as possible about how the brain—the learning organ—and the cognitive system work. Since 1990, neuroscientists have been discovering more about the brain than had ever been known before. Yet being familiar with the research is not enough to help teachers understand how to apply this knowledge in their classrooms.

The problem with studying and trying to apply the brain research is that the wealth of complex information about the physiological, chemical, and biological functions of the brain can leave educators at a loss about how to use these facts to help their students learn. Typically, educators who are knowledgeable about brain research choose only various isolated elements to incorporate into their teaching. For example, because emotions have a chemical effect on the brain's learning, thinking, and remembering processes (discussed in Chapter 3), some educators quite rightly recommend that teachers take students' emotions into account by creating a supportive and respectful classroom environment. They might also enrich their classes with music, art, and group projects because brain research shows these activities have a positive affect on brain processes.

Teachers who want to do brain-compatible teaching often have lists of brain-compatible strategies, tips, and practical suggestions to guide them. These can certainly be fruitful and useful lists. Unfortunately, however, lists do not provide a coherent, theory-based method for developing comprehensive curricula for teaching whole units, courses, and programs. With such a method, educators would be able to teach every topic, skill, concept, and body of knowledge for any subject at any level so that students would learn naturally and successfully, the way they were born to learn.

In short, what has been missing is a research-based, theory-based method to help educators know how to put what is known about the brain squarely and productively in the curriculum of every classroom.

THE RESEARCH-BASED STAGES, CURRICULUM, AND LESSON PLANS

This book proposes an approach to developing curricula and lesson plans based on both natural-learning and brain research. The convergence of these two areas of research leads to a multistage learning process. When lesson plans and curricula comprise these research-based stages, students are able to learn as they were born to learn—with motivation, naturally and successfully.

How People Learn 2

The Natural Human
Learning Process (NHLP)

The mind is fire to be kindled, not a vessel to be filled.

Plutarch

CRITICAL AND CREATIVE
THINKING BY INFANTS AND CHILDREN

Students are perfectly able to do critical thinking in all their classes. This view may seem to contradict the apparent inability of some students to think critically in their courses. Because some students do succeed, we might assume that the failure to meet the objectives of the course rests with the students, that there must be something wrong with them or what they are doing.

Some educational theorists believe the lower-achieving students have been slower to develop intellectually than the higher-achieving students and, thus, are simply less mature. Some theorists believe the lower-achieving students have low motivation, a poor attitude, less intelligence, or less aptitude for particular subjects or for school work in general than the higher-achieving students.

Any or all of these causes might explain why certain students do not demonstrate a high level of thinking or achieve success in their courses. But could it be possible that all these students really are able to do critical thinking in their courses—and would be glad to do so—except that some external obstacle prevents them from doing so? This possibility cannot be overlooked.

After all, if they can speak—and they probably learned to speak when they were about 2 years old—they have been operating at a high level of abstraction, skillfully using their critical and creative faculties, since they were infants. In fact, research now seems to show that infants as young as 9 months old perceive patterns and do what appears to be critical and creative thinking.

> Experts can now say with some conviction that by the time babies are all of nine months old, they are performing *statistical analyses* of the language they hear. Through this knowledge they can figure out that "big baby" must be two words, "big" and "baby," and not three words, "bi," gba," and "by." The sounds "gba" never occur together in English. By knowing the possible sequences of sounds, infants discover where words begin and end. . . . They attend to those cues—the sounds, the order of the sounds, and the stress patterns—to locate the building blocks of language. (Golinkoff & Hirsh-Pasek, 1999, pp. 76–77)

To learn language, one of the most complex skills—if not the most complex skill—children have to learn abstract language rules and structures. This requires the innate ability to perceive patterns and then use those perceived patterns to create new forms (new words and new sentences); these are critical and creative thinking activities that children do naturally, without deliberate or conscious effort. For example, ask a two-year-old child, "Did you run around in the park yesterday?" The child will probably answer, creating a new word and a new sentence, "Yes, I runned around there."

Some educational psychologists have said the creation of new words such as "runned" is an overgeneralization or overregulation and see it as characteristic of a child's immaturity. For example,

> children frequently overregularize, that is, use word forms that follow a rule rather than recognize an exception to it. For example, a child may overregularize the rule that says past tense words end in -*ed*, by saying "I goed home." Yet children typically have never heard the overregularizations they produce. . . . [C]hildren will learn to speak and write better if they are given good models to learn from. (Sternberg & Williams, 2002, p. 68)

This assumption that children make mistakes because they do not know any better might be missing the point. Leslie Hart (1999) offered a different explanation. It is his view that children create unheard-of words like "goed" and "runned" not because they are immature or ignorant but, rather, because they are natural-born independent pattern seekers and critical and creative thinkers. Instead of focusing on the incorrectness of children' speech and their needing to learn from correct models, Hart focused on the ability of children to be innately and brilliantly perceptive and creative:

> The brain is, by nature's design, an amazingly subtle and sensitive pattern-detecting device. The brain detects, constructs, and elaborates patterns as a basic, built-in function. It does not have to be taught or motivated to do so, any more than the heart needs to be instructed or coaxed to pump blood. (Hart, 1999, pp. 115–116)

Hart went on to say that what is "amazing is the obvious ability of preschool children to extract rules about language from the quite random speech they hear about them and engage in" (p. 125). Two-year-old children have all by themselves discerned there are *action words* such as "go" and "run" in utterances. And not only have they perceived which exact words are the action words, they have also perceived the common difference between the past and the present forms of action words. Using all this knowledge, they know to add *-ed* to an action word when they want to talk about a past action.

Thus, they create words they have never heard because the "brain is by nature a magnificent pattern-detecting apparatus, even in the early years" (Hart, 1999, p. 127), not because they are making the mistake of overgeneralizing. They are not merely imitating or learning to speak correctly by what behaviorists see as reinforcement, being consistently rewarded for speaking correctly (Skinner, 1957) or by having good models to follow. Instead, on their own they are discovering subtle and complex patterns and are creating new forms that follow the patterns they have perceived. That is how brilliant they are: They make up words such as "goed" and "runned" not because they are doing something wrong, but because they are doing something very right. Their brains are discovering, thinking, creating. When they are a little older and more experienced in life, they will observe, or be taught, that, as illogical and improbable as it is, "went" is the grammatically correct past tense of "go" and "ran" is the past tense of "run." This information has to be memorized. Logic is not useful here; it is even counterproductive.

Young children are, in fact, using logic even without enough life experience or knowledge to judge whether their logical conclusions are realistic. For example, on the day before his fourth birthday, my grandson Jesse received in the mail a pair of new shoes from his uncle who lives across the country. When Jesse tried on the shoes, it was clear that they were too large. "It's okay," Jesse said. "Tomorrow I'll be bigger and then they'll fit." If he will be older, then he will be bigger; therefore, the shoes will fit—an excellent example of deductive reasoning.

Gopnik, Meltlzoff, and Kuhl (1999) reported that "babies *are* brilliantly intelligent learners" (p. 10). Other researchers have also reported that "[i]nfants are outstanding pattern seekers" (Golinkoff, Mervis, & Hirsh-Pasek, 1994, p. 19) and problem solvers (e.g., Barrows & Kelson, 1996). They might "lack knowledge and experience, but not reasoning ability. Although young children are inexperienced, they reason facilely with the knowledge they have" (Bransford, Brown, & Cocking, 1999, p. xiv). Wynn (1992) found that infants are even capable of doing mathematics.

Healy (1994), in reviewing the research, came to the same conclusion: Human beings are natural and apt pattern seekers, thinkers, and learners from birth; and the brain uses the same innate processes throughout life (also see Freeman, 1995; Jensen, 1998; MacDonald, 2002).

AN EXAMPLE OF CHILDREN'S CRITICAL AND CREATIVE THINKING

Young children "think, observe, and reason. They consider evidence, draw conclusions, do experiments, solve problems, and search for the truth" (Gopnik et al., p. 13). As an illustration of children's ability to search for the truth and solve problems, here is a search for the truth to solve a problem conducted by two boys, my grandson Rome (then 4.9 years old) and his friend Marley (then 3.11 years old). They were looking at a card with pictures of many Ninja Turtles on it.

Marley pointed to a picture of a blue-garbed Ninja with a backpack and said to Rome, "This is the Ninja you have."

Rome replied that, no, he had the Ninja in the orange suit.

Marley calmly persisted, "This is the one you have."

Rome replied with equanimity, pointing to the picture of the orange-garbed Ninja, "No, this is the one I have."

Marley, equally serious and composed, said, pointing to the blue one, "This is the one you have."

Rome, unruffled, in the spirit of scientific inquiry, got up and left the room, telling Marley that he will get his Ninja and show it to him.

When he returned with the Ninja in the orange costume, Marley said, revealing the evidence and logic he had been using to form his thesis, "You do have the orange one. But this one [pointing to the orange Ninja's picture] doesn't have a pack on its back, and yours does."

Serious and thoughtful, the two boys leaned over the picture and looked back and forth between it and the Ninja in Rome's hand. They were trying to reason out the incongruity between the picture and the reality. Rome did, indeed, have the orange one and his had a pack on its back; but the orange Ninja in the picture had no pack. They were trying to solve this problem. Unfortunately, I jumped into their scientific investigation prematurely to point out that the orange Ninja in the picture was facing us but did have a backpack; "See, just the tip of it is showing over his shoulder in the picture."

Marley pulled the picture away and told me, "You don't know anything about Ninjas. You don't have a Ninja."

This is a brilliant assumption—that one first needs to have experience in order to have knowledge about that experience, and only then can one understand an anomalous phenomenon about that experience. And wouldn't any scientist or scholar agree? The only relevant difference between me and the boys was not that I was more intelligent or a better thinker; it was only that I had the advantage of many more years of experience to inform my understanding.

CRITICAL AND CREATIVE THINKING IN SCHOOL

Does the innate intellectual ability of children disappear as they get older, or are there reasons for their not being able to use this ability in the classroom? Why would students not be able to do the same kind of logical and creative thinking in school that they did as infants and preschoolers? A major reason is that, as noted earlier, some researchers and educators believe that young children are not capable of critical thinking. Consequently, these educators do not give them sufficiently challenging creative-thinking, critical-thinking, and problem-solving tasks. In other words, educators who believe children are functioning at a low intellectual level "dumb down" the curriculum to that assumed low level.

However, the research that has been conducted in the 1990s and beyond reveals how intelligently infants and children actually think and learn. In 1999, the Committee on Developments in the Science of Learning (with the Commission on Behavioral and Social Sciences and Education along with the National Research Council) published an evaluation of new developments in the science of learning, *How People Learn: Brain, Mind, Experience, and School* (Bransford et al., 1999). For example, they report that at 2 months, infants

pay attention to the features of speech such as intonation and rhythm, that help them obtain critical information about language and meaning. As they get older, they concentrate on utterances that share a structure that corresponds to their maternal language, and they neglect utterances that do not. (p. 81)

By about 1 year, babies are babbling in their own language:

Babies from different cultures, learning different languages, start to make the distinctive noises of their own community. ... The Chinese baby starts to babble in a way that sounds Chinese. . . . Swedish babies babble in a way that sounds distinctly Swedish. (Gopnik et al., p. 111)

In other words, here are babies perceiving, discerning, learning. Bransford et al. (1999) reported that 5-month-old infants are capable of numerical representation; that is, they are aware when the quantity of objects change, when one item is added or taken away from a group of objects (p. 79). Also, children

as early as 3–4 months of age . . . understand that objects need support to prevent them from falling; that stationary objects are displaced when they come into contact with moving objects; and that inanimate objects need to be propelled into motion. (Bransford et al., p. 72)

No one teaches or models these phenomena for infants; infants observe them and, all on their own, understand the physical laws that are at work.

Each student comes to school able to do critical and creative thinking. How can teachers make it possible for students to use these innate powers in school? Answering that question is a major focus of this book. The first step is to look at how the human being and the brain naturally learn.

THE NATURAL HUMAN LEARNING PROCESS AND SCHOOL

Our Brain Is Our Survival Organ

Our brain is our survival organ. It is born with the natural impulse and ability to figure out—through logic, through seeking patterns and solving problems—how the world works so we can survive. Look around you, at the features of the room you are in, for example, at your chair, your book, your lamp, your clothes, the coffee or tea in your cup: All are products of our brain's need, desire, and ability to figure things out, to think, to learn, to discover, to create so that we not only survive but also thrive.

A major theme of this book is that human beings have an innate learning process, which includes a natural motivation to learn (Chapter 4). Outside school students constantly engage in learning, teaching themselves and each other to be, among other things, electronic game and computer masters, popular culture savants, streetwise survivors, sports experts— and they do this complex learning with attentiveness, determination, and perseverance.

When students are not motivated in school, perhaps it is because they are not given the opportunity in school to learn naturally. Although the brain innately knows *how* to learn, the knowledge, skills, or concepts the brain acquires by means of its innate learning process depends on the learner's experiences and environment. When human beings have the opportunity to experience activities and environments that are compatible with the brain's natural learning process, they learn naturally, successfully, and with motivation.

The Traditional Classroom

On the other hand, some learning experiences and environments are not compatible with the brain's natural learning process. One such environment is the traditional classroom in which students are sometimes asked, especially in these days of standardized tests (Chapter 4), to accept or memorize the "one right answer" to specific questions and practice the "one right way" of doing specific tasks.

Moreover, in the traditional classroom, teachers impart knowledge by lecture and demonstration while students take notes, observe, do drills, memorize, take tests, and later try to use or apply the imparted knowledge in other situations and settings. Often teachers expect that students are able to do this even though the transfer of knowledge, especially imparted knowledge, to new uses and situations is highly problematic (see the discussion in Chapter 7 about the transfer of learning). Some students, of course, do well in traditional classrooms. For example, students who are well prepared with study and test-taking skills, who have relevant prior knowledge, and who have been socialized to behave appropriately (obediently and quietly) can perform successfully in such classrooms. Although some of these students enjoy knowing how to get good grades, other well-prepared students do not enjoy the exigencies of the traditional classroom. In any case, students who are not well prepared are always at a grave disadvantage (Heath, 1982, 1983). Moreover, students who share the same culture as their teachers have an advantage over students who do not (Delpit, 1988; Spindler & Spindler, 1982).

However, all students could use their brains' natural learning process to be successful critical and creative thinkers and learners in school—if they were given the opportunity to do so. Thus, when we see students who seem unable to learn, who do not want to learn, or who are apathetic or rebellious in school, we are seeing students who are not enjoying their birthright to be natural—and naturally motivated—learners. As Leslie Hart (1999) wrote,

> [W]e know that as the consequence of long evolution, the brain has modes of operation that are natural, effortless, effective in utilizing the tremendous power of this amazing instrument. Coerced to operate in other ways, it functions as a rule reluctantly [and] slowly. (p. xi)

Under coercion, learners might also function as depicted in Figure 2.1.

The challenge for educators is how to develop curricula and select pedagogical strategies that will most effectively help students learn by using their brain's innate learning process. When teachers duplicate in the classroom the same conditions and processes by which students learn outside the classroom, students are able to experience the same motivation, enjoyment, and success with school subjects in the classroom that they experience with activities outside the classroom. (See "A Chicken or Egg Question" in Chapter 3 for more on this point.)

Students Who Have Special Needs or Who Learn Differently

Some students are diagnosed with what are called learning problems, such as dyslexia, attention-deficit disorder, and attention-deficit/hyperactivity disorder. They can and do learn, but their brains learn differently. Although they can benefit from the NHLP (brain-based, natural-learning) approach, they might also need special help. Some resources for teachers, parents, or students are *A Mind at a Time* (Levine, 2002), *How the Special Needs Brain Learns* (Sousa, 2001), and *Wall of Fame* (Freedman, 2000).

These books give hope to those who fail to learn in the traditional classrooms or who are thrown away or lost because they are labeled—by others and themselves—as deficient or a failure. As Levine pointed out, every student has a strength. If students were recognized and praised for their strengths rather than shamed for their "weaknesses" and were helped to use their strengths to compensate for and possibly overcome their weaknesses, they could enrich their homes, schools, and communities with their strengths and gifts.

Figure 2.1   Coercive Learning

Sousa (2001) provides educators and parents with information and strategies to help them understand, assist, and support special needs students in their efforts to learn and achieve. Although this book does not focus on special needs students, Chapters 6 and 7 describe brain-based, natural-learning curricula and pedagogy, which make it possible for all students to learn.

THE NATURAL HUMAN LEARNING PROCESS RESEARCH

As noted in Chapter 1, my own NHLP research, carried out with more than 5,000 people, reveals the common experience human beings have when learning something new. Moreover, every student I have worked with, or heard about from other teachers doing this research, has enjoyed participating.

Many teachers tell me they have done this activity with their students, but I do not know how many people altogether have participated.

Participating in the Research

Before reading on, if you participate in the research yourself, you will be able to make a personal connection with the findings described here. Also, when you look at those findings, you will see how your own learning process is similar to or different from the thousands of others who have also participated in this activity.

First, think of something you learned to do well outside school. It could be a sport, a hobby, an art, a people skill, or something you did as a youngster but do not do any more; it could even be driving a car. Second, just write down how you got from not knowing how to do this one thing to becoming good at it—not necessarily the world's best expert, but reasonably good at it.

When you have finished, continue on to see how to conduct this research with others and what the research has found.

Conducting the Research

Here is the research or survey protocol introduced in Chapter 1, which any teacher–researcher can use with his or her students. The research procedure lasts approximately 30 to 40 minutes and is best done early in the term, perhaps even on the first day, because it is an excellent way for students, and for students and teacher, to get to know each other and to begin forming a learning community. This research can also be done with colleagues in faculty development workshops. This same protocol has been used with all the participants in the research reported here.

1. The teacher tells the students they are going to look at how they learn and then begins the activity. (*Note:* All the remarks addressed to students here and in the numbered items that follow are only suggestions. They are not meant as scripted speeches.)

Think of one thing you're good at that you learned to do outside school. It could be a sport, a hobby, an art, a people skill, something around the house; it could be something you did when you were younger but don't do any more; it could be anything. When participants are over 18 years of age, "driving" can be included. *I know everybody's good at something; so if you can't think of anything, raise your hand and I'll come over and help you.* It is imperative that every participant identify something so that everyone will be able to participate in the next activities.

Think back to before you knew how to do it. Write down how you started learning it and then how you got from not knowing how to do it to being good at it. These aren't to hand in. They're just notes to help you remember. If some finish quickly, they can be asked to go back and see whether there is anything else they can add.

2. When most are finished, the teacher proceeds to the next phase. *Get together with two or three others, introduce yourselves, say what you're good at, tell each other how you got to be good at it, and see whether there is anything similar in how you all got to be good at your different specialties.* This is an excellent way for participants, whether children, adolescents, or adults, to introduce themselves: "Hi, I'm Eli, and I'm good at rock climbing." "I'm Rose, and I'm good at designing and making clothes." "I'm Louis, and I'm good at acting." If some groups finish early, the teacher goes to those groups and asks whether they found anything similar in how they learned their different things and what their different things are. When most groups are finished, the teacher proceeds to the third stage.

3. Ready to write their contributions on the chalkboard, flipchart, or overhead transparency, the teacher reconvenes the class and asks the students to report. *What happened at the beginning of your learning your new skill?* As students call out what happened, the teacher lists their contributions verbatim on the board, flipchart, or transparency. Invariably, participants stop after telling what happened at the beginning, as in the example in Chapter 1. (See Stage 1 in Figures 2.5–2.8.) *Anything else at the beginning?* When no one adds anything else, the teacher can go on. *Okay, we'll call this "Stage 1."* The teacher writes this number at the top of the list and draws a line below or to the side of it for the next list (Stage). *Then what happened next?* Same as before—students call out comments and then stop. This process continues until there are no more contributions and no more stages.

If a student calls out an item that probably comes later (e.g., saying "teaching" at the first or second stage), the teacher can ask, *Does that go here, at this point, or later?* and lets the student make the decision.

During one session at a community college, a student asked me how many stages there are. I said, "This is research. You're going to tell me. It's however many stages you all say there are." As almost every other group has done, any group will probably also come up with similar four, five, or six stages. (See the representative samples in Figures 2.5–2.8.)

Other teachers have reported to me only one class that came up with less than four stages. In this case, the teacher said the three stages were, nevertheless, similar to the usual four to six stages.

4. After students have no more to contribute, the teacher provides closure to this phase of the activity. *Now I'm going to read all this. Let me know if you want to add, subtract, or change anything so it is closer to the learning process that you went through. Then I'm going to ask whether you learned your thing more or less this way, not every word in this exact order but, generally, more rather than less.* The teacher reads over the list given by the students. If someone wants to change something, the person who contributed the original point has to agree, or else the new point is just added to the list. If someone wants to subtract an item, it remains; but a question mark is placed after it to indicate that someone does not agree with it. Sometimes participants will agree that a particular item was present for more than one stage (e.g., practice). Then a line can be drawn between the relevant stages to represent that fact.

5. After the reading, and after everyone has had the opportunity to add or change anything, the teacher proceeds. *Raise your hand if you learned your thing more or less this way, not every word in this exact order, but more rather than less this way.* The teacher waits for the response; most students, sometimes all the students, raise their hands.

Raise your hand if you didn't learn your thing at all this way. Few students, sometimes none, raise their hands. The teacher then asks those students who did not learn their thing this way how they did learn it. Usually the person says, "Because I was good at it from the beginning." This person has an aptitude, which should be explained to the students: *This person has a natural talent* (Chapter 4). Occasionally, when people say how they learned their skill differently, they are actually close to the stages and process the group came up with, which can be pointed out with the reminder that the question was whether the way they learned was more rather than less like this, not exactly like this.

6. Then the teacher can look into his or her students' eyes and encourage them with heartfelt conviction. *You are all natural-born learners. You were born with a brain that knows how to learn. You are all very smart.*

If a teacher–researcher is working with a nonstudent group, for example colleagues at a faculty development workshop, it is probably not necessary to add, "You are all very smart." It is wonderful, though, when students hear this, especially students who have had difficulty in school and perhaps feel they are not smart. And, of course, it is true that they—we—are all natural-born learners and can and do learn. In other words, we are all smart (Chapter 4 discusses intelligence).

The teacher then can tell how she or he will contribute to the students' learning in the course. *It will be my responsibility to provide the same kind of natural-learning opportunities in class that helped you learn outside school. Then you will be able to learn as successfully in this course as you learned outside school.* The teacher can then point to the evidence of their successful learning, displayed before the class on the board, flipchart, or overhead transparency. The teacher might also explain that even though some students would probably not want to pursue the subject beyond that term, they would, however, enjoy learning it for those months because they would be using their natural learning process, which is always an enjoyable experience.

7. After that, the teacher asks each person to say what he or she is good at. It is usually a great array of accomplishments. *And you all learned your different things pretty much by this same process? This research has been done with more than 5,000 people, and they have all come up with the same four to six stages. So we might say this is the natural human learning process.* This convinces the students—and the teacher as well—that there is, indeed, a natural human learning process and that this is it.

After this activity, students often look around and realize that they are in a classroom of people of accomplishment and that all the students in the class, including themselves, are successful learners—as proven by the research and believed by the teacher. This adds to the positive emotion that is essential if students are to learn well. Chapter 3 explains why positive emotions are chemically necessary for learning.

8. Finally, to translate their self-reports into a concept that will be invaluable to them as self-aware and self-confident learners, the teacher can present the diagram in Figure 2.2 on the board, flipchart, or overhead.

I've listed six stages because those are the most people usually come up with. Then, drawing the upward arrow, asks this critical question: *What are two or three words that tell how you got from not knowing how to do your thing up to being good at it?*

Students will probably volunteer such processing activities as "practice," "effort," "time," "support," and "perseverance." Whatever they answer is fine because it is true for them. There is no one right answer. There is, instead, a focus on their being introspective and gaining metacognitive knowledge (thinking and knowing about how they learn,

Figure 2.2   Six Stages

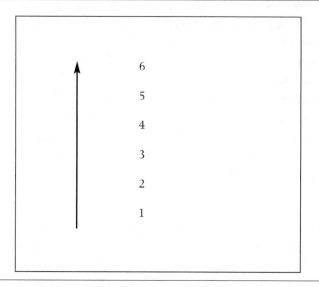

about how they know). This is critical if they are to be self-aware, self-empowered learners. The teacher can then add their answers below the diagram (Figure 2.3) and show how they affect the students' progress by drawing the diagonal "ceiling level" arrow and the bottom axis line, explaining that the ceiling level is how much skill and understanding students have at any point in their learning process as a result of the work they are doing.

The teacher can also say the ceiling level is "iron" because people can know more about something they are learning (increase their knowledge, skill, and understanding) only with more work on it. Only by their own efforts can they raise their ceiling level, their skill, and knowledge level.

Can Learning Stop?

Does a learner's ceiling level (the level of skill and understanding for an object of learning) ever stop moving upward? Yes. If a person stops practicing, thinking about, or using a skill, concept, or body of knowledge, the ceiling level for it might not merely stop moving higher, it might, more likely, decline. The result would be a diminished level of skill or understanding. In other words, use it or lose it (Chapter 3).

Differential Learning

Figure 2.4, "Model of Differential Learning and Individual Differences," shows that an individual might learn one skill, concept, or

Figure 2.3   Ceiling Levels

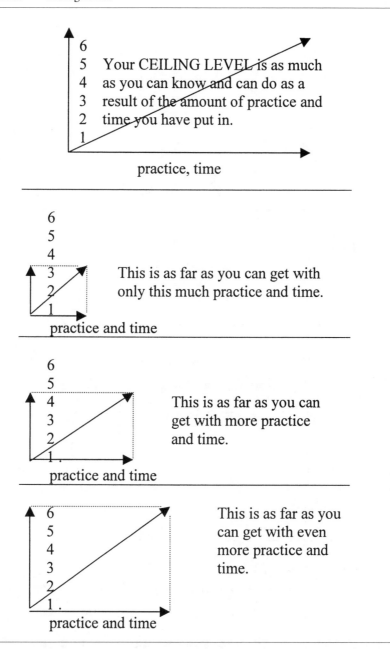

body of knowledge more quickly and easily than that person might be able to learn another skill, concept, or body of knowledge. It is unlikely that any single person will be able to learn everything with the same amount of practice and time.

Similarly, Figure 2.4 indicates that because everyone is different, with different aptitudes, interests, and opportunities, different people are able

Figure 2.4   Model of Different Learning and Individual Differences

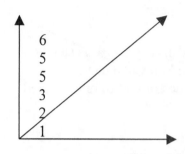

The Model in general

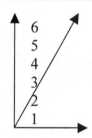

Someone with an aptitude for this skill

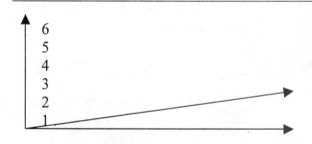

Someone who finds this skill hard to learn

**People learn different skills with different amounts of
practice and time, learning some skills more or less
quickly and easily than others.**

to learn different skills or concepts or bodies of knowledge with different
amounts of time and degrees of effort. For example, someone with an
aptitude for a specific skill or concept might reach a high level of expertise
in that skill in a relatively short time. Someone else might practice a lot

over a long period of time and never reach a high level of expertise for a particular skill or concept. With enough time and practice, however, that person will certainly be able to learn something about it. At the same time, that individual might be able to reach a high level of expertise for a different skill or concept or body of knowledge.

For example, Einstein reached his extraordinarily high level of expertise in mathematics with less time and effort than it would take someone with less aptitude to reach even a lower level of expertise. However, Einstein apparently did not reach as high a level of expertise in other areas. Perhaps he did not put in a great deal of effort and time to learn those skills, or perhaps he did not have an aptitude for them.

AFTER THE RESEARCH IS OVER

Students can use handouts of Figures 2.3 and 2.4 to remind them that they are self-empowered, able learners. This metacognitive knowledge of the relationship between the students' own self-reported learning stages and what the students themselves do when learning take the mystery out of how to be successful learners. Most important, it proves to the students that they are responsible, by their own admission and experience, for their own learning. They are the ones who have to do the learning stage by stage from the bottom up; and, because they have done it before, they can do it again and always—because they are natural-born learners. (Chapter 5 shows how these diagrams can be powerful tools for the teacher's evaluation of students as well as for students' self-evaluations.)

The teacher then explains to the students how their brain learns. Chapter 3 provides the information and visual aids for this presentation, which participants at every age invariably find fascinating and inspiring.

RESEARCH REPORTS

Again, as described earlier in Step 3 of "Conducting the Research," the words in all the following reports were contributed by individual participants recounting their own experiences.

Four-Stage Learning Process

Following are verbatim reports from three representative groups who reported a four-stage learning process (Figure 2.5). The groups are as follows:

1. An evening class of high school students who attend school during the day and then attend classes after school to make up credits lost by having failed their regular courses (Chapter 6)

Figure 2.5   Groups Reporting a Four-Stage Learning Process

Evening High School Students	College of Education Students	Faculty at a Professional Conference
STAGE 1		
Worked at it Someone helped Signed up Observation Initiated it Tried it Had to practice Learn the basics Had to learn names Took lessons Learn the rules & regulations	Watching Wanting Listening to instructor Excitement Tried it Practice Didn't like it Interest Survival Making mistakes	Interest Watched/Saw Observation Experimentation Hands-on Took a class Read about it Imitation Practice, practice, practice Watched a video It was in the environment Trial and error Talked about it
STAGE 2		
Perform (well if you had a natural ability but not well if you didn't) Keep doing it Practice	Determination Dedication Practice and more practice Experimenting Some skill building Liking it better Having patience	Tried it on my own Got good feedback Fell down and did it again Learned from my mistakes Helped somebody else do it
STAGE 3		
Practice, practice, practice Perform better	More practice Began to teach it Wanted to be the best at it Started having fun Learning more about it	Watched again Read more/Classes Practice, practice, practice Expert instruction Fell down less Refinement
STAGE 4		
Stop/Conclusion Succeed Quit Contribution Looking for new challenge Start using it to get money	Started sharing after got good at it Altering and trying new skill Advancing Competing	Became expert Got paid Changed directions Became independent Took on greater challenges

2. Students majoring in education at a university college of education

3. College faculty members attending a session at a national professional conference

The groups reporting five stages and six stages are similarly diverse, as shown in the following figures.

Five-Stage Learning Process

Figure 2.6 shows three representative groups reporting five stages.

Six-Stage Learning Process

Figure 2.7 comprises three representative groups reporting six stages.

Elementary School Students' Learning Process

In Figure 2.8, two sixth-grade classes, a fourth-grade class, and a second-grade class all report five or six stages.

Summary of Research Reports

Whether there are four, five, or six stages, the process is similar and might be summarized as shown in Figure 2.9.

Although not all the groups had six stages, in every group's first stage all had had similar experiences, as listed in the summary (Figure 2.9). Moreover, interestingly, the groups who reported only four stages had five- and six-stage-like experiences in their fourth stage, for example, "succeeded," "dropped it," "looked for new challenges," "became expert," and "taught others." Furthermore, between their first and last stages—whether there were two, three, or four intermediate stages—all groups had similar learning experiences, including some of the following: "more practice," "feedback," "gaining confidence," and "continuing improvement." Thus, this qualitative research strongly suggests that there is a four- to six-stage natural human learning process.

To my knowledge there has been only one other report of a learning process that was less than four stages. It was given by my grandson Jesse, who, by the time he was 3 years old, had a huge collection of train tracks that he could arrange and rearrange any way he chose and scores of toy trains of different types. He created track designs

Figure 2.6   Groups Reporting a Five-Stage Learning Process

Inner City Community College Class	College of Education Graduate Students	Faculty at a Faculty Development Workshop
STAGE 1		
Desire/Need/Interest Challenge Curiosity Feel the need to succeed Practice? Instruction Requirement Observation Persistence? Natural talent and being exposed to it Determination Releasing of frustration In the surroundings	Started out very simply Seeing other people doing it Natural interest A need or a want Practice Parental support Trial and error	Someone demonstrated Had the opportunity Doing it Practice ? Reading books Watched Persistence Inspiration Talking to people who said this is fun Tried it Play Was easy
STAGE 2		
Practice, practice, practice Discipline, self-control Patience Questions Confidence Start and stop Consulting others Trial and error Making mistakes Imitate Research Seek a mentor Feel successful Receiving info. from class Keep a journal, notes	Became enjoyable Researched Total absorption and concentration Repetition Practice Spending money on equipment	Practice, practice, practice Advice and counsel Evaluation Fail and try again, fail and try again–making changes in the process, gathering more info. Do it/Don't give up Reading Networking and resources Notice what works and what doesn't Make an investment, commit
STAGE 3		
Perfect it with practice Evaluate your practice Analyze your practice Critiques from others Demonstrating Study/Research Expanding what you know Self-confidence More technical Seek a mentor Practical application of the things you've learned to see if they work Performing Good practice habits	Being shown how Formal teaching Asking questions Getting feedback from others Gaining confidence to share your activity with others Positive results Socializing with others who are good at it Making money	Practice, practice, practice Try different ways and things, tools, techniques Review, reflections, reassessment Enjoy it

Figure 2.6 *(Continued)*

Inner City Community College Class	College of Education Graduate Students	Faculty at a Faculty Development Workshop
STAGE 4		
Look back at what you've achieved–reflection A feeling of success Total evaluation Confidence Come up with end product	Willing to starve for it Acquiring experience Ease–not hard any more Habit Potential to share this knowledge with others	Move on to higher levels with better equipment, skills, more knowledge and money Might stop Show someone else how to do it Feeling of success Participate in this with someone who is better than you to continue to grow
STAGE 5		
Teaching others Find a new challenge Reach for higher heights Continuous study to succeed on what you started out with Repeat the cycle at a higher level or with new things	Quality of life got better Stagnation Specialization Prioritizing to figure out how to fit it into the rest of your life Gets more challenging Going to higher levels	Quit Retire Die

and selected sets of trains to run on them. He was the master of his railroad world.

I asked him how he had learned to be good at playing with trains. He looked aside and thought for a moment. Then he gave the following report:

"I did it myself. . . . I played in my sandbox. . . ." Then, looking up, he ended emphatically, "I'm good at it." These were his three stages: beginning practice, more practice, mastery.

THE IMPORTANCE OF MAKING MISTAKES

One of the most important insights to be gained from this research is that, essentially, people learn by making and correcting (with feedback from others or themselves) their own mistakes, that is, by practicing, through trial and error. When teachers, parents, and students come to accept, and even value, this making of mistakes by learners, one of the greatest barriers to learning is eliminated. The positive effect of removing this obstacle was illustrated to me when, in one of my basic grammar courses for adults

Figure 2.7   Groups Reporting a Six-Stage Learning Process

Community College Basic Skills Class	College of Education Students	Faculty at a Professional Conference
STAGE 1		
Watch Listen Necessity Desire Discover something	Desire Interest ? Curiosity Made me do it	Initial instruction Observation Motivation Interest Practice Reinforcement Investigating Trial and error Encouragement Non-judgemental Role model Overcoming fear Curiosity Risk taking
STAGE 2		
Imitate Fascination Explanation Knowledge of where I was at and what I needed to know Practice	Introduction to the subject Instruction Basics/Guidelines Trial and error Observation, watching Questions	Practice Lots of practice Explore Trial and error Study Play Ask questions Continuous reinforcement Listening to others Self-evaluation of progress Discussing with others Plenty of available time
STAGE 3		
Getting encouragement Practice Repetition Supervision Experiment Questions answered	Reading Trial and error Mistakes/Learn from your mistakes Practice, practice More experimentation Having the right tools Support Asked advice Sharing info. with others Letting go of your apprehensions Some sort of structure Positive attitude Just go for it/Jump into it Process of elimination	Imagining yourself being good at it Attention to detail Setting goals Motivation from success Control

Figure 2.7 *(Continued)*

Community College Basic Skills Class	College of Education Students	Faculty at a Professional Conference
STAGE 4		
Creativity Correction and confirmation by others	Time and practice Success Increase of excitement from success Positive reinforcement Sharing of knowledge Loss of interest Self-drive Continued application	Improve self-concept Feeling good about yourself Pleasing others In some cases a finished product Teaching others
STAGE 5		
Never totally good Room for improvement Can always be better Family criticizes so you try harder Self-confidence Schooling	Other people watch *you* Mastery Desire and compensation for doing it Teaching it/Passing it on Start making changes to make it your own, alter it Develop your own style	Validation by others Continuing to develop the interest Springboarding to other things Ownership
STAGE 6		
Teaching others Total participation from others Hands-on experience Feedback Getting good and better and better at it	Completely reinvent and start over Feeds into other interests	Mastery

reading and writing at the fourth- to sixth-grade level, a student came to the chalkboard to write one of his practice sentences and said, as he walked to the front of the room, "I'm probably going to make some really good mistakes here"—and the rest of the class burst into spontaneous applause. He did make some mistakes, mistakes that many of the other students had also made. As a result of the ensuing class discussion, everyone learned more. The applause was justified.

MORE RESEARCH

More information is needed to help educators know how to use the natural-learning research reports to develop and implement complete,

Figure 2.8 Groups Reporting a Five- or Six-Stage Learning Process

Second-Grade Class	Fourth-Grade Class	Sixth-Grade Class 1	Sixth-Grade Class 2
		STAGE 1	
I wanted to do it I wanted to learn how I liked it I saw pictures and wanted to do it And I wanted to do it Everybody said it was easy	My parents told me we were going to ski I wanted to I saw pictures and wanted to do it, too I thought it was cool so I started lessons I thought it was fun I thought it was cool I started taking lessons and wanted to	Someone showed me the basics and I tried them and practiced them Tried to Wanted to and kept failing and tried different approaches and finally started to get it Tried it and horrible so read about it Slipping and falling Lots of practice Dad showed me examples Just kept trying for a long, long, long, time	Someone told me Someone showed me Practiced Did it over and over Imitated; did it together with an instructor Someone walked me around and showed me how it felt Played follow the leader, imitating the coach Kept falling Dad helped me Tried something new Just did it
		STAGE 2	
I started riding with training wheels I bought a tip book, but I did better without it I started with the 2nd bar then moved to the 3rd My mom helped me I got frustrated but I didn't give up My friends helped me I asked my mom to show me	I started to bounce and then started dancing I went with my Dad and he told me to lean forward My family taught me how	Then learned, tried more difficult stuff and practiced till I got good Date took me on harder courses and took riding lessons Failed miserably and then practiced a lot Learned skate-boarding was different from running Practiced hard Just practiced a lot Was determined to do tree climbing and went higher and higher and got better	Started to use my arms and legs on my own to swim Practicing Was showed new stuff Reviewing to make sure I got it down After I practiced for a long time, I got better; and then I tried new things Started with simple tumbling with the coach spotting us Just rode around with help and then without help Just practiced a lot and got pretty good

Second-Grade Class	Fourth-Grade Class	Sixth-Grade Class 1	Sixth-Grade Class 2
		STAGE 3	
Went to a 2-wheeler with help	After I got bigger and better he taught me to turn (ski)	Learning how to ride English	Practicing a lot and got better
I went to lessons	As I got older, I got more tips	Got better and practiced	Got used to doing the basics by doing it over again; then started playing
I practiced a lot	I walked on the ice, holding on to the sides	Got better and did it a lot	Read stuff about it, got tips, went out and did it
If I keep moving I won't fall	I went slow at first	Tried different types of drawing	Worked on my own technique
I practiced again and again		Dad took me on a harder course and went faster	Just practiced over and over and over again
		Learned new skills and fancy stuff	Practiced and moved on to more complicated stuff
		Started going off jumps	Started lessons and learned some new things
		Can do about 1,000 pogo stick jumps	Learned basics and could do it on my own from practice
		Playing M (the harder computer) game	Played games and used my experience to teach myself better
		STAGE 4	
I taught myself how to get better	I kept practicing	Won 5 ribbons (in riding shows)	Started competing and doing routines my coach gave us
I taught myself to ride no-handed	I kept practicing and I learned more	Tried to teach my brother	Played in a game and learned some things from other people
I went on the swim team	I practiced and got useful tips	Got better and better and faster and faster and could beat all my friends	My coach showed us tricks; we knew the basics
I saw other kinds doing tricks and I tried them, too	I tried it four times	I have to do (pogo sticking) by minutes instead of counting past 1,000	Taught myself tricks, went to skate parks
I figured out how to turn; it was my favorite part	I went to class	Going to state parks and doing grinding rails (on skateboard)	Just doing it for fun and then started teaching people
	I have to go to class	Set harder goals to make a certain number of tackles during a game	
	I do it the same as in class so I can practice		

Figure 2.8 (Continued)

Second-Grade Class	Fourth-Grade Class	Sixth-Grade Class 1	Sixth-Grade Class 2
STAGE 5			
I learned different strokes I tried them and learned to do them I do it different from both my Mom and Dad	I do it differently I only use one foot to push I always start at the beginning level I will do it differently because I am a different person	Jumping horses Trying to break 2 hours (on the pogo stick) Trying for new tricks in the air (skate-boarding) Trying to go high enough (tree climbing) to see beyond the leaves	Started making up my own routines Make up my own moves, combining moves I've already learned Improved with getting my own horse–sort of specialized for me
STAGE 6			
Breast-stroke is my favorite stroke I haven't learned my favorite trick yet, but I know what it is			Teach others

Figure 2.9   Summary of Natural-Learning Stages

STAGE 1: MOTIVATION/Responding to stimulus in the environment: watched, observed, had to, interest, desire, curiosity
STAGE 2: BEGINNING PRACTICE/Doing it: practice, practice, practice, trial and error, ask questions, consult others, basics, make mistakes, lessons, some success
STAGE 3: ADVANCED PRACTICE/Increase of skill and confidence: practice, practice, practice, trial and error, some control, reading, encouragement, experiment, tried new ways, positive attitude, enjoyment, lessons, feedback, confidence, having some success, start sharing
STAGE 4: SKILLFULNESS/Creativity: practice, doing it one's own way, feeling good about yourself, positive reinforcement, sharing knowledge, success, confidence
STAGE 5: REFINEMENT/Further improvement: learning new methods, becoming second nature, continuing to develop, different from anyone else, creativity, independence, validation by others, ownership, habit, teaching
STAGE 6: MASTERY/Broader application: greater challenges, teaching it, continuing improvement or dropping it, feeds into other interests, getting good and better and better, going to higher levels

coherent curricula. Chapter 3 provides neuroscience research that explains how the brain learns. That information converges with the information in this chapter about the NHLP. Chapter 6 then shows how to use the converging information in these two chapters to develop natural-learning, brain-compatible curricula, curricula that help students become motivated, successful, natural learners in every classroom.

How the Brain Learns

3

The Brain's Natural Learning Process

INTRODUCING THE BRAIN

Human beings are born with a brain that learns by natural, innate processes. Teachers who understand these processes are better able to help their students be the successful natural learners they were born to be.

There is one major problem, however, with studying the brain for the purpose of helping students be successful learners. The problem is that our three-pound, Jell-O–like brain has been described as "a structure of the utmost complexity" (Thompson, 1985, p. 250), "staggering in its intricacy and diversity" (Edelman, 1992, p. 21), and, "[a]rguably, the most complex system known to science" (Ratey, 2001, p. 358).

Even though neuroscientists say they do not know, and perhaps never will know, everything about the brain, they have written books and more books on various aspects of the brain, its 100 billion or more nerve cells (neurons), the 10,000 connections that any one neuron might be making with any other of the 100 billion neurons, that "[t]here are more possible ways to connect the brain's neurons than there are atoms in the universe" (Ratey, 2001, p. 20), and that if you "start counting connections in just [the] higher-thought area alone, at the rate of one connection per second, [you] wouldn't finish counting for 32 million years" (Khalsa & Stauth, 1997).

They have reported on the many chemicals circulating in the brain, the complex actions and reactions of these chemicals, and the electrical–chemical interactions going on in different parts of the brain. They have also described the many structures of the brain and the complex actions of and interactions between these structures (e.g., Calvin & Ojemann, 1994; Goldblum, 2001; Greenfield, 1997; Morowitz & Singer, 1995; Restak, 1994; S. Rose, 1992).

Fortunately, we do not need to know about all these chemicals, structures, and interactions to create and deliver effective curricula. This chapter provides an account of only those facts that help us understand how to do this.

Please share everything here with your students, colleagues, friends, and family. Everyone seems to love knowing how her or his brain learns.

GETTING TO KNOW THE BRAIN

The Brain's Innate Functions

Our brain is an organ in our body, like the heart, the lungs, the stomach. All the organs have been evolutionarily developed to perform specific functions and are born knowing how to perform them. In fact, some organs are performing their functions even before birth. The heart, for example, is beating before birth and causing the blood to circulate through the body. Immediately after birth, the lungs begin to breathe and also know what to do with the oxygen they take in. Soon after birth, the complex digestive system is also working by innate chemical and physical processes, including the baby's instinct for sucking. The brain is also functioning before birth, for example growing brain cells (neurons) and moving them to specific locations by an innate process. If the organs do not innately and naturally know what to do, the baby will die without—and perhaps even with—medical assistance.

On the other hand, we cannot, and do not need to, teach the normally functioning heart how to beat, the lungs how to breathe, the stomach how to digest food; by the same token, we cannot, and do not need to, teach the normally functioning brain how to perform. Moreover, across gender, race, culture, age, all the organs of the body have similar functions and processes.

Our Self-Empowering Brain

The brain has many functions. Among them, and perhaps of most interest to educators and students, are those of learning, thinking, and remembering. The brain is performing these functions, as most other organs are performing theirs, even before birth. For example, recent research finds that a newborn recognizes the mother's voice, showing that the fetus, innately and naturally, without instruction or example, hears and then remembers this particular voice.

Other research shows that infants are able to think soon after birth. In *How People Learn: Brain, Mind, Experience, and School*, Bransford et al. (1999) found in their 2-year evaluation of new developments in the science of learning that even 5- to 12-week-old infants are

> capable of perceiving, knowing, and remembering. . . . The answers about infant understanding of physical and biological causality, number, and language have been quite remarkable. These studies have profoundly altered scientific understanding of how and when humans begin to grasp the complexities of their worlds. (p. 72)

Learners are "biologically driven to make sense of their world" (Caine & Caine, 1991, p. 50). Perhaps this is what impels 2-year-old children to want to find out about everything and do everything by themselves. Some people see this innate and natural desire to understand and to be empowered ("How does the world work and how can I make it work for me?") as the defining characteristic of the misnamed "terrible twos."

My two-year-old grandson was visiting us, and I took his hand to help him up our front steps. Part way up, he pushed me away and said, "Jesse do it!" Then he climbed back down to the bottom and started up the steps again on his own. My daughter put her head in her hands and exclaimed, "Oh no, the terrible twos are here!" But, no, these are the twos that guarantee that civilization—its art, science, and technology—will continue to develop.

HOW THE BRAIN LEARNS

One challenge for educators is to learn about the brain's innate and natural learning, thinking, and remembering processes if they are to teach the way the brain naturally functions.

Brain Facts

Figure 3.1 shows how the brain, which is soft, like intestines, sits in the skull. The adult brain weighs about 3 pounds and could be held in one hand. Figure 3.2 shows the sections (lobes) of the brain.

Figure 3.1   The Brain in the Skull

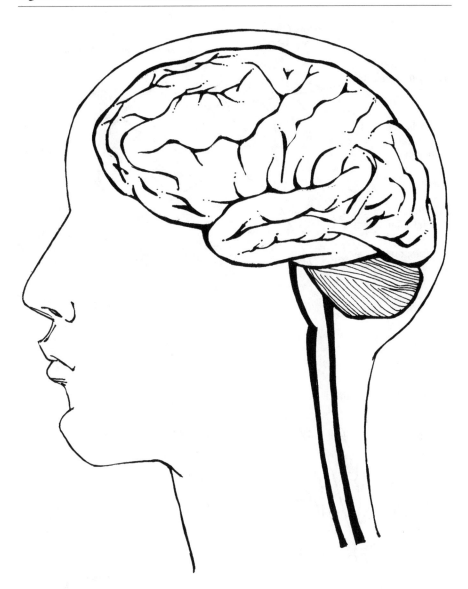

Neurons

Figure 3.3 is a picture of a brain nerve cell (neuron), and Figure 3.4 is a photograph of a neuron magnified 1,000 times. As noted above, we have about 100 billion (100,000,000,000) neurons in our brains.

There are many kinds of neurons, but generically they are the same. They have a body and from the body grow fibers called dendrites, which means "treelike." If you look at deciduous trees in the winter or pull out a bush and look at its roots, you will see for yourself how dendrites look.

Figure 3.2 The Sections of the Brain

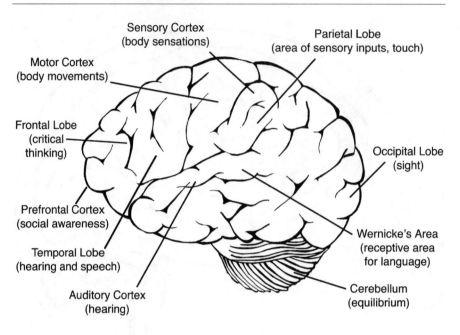

Figure 3.3 A Neuron

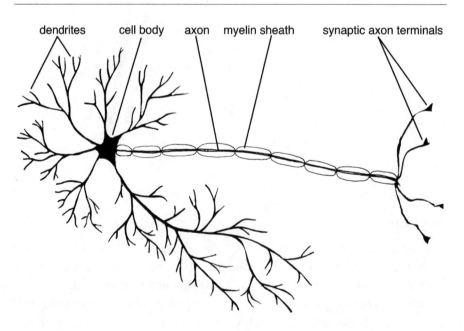

Figure 3.4   Neuron Magnified 1,000 Times

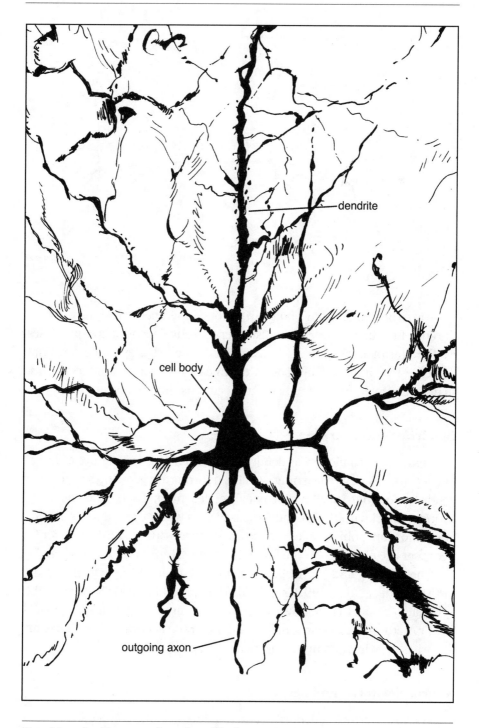

Note: Many dendrites grow from the cell body in every direction.

Figure 3.5 Growing Dendrites = Learning

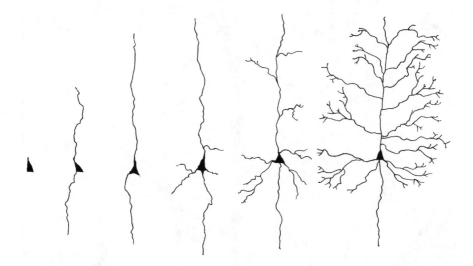

Also from the neuron's body grows one long fiber called the axon. At the end of the axon are dendrite-like fibers called teledendrites or processes. At the end of each process is a tiny bulb, called a synaptic terminal. Synaptic terminals are filled with chemicals (neurotransmitters). These structures are discussed further in the sections that follow.

Dendrites and Learning

Figure 3.5 is a picture of dendrites growing. This is a picture of learning because, as we are learning, specific neurons are growing specific new dendrites for that specific new object of learning. Then other neurons' axons connect with these dendrites, as well as with other neurons' bodies, at connection points called synapses (Figures 3.6A, 3.6B, and 3.6C). Synapses are discussed in the "How the Brain Thinks and Remembers."

The growing and connecting of dendrites *are* learning (e.g., Borklund, 2000; Gopnik et al., 1999; Greenfield, 1997; Restak, 2001; S. Rose, 1992; Sylwester, 1995). In fact, as we feel ourselves learning, instead of saying, "I feel I'm getting it; I'm learning it," we could more accurately say, "I feel my dendrites growing and my synapses connecting."

Neural Networks and Learning

As we are growing dendrites and making synaptic connections—that is, as we are learning—neurons are being connected into networks. In Figure 3.6C, we see several neurons connected in what is called a neural network.

Figure 3.6A Synapses

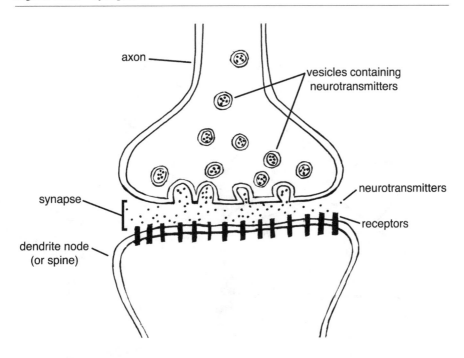

Figure 3.6B Drawing of Single Neuron With Synapses on It

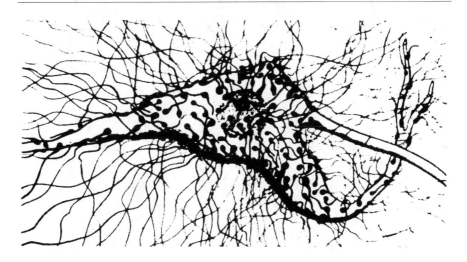

In Figure 3.6C axons from two neurons are approaching another neuron (in the middle). One of these axons is putting a "synaptic terminal" next to one of the "receiver" neuron's dendrites to form a synapse. The other neuron's axon is putting a synaptic terminal next to that same "receiver" neuron's body (soma) to form another synapse. The axon from

Figure 3.6C   Neural Network

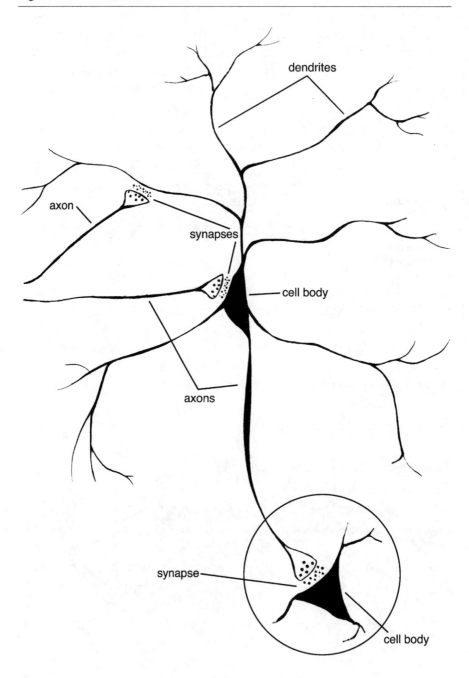

the "receiver" neuron is also moving out to a fourth neuron's soma (at the bottom). These four neurons are now connected in a neural network.

Neural networks can be inconceivably complex and numerous. Again, any one of a person's 100 billion neurons could be connected to as many as 10,000 other neurons. "A square centimeter of the brain's cortex, or outer layer, has a million neurons with over one billion interconnecting fibers, called dendrites" (Johnson & Brown, 1988, p. 39). Furthermore, "the theoretical number of different patterns of connections possible in a single brain is approximately 40,000,000,000,000,000—forty quadrillion" (Ratey, 2001, p. 9). These uncountable networks are interacting or parallel processing: "The 100 billion neurons in the brain all perform operations simultaneously, . . . [in an] enormous tangle of interconnections" (Johnson & Brown, 1988, p. 39). This results from learning, is how we think and remember, and, according to LeDoux (2002), is who we are.

Pruning

We can surmise from the research that one of the rules of how the brain learns is that *dendrites, synapses, and neural networks grow for what is personally, actively, specifically experienced and practiced.* That is, they grow for what is processed (e.g., attended to, explored, experimented with, thought about). However, if these particular structures and connections are not used subsequently, because that skill or idea is not used or practiced, they can be "pruned." That is, the brain apparently is economical: If a dendrite or synapse is not being used for a period of time, it can be eliminated. Thus, we come to a widely acknowledged, well-documented second rule of how the brain learns (and forgets): *use it or lose it.* This and other rules are discussed later in this chapter in "Five Rules of How the Brain Learns."

Experience and Brain Growth

"Researchers have . . . accumulated a substantial amount of data indicating that the brain will grow physiologically if stimulated through interaction with the environment" (Caine & Caine, 1991, p. 28). Marion Diamond (1967, 1988) and other researchers (e.g., Greenough, Black, & Wallace, 1987; Renner & Rosenzweig, 1987) have done numerous experiments with rats, whose neurons are similar to human neurons (Ratey, 2001, p. 22). The researchers have found that rats who live even 2 weeks in what Diamond called an "enriched environment" (with other rats, toys, and mazes) have heavier and larger brains than rats who live in an "impoverished environment" (nonactive, noninteractive). Their brains are bigger because they have more dendrites, a thicker cerebral cortex, more synapses, and more and larger neural networks. The researchers' conclusion is that this disparity in brain structures results from the one variable that is different between the two groups: The rats in the enriched environment have the opportunity to experience a greater amount of activity and interactivity than the rats in the impoverished environment.

Figure 3.7   Convergence of Brain and Natural Learning Research

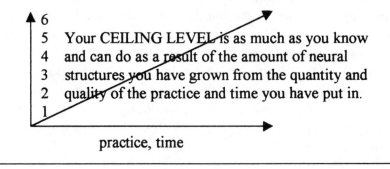

Your CEILING LEVEL is as much as you know and can do as a result of the amount of neural structures you have grown from the quantity and quality of the practice and time you have put in.

practice, time

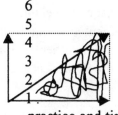

This is as far as you can get with only these few neural structures from only this little amount of practice and time: low ceiling level.

practice and time

This is as far as you can get with more neural structures from more practice and time: higher ceiling level.

practice and time

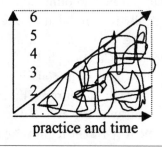

This is as far as you can get with even more neural structures from even better quantity and quality of practice and time: very high ceiling level.

practice and time

Similarly, Jacobs, Schall, and Sheibel (1993), studying human brain tissue, found that "dendritic systems proliferate in response to active interaction with novel and challenging environments" (p. 109).

From a great deal of converging research, it is now taken for fact that activity and interactivity stimulate the brain to grow dendrites, synapses, and neural networks, constituting an increase of knowledge and skill. There is more about increase of brain size and increase of knowledge and skill in the "A Chicken or Egg Question" section later in this chapter.

This research leads to yet another rule of how the brain learns: *dendrites, synapses, and neural networks grow from stimulating experiences.* Chapter 4 looks at what happens when those stimulating or challenging experiences are negative or abusive.

CONVERGENCE OF CEILING LEVELS AND NEURAL NETWORKS

A ceiling level is as much as a person knows and can do. Figure 2.3 in Chapter 2 shows that a learner's ceiling level (knowledge, understanding, skill) rises with more practice and processing (attending to, exploring, experiencing, experimenting with, thinking about an object of learning). Figures 2.9 and 3.7 show the convergence of how people naturally learn. And how the brain naturally learns. Specifically, the learner's ceiling level is rising (the learner's knowledge and skill are increasing) and the learner's dendrites, synapses, and neural networks are growing at the same time. The ceiling level is rising *because* and *as* the brain structures are growing, which is happening *because* and *as* the learner is experiencing, practicing, and processing.

CONSTRUCTIVISM

Jean Piaget (1896–1980), Swiss biologist, child psychologist, and epistemologist, originated the learner-centered theory of learning known as constructivism. Piaget said that learning starts with the infant's complex reflexes, such as sucking, and subsequent learning is constructed stage by stage from those original foundations (Piaget, 1973, p. 66; Piaget & Inhelder, 1969, pp. 7, 16, 20). Gopnik et al. (1999) called this "bootstrapping": "Babies take what they already know and use this as a basis to learn more: they pull themselves up by their own bootstraps" (p. 131). They also compare babies with scientists: "They never start from scratch; instead, they modify and change what they already know to gain new knowledge" (p. 151). Goldblum (2001) took this constructivist view into the classroom:

> [N]o one can learn anything completely new. This means that anything we teach must link up with something that the learner already knows, elaborating it or changing it in some way. Whether we are parents of a young child or teachers of older

children or adults, we must try to figure out what they already know and add the new knowledge to the old. (p. 110)

This statement invokes a constructivist rule of how the brain learns: *new and higher-level neural structures have to connect to or grow from structures (knowledge) already there.* Chapters 6 and 7 show how to help students construct new knowledge—start learning something new—from the knowledge they already have.

Prerequisites

Picture a tree with many delicate twigs high up growing off lower twigs; these twigs grow off branches and those branches grow off the trunk. Just as twigs do not grow out of nothing but only out of a lower twig or branch, each higher level of dendrite and neural network growth, each higher level of knowledge, can grow only from a prerequisite lower level of neural structures, a prerequisite lower level of knowledge. Each higher level of neural growth is the embodiment of a higher and more complex, refined, sophisticated, and in-depth level of understanding and skill than the learner had before.

This is borne out by the research that shows the dendrites farthest away from the cell body—therefore those embodying the most learning, knowledge, and skill—are "remarkably sensitive to environmental influences" (Jacobs et al., 1993, p. 108).

> A particular neural network is the physiological embodiment of the complexity and expanse of a person's understanding about a particular object of learning.

Learning Takes Time and Practice

Apparently for all learners, "[i]n all domains of learning, the development of expertise occurs only with major investments of time . . . [and] a great deal of practice" (Bransford et al., 1999, p. 46).

Julia H. Bonkowski, a faculty member at Ferris State University, told this story about her grandson, D. J., who at age 5 already understood the following:

D. J. is five years old. He is bright, active and curious. A perfume atomizer caught his attention while his mother and I were dressing his four-year-old brother. Suddenly, D. J. grabbed the bottle and ran to the other room. His mother warned him that he could get hurt and that he needed to bring it back to her—pronto! Within seconds we heard a scream followed by frantic crying; D. J.'s footsteps were rapid as he ran back to seek comfort from his mother and me. As grandmother, I hugged him but reminded him of his mother's warning. He rubbed the tears from his stinging eyes and looked straight at me. "But, Nana, I am just a little kid—I have not had time to learn about this yet." It was difficult to keep our composure during this precious, teachable moment. (Personal communication, April 30, 2002)

Learning takes time because it requires growing new dendrites, synapses, and neural networks. These are physical structures and physical structures ordinarily do not grow instantaneously. However, people with an innate aptitude or preference or intelligence (Gardner, 1993; also see Chapter 4) for a skill or subject will need less time and practice than other people to learn how to do or understand that skill or subject (Figures 2.4 and 3.8).

On the other hand, as noted in Chapter 2, any one individual might need different amounts of time and practice to learn different skills and concepts (also Figure 3.8), not only because of different aptitudes for or attitudes about, the different objects of learning but also because of different quantities and qualities of prerequisite neural structures from prior experience.

For example, a student with an aptitude and preference for math might not need much time and practice to understand math concepts well. In contrast, she might need a lot of time and practice to understand literary concepts if she does not have an aptitude for, or a positive attitude about, interpreting literature.

Then again, if it is a powerful emotional experience, a person might never forget it even after only one exposure to it. The amygdala, a small discrete cluster of brain cells deep in the center of the brain, immediately stores this kind of experience and keeps the memory of it for a long time, sometimes for as long as the person lives. Except for those extraordinary experiences, learning takes time and practice.

Prebirth and Infant Learning

Figure 3.9 shows learning over time, from birth to 15 months.

If dendrite growth means learning, what can the fetus have learned before birth to have grown these dendrites? We now know that infants are born having learned the sound of their mother's voice. They have also experienced what it feels like to move their arms, legs, and body in a liquid environment. (After they are born, it will take awhile for them to learn about their new and strange nonliquid environment and how to move

Figure 3. 8   Individual Differences

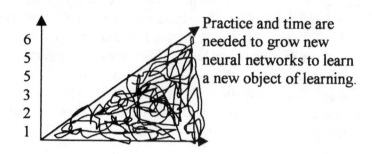

6
5
5
3
2
1

Practice and time are needed to grow new neural networks to learn a new object of learning.

The Model in general

6
5
4
3
2
1

Less practice and time are needed because this person's neural networks grow more quickly for this particular object of learning.
AND this person can learn this skill more easily and quickly than the skill below.

Someone with an aptitude for this skill

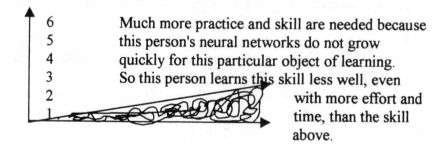

6
5
4
3
2
1

Much more practice and skill are needed because this person's neural networks do not grow quickly for this particular object of learning.
So this person learns this skill less well, even with more effort and time, than the skill above.

Someone who finds this skill difficult to learn

around in it.) Some infants are born sucking their thumb, another skill learned before birth. Perhaps there are even more things they have learned from their in utero experiences that we do not know about yet. By 15 months, however, babies have learned a great deal, that is grown many new dendrites, synapses, and neural networks about this new place, its

Figure 3.9   Learning Over Time

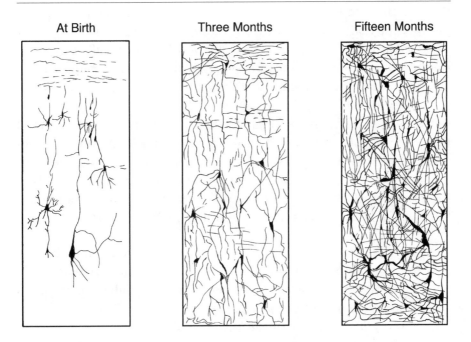

At Birth   Three Months   Fifteen Months

Figure 3.10   Disappearing Dendrites, as in Alzheimer's Disease = Forgetting

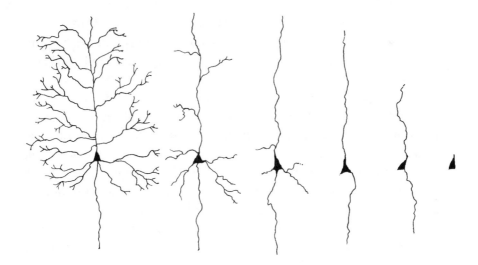

things and people, how it works, and how to negotiate in it (Chapter 2, "Critical and Creative Thinking by Infants and Children").

Alzheimer's Brains

In contrast to growing dendrites when learning, Figure 3.10 shows the loss of well-grown dendrites in Alzheimer's disease.

This loss of dendrites in Alzheimer's disease is caused by "sticky globs that attach themselves . . . to the outside of cells [and then] disrupt the normal functioning of the neuron, setting off a chain of events that destroys the neuron itself" (Restak, 2001, p. 173). The result of the deterioration of neurons' dendrites and synapses in Alzheimer's patients is the deterioration of their thinking abilities and memory: lose dendrites and synapses, lose knowledge and memory.

A study of elderly nuns who had resisted Alzheimer's disease showed that they had more and healthier neural structures than nuns who had succumbed more quickly to the disease. A significant difference between the two groups of nuns is that those who had not succumbed so quickly to the disease had had more intellectually stimulating experiences than those who had succumbed earlier. According to Ratey (2001),

> Snowdon [the author of the nun study] . . . maintains that the axons and dendrites that usually shrink with age branch out and make new connections if there is enough intellectual stimulation, providing a bigger backup system if some pathways fail. . . . [A]ny intellectually challenging activity stimulates dendritic growth, which adds to the neural connections in the brain. (p. 43)

Thus, although the healthier nuns had lost some of their multitudinous neural connections, they did not suffer a great loss of knowledge and skill: more learning, more neural structures, more long-term knowledge and memory.

Snowdon (2001), reporting further on his nun study, wrote that perhaps even more predictive of who will suffer from Alzheimer's disease and who will not is the degree of "high idea density" in their writing. He describes such writing as "vivid, almost poetic, in the way [sentences] link together complex ideas and events" (p. 116). The writing samples in his study were 93 autobiographies written a few days before the nuns, now in their 80s, took their vows 60 or so years earlier. "An amazing 90 percent of the women with Alzheimer's disease had low idea density in their autobiographies, as compared to only 13 percent of the healthy sisters" (p. 114).

HOW THE BRAIN THINKS AND REMEMBERS

The previous section focused on learning and on dendrites growing, synapses forming, and neural networks being constructed. This section focuses on thinking and remembering, which happen when the brain communicates with itself through the synapses and synapse-connected neural networks.

Figure 3.11 Neural-Chemical Ion Channels in the Axon

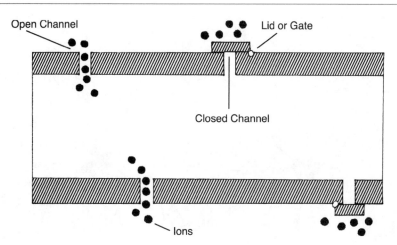

Synapses

Here is a step-by-step description of how synapses work, how neurons communicate with each other, and how we think and remember. Even if we do not understand how the brain knows what to do and how to do it, this is, as far as we know, the way it does it.

1. The brain is stimulated by something. It could be a sensory experience like light on the eye or sound in the ear or something touched. Or it could be a stimulating emotional, intellectual, physical, spiritual, aesthetic experience—any sort of experience, including, importantly, the stimulation of interacting with others.

2. Specific neurons are stimulated by different experiences. For example, if it is a visual experience, neurons at the back of the brain in the visual cortex or occipital lobe (see Figure 3.2) will be stimulated.

3. A neuron, when stimulated, causes its body or axon, which is a tube, to open up portals called "ion channels" in its sides (see Figure 3.11).

4. There are chemicals, including sodium and calcium, in the natural fluids in the brain. When the ion channels open, the right amount of the right chemicals enters the neuron and interacts with the potassium inside the neuron. The resulting chemical reaction creates an electrical current called an action potential.

Figure 3.12   Electrical-Chemical Communication at a Synapse

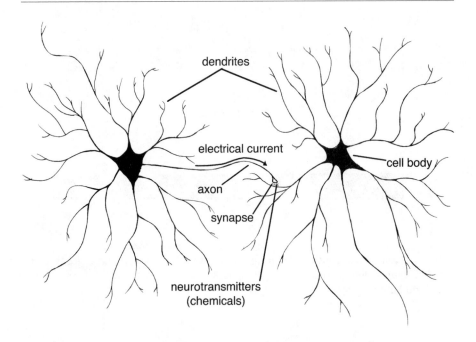

5. This electrical current then speeds down the axon tube to the synaptic terminal(s). The speed of transmission depends on whether a fatty material, myelin, is coating the axon. Some believe myelination occurs from practice or frequent use of a particular connection between neurons: the more practice, the more myelin, the speedier and more automatic the action. With myelination, the "effortless rapidity of our brain processes and our movements can be explained by the speed of nerve conduction, up to approximately 220 miles per hour!" (Greenfield, 1997, p. 73). Certain diseases, however, such as multiple sclerosis, cause the myelin sheath to deteriorate, resulting in less-efficient communication between neurons (Greenfield, pp. 72–73).

6. One axon might have many synaptic terminals, which means it can form synapses with many neurons at the same time. During the learning process, just the right terminal moves next to just the right receiving dendrite or body of just the right other neuron to form the synapse.

7. When the electrical current reaches just the right axon terminal, it causes the terminal bulb at its end to release just the right amount of just the right chemicals (neurotransmitters) into the tiny synaptic space between it and the receiving dendrite or body (Figure 3.12). This is the first thing that happens at a synapse between two neurons.

8. Then these chemicals move across the synaptic space and stimulate the receiver neuron's dendrite or body. This is the second thing that happens at a synapse. "Synaptic firing" is the name for the double action in a synapse of (a) neurotransmitter release by the sender neuron and (b) stimulation by the neurotransmitters of the receiver neuron.

9. When the synapse fires, neurons are communicating, which causes thinking and remembering. These chemical–electrical actions and reactions (Figures 3.12 and 3.13) can rush through the hundreds or thousands—perhaps even as many as 10,000 or more—neurons in one network at about 220 miles per hour or in "milliseconds to seconds" (Sylwester, 1995, p. 447). Additionally, the more times those particular synapses fire, the more new synapses will appear, making the remembering and thinking about and use of that skill, concept, or body of knowledge even faster, more automatic, more natural. Myelination would also be occurring during these activities.

The Brain Knows What to Grow and Where

Fortunately, to learn something new—to acquire new or better knowledge and skill—we do not consciously have to decide which neurons' dendrites to grow and how many and how long or which synapses we need to form to connect which neurons with which other neurons. Neuroscientists say they do not know how the brain knows how to make these unimaginably complex decisions; but the brain, not the conscious mind, knows what to do and how to do it. (One of the major topics of investigation and discussion among brain researchers continues to be what the conscious mind is and how the brain and mind interact, e.g., Damasio, 1999; Eccles & Robinson, 1984; Goldblum, 2001; Hunt, 1982; LeDoux, 2002; Ornstein, 1991; Vedantum, 2002).

Nourishing the Brain

The brain is less than 3% of the body's weight. However, it uses 20% of the body's energy or fuel. There are two sources of this energy or fuel: the glucose in the carbohydrates we eat in food and the oxygen we breathe in from the air and drink in water. It burns this energy "at ten times the rate of all other body tissues at rest" (Greenfield, 1997, p. 27). The brain needs this disproportionate amount of the body's fuel because it is the hardest-working organ in the body. Moreover, when it is working especially hard, as when solving a problem or doing a complex critical- or creative-thinking activity, it uses even more energy and fuel.

Figure 3.13   Synaptic Firing

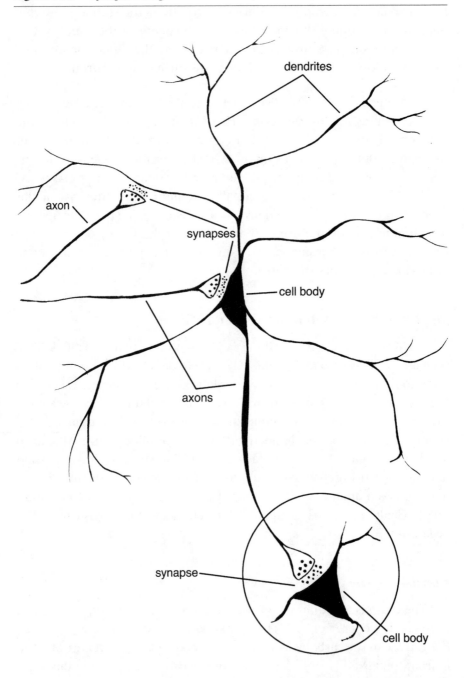

It is essential, then, that we ingest enough glucose and water to provide the energy the brain needs to work well. Exercising is another way to increase our intake of oxygen. We also need certain vitamins and chemicals, for example calcium, sodium, and potassium, which are essential for synaptic firing. Moreover, "[o]ur brain craves nutrients based on its evolutionary history, such as fruits, vegetables, nuts, legumes, lean meat, eggs, fish, and shellfish" (Carper, 2000, p. 42).

THE BRAIN'S INNATE RESOURCES AND RULES

The brain's innate abilities and processes, discussed in Chapter 2, constitute the brain's innate resources for learning.

The Brain's Innate Resources

- The brain has a natural learning process.
- The brain has an innate sense of logic.
- The brain is an innate pattern seeker.
- The brain is an innate problem solver.
- The brain is innately imaginative and creative (can see in new ways).
- The brain is innately motivated to learn.

> Curricula that give students the opportunity to use their brains' innate resources give them the opportunity to be the natural learners they were born to be.

Five Rules of How the Brain Learns

Four of these rules were introduced earlier and are explained in more detail here; the fifth rule is discussed in Chapter 4.

1. Dendrites, synapses, and neural networks grow only from what is already there. We learn by connecting new learning to something we already know and then constructing new levels of neural/knowledge structures, level by level, twig by twig, from that prerequisite foundation. Thus, to teach or learn something new, we must always start with something familiar as the foundation from which to construct the next level of knowledge or skill. Chapter 6 discusses and illustrates how to start each piece of curriculum or each lesson plan with such a foundation.

2. Dendrites, synapses, and neural networks grow for what is actively, personally, and specifically experienced and practiced. As people actively practice an object of learning, they get better at what they are practicing because their brains are growing more dendrites, synapses, and neural networks for that specific object of learning. The larger the networks get, the more naturally and automatically they can think about, remember, and use that object of learning. Unfortunately, in the same way, if an experience is negative or abusive and it is repeated—practiced—often enough, that network will get stronger; and learners will become better at (become more and more accustomed to) being abused (discussed in Chapter 4).

3. *Dendrites, synapses, and neural networks grow from stimulating experiences.* Because learning, thinking, and remembering are active physiological, chemical, electrical phenomena, stimulation is needed to arouse the brain to grow new neural structures and fire synapses. For example, a stimulating experience would be processing with others, as when getting and giving feedback about an object of learning. Stimulating experiences also arouse the brain to use its innate resources, that is its impulsion to seek patterns, solve problems, and understand how the world works and how to make it work. These are activities that cause neural structures to grow and connect. And, again, even negative and abusive experiences are stimulating because they impel us to see how that abusive world works and how to act and survive in it.

4. *Use it or lose it.* If people stop doing something that they had previously learned, even if it is enjoyable or useful, after a while they might, because of neural pruning, forget some or all of it:

a.   A boy takes skiing lessons for 3months when he is 8 and then does not ski again for 10 years. He might have to start over again from the beginning because he will probably have lost the small amount of dendrites, synapses, and neural networks he had grown in those earlier few months. As noted above, the brain prunes structures that are not being used.

b.   A girl rides her bike every day from the age of 8 until she goes to college 10 years later and then does not ride a bike for the next 10 years. She might have trouble starting again after that hiatus, but it will not take long before she recovers her skill because she will not have totally lost the vast volume of dendrites, synapses, and neural networks she had previously grown. Although the brain prunes unused structures, when those structures are vast and deeply embedded from years of constant use, pruning will have less of an effect.

c.   A student takes a first-level math course during the spring term and does not think about math all summer. The following fall, in the second-level math course, she cannot remember everything she knew from the previous spring term.

d.   A young man who had been emotionally abused as a child is always repeating, as negative self-talk, what his alcoholic father had told him, that he is stupid, a loser, worthless. But the young man, seeking help, joins a therapy group. In this group, he comes to understand where his negative self-image and self-talk came from and that, by understanding and using the "use it or lose it" rule, he can lose that negative network by not repeating its negative words, by rejecting them. He also starts to practice positive self-talk in order to grow a new, positive neural network. The more he practices the positive self-talk and ignores and rejects the negative talk, the stronger the positive network will grow and the weaker the negative one will become, perhaps atrophying altogether over time. Chapter 4, "Negative and Positive Self-Image Networks," explains this phenomenon further.

5. *Emotions affect learning* (explained in Chapter 4).

Chapters 6 through 9 present a method for creating curricula that comprise these rules. The result is that teachers can make it possible for their students to be motivated and successful learners in every classroom.

CHILDREN'S BRAINS AND ADULTS' BRAINS

Recently I was working with a sixth-grade class. First we did the natural human learning process (NHLP) activity (Chapter 2, Figure 2.8, Sixth-Grade Class 1). Then I showed them pictures of the brain, and we talked about how the brain learns. I said to them, "Your brains are no different from the brains of adults in the way you learn. You are just as capable of learning as adults are. The only difference is that adults have lived a longer time and, because of that, have had more opportunities to learn from more experiences. This means they have grown and connected more dendrites and synapses so they know more. That's the only difference. Your brains want to learn, know how to learn, and are, in fact, learning all the time, just like adults' brains."

A strange thing happened as I spoke to them. I began seeing them as I had just described, as small beings with adultlike brains eager and ready to learn, but not yet having had the time and opportunity to grow and connect as many dendrites, synapses, and neural networks as adults. So, of course, they knew less.

They seemed transfixed by what they had been hearing about how the brain learns; they were intensely attentive and alert. When some of them came up afterward to ask more questions, I looked down at their faces and saw their intelligence and intellectual excitement. I had theorized before that the child's brain is similar to the adult's brain in its nature and capabilities, but now I really knew it.

The Brain Is a Work in Progress

The brain of a child must grow trillions of dendrites on, and synapses between, billions of neurons to learn about the world, what is going on in it, how it works. This includes learning about life, self, other, language, communication (verbal and nonverbal), cause and effect, things, quantity, emotions, social interaction, ad infinitum. Everything. The child does this from personal experience.

The child's brain, apparently operating with the same power as the adult brain, grows dendrites, new ones constructed on prerequisite ones. Over time this learning produces a brain filled with networks that are complexly interrelated.

We are seeing a work in progress when we watch a child negotiate the world, trying to see how to be empowered in it, feeling, acting, reacting, interacting, communicating, playing, trying to figure something out, or solving a puzzle at the level of network growth the child has thus far achieved.

If these learning drives and capabilities seem to disappear when children get older, it is only because the children are somehow prevented from enjoying them. If they seem to disappear in school, while the students, young or old, are learning with interest and motivation outside school, perhaps there is a lack of opportunity in the classroom to use their innate resources and some of the brain's rules for learning, to think, explore, experiment—in short, to be the natural and naturally motivated learners they were born to be.

A CHICKEN OR EGG QUESTION

As Bransford et al. (1999) described it, one view of learning is that children's brains have less memory and mental space than adults' brains and, therefore, children cannot remember as much and cannot think as well or as complexly. "A second view is that children and adults have roughly the same mental capacity, but that with development children acquire knowledge and develop effective activities to use their minds well" (p. 84).

The Biological Clock

Some neuroscientists believe the brain grows according to a biological clock. They believe, for example, that the prefrontal cortex grows large enough to be capable of thinking and feeling more maturely only at or approaching adolescence. The prefrontal cortex (the surface of the frontal lobe, Figure 3.2) is the location of the "ability to delay gratification and to act on the basis of complex understanding and with compassion and empathy" and the ability to think, plan, and act realistically and responsibly (Caine & Caine, 1997, pp. 60–61).

Growth Spurts

Robert Thatcher, University of Maryland neuroscientist, and Bill Hudspeth, Colorado State University neuropsychologist, used a computerized brain-wave technology (neurometric analysis) to measure synapses in the brains of children in both the United States and Sweden. They found that, in both groups, there were five age-related growth spurts or stages in the brain from birth upward. Thatcher said, "Different parts of a child's brain turn on at different times [and each spurt] is marked by a sudden proliferation of connections between brain cells" (in Schwarz, 1988, p. 5). Moreover, according to Thatcher, "[t]hese brain stages . . . correspond to Piaget's famous cognitive stages" (Schwarz, 1988, p. 5). Thus, their view is that a biological clock causes the brain to start growing and connecting dendrites and synapses at certain approximate ages.

Effect on Curriculum of the Biological Clock Theory

Belief in the biological clock leads to the "dumbing down" of curricula for young students—not providing them with activities that would challenge them to use their innate pattern-seeking, problem-solving, logical thinking, and creative capabilities. Given the opportunity to explore, experiment, discover, and create, they would be challenged to make sense of their world, to learn how the world works, and to see how to make it work for them. Such opportunities also would naturally motivate them and gain and keep their attention. However, teachers who believe children are not yet capable of these higher-level mental operations do not provide opportunities for students to use their brains' innate resources and rules. This can thwart students' readiness and eagerness to learn. Depending on personality and family or cultural expectations about, and socialization for, school, students in this situation might be obedient, bored, lazy, apathetic, or rebellious.

Constructivist Learning

An alternative to the biological-maturation view is that the prefrontal cortex grows larger not as a result of biological maturation but—also, or perhaps only—as a result of learning from one's experiences, that is from having the opportunity and time to construct more neural networks, which add volume and weight to portions of the brain.

Ornstein and Thompson (1984), reviewing Diamond's seminal research with rats in enriched and impoverished environments (1967), describe in constructivist terms what she found:

> An analysis of the [rats'] brain growth showed that specific changes in the brain took place in the dendrites of each nerve cell, which thickens with stimulating experiences. It is as if the forest of nerve cells became literally enriched, and the density of the branches increased; this is what produced a bigger brain. (p. 167)

Thus, the constructivist view is that when children are exploring, experimenting, making their own discoveries, as they are innately impelled to do, their neural structures are growing and connecting. These physical structures *are* the new higher-level knowledge and skill they are acquiring, and these new knowledge-related physical structures are what make their brains increase in volume, no matter what the child's age.

According to this view, the critical factor is the time it takes a child to have enough experiences to grow enough connections between brain cells to make the brain observably heavier and bigger. If the critical factor is time, it might explain why there are observable increases in the volume and weight of structures (dendrites and synapses), or "brain spurts," occurring at similar approximate ages.

Does a biological clock cause the brain to turn on and suddenly grow new structures (out of what? how?) for new learning? Or do the structures, which grow as a result of experience, finally reach a large enough or critical mass to then be observed as constituting a bigger brain? With a larger mass of experience-based structures, the brain would not only increase its volume, it would also attain a higher level of knowledge and skill. Furthermore, the learner would now have a larger mass of neural foundations (knowledge, understanding, and skill) on which to construct new neural structures (new learning) at a higher level.

Research using brain-scan investigations to compare the responses to single-word cues by children and adults shows that

> [a]dults displayed greater activity than children did in a section of the frontal cortex, indicating the use of a more complex thought process. . . . The researchers[, however,] couldn't discern from these brain scans whether the observed changes . . . stem from specific physical changes that occur in brain maturation or from a general superiority in word knowledge among adults. (Bower, 2002, p. 326)

A "general superiority in word knowledge among adults" could be the result of adults having had more learning from more experiences over more time than children.

As yet there is no definitive answer to the question about whether it is maturation, as a result of the ticking of a biological clock, or experience that causes observable changes in the brain.

Or Is It the Genes?

Some believe genes control the size of the brain, when it grows, and how much. Plomin and Kosslyn (2001), reviewing research on the influence of genes on the brain's structures, reported that the volume of the gray matter (the neural cell bodies) seems to be genetically controlled. On the other hand, the white matter, which consists of the connections between neurons, "might be expected to differ among individuals as a result of experience" (p. 1153).

Allman (1989) also saw experience rather than genes as the producer of connections between neurons and, hence, the size of the brain or portions of it:

[I]n the human brain, the number of synaptic connections is millions of times greater than the number of human genes. It is virtually impossible for genes to encode the entire wiring diagram of a human brain—or even those of less brainy animals. One particular species of tropical fish, for example, reproduces by cloning; that is, each fish makes an identical copy of itself. Though a cloned pair of fish have exactly the same genes, no two of them have the same synaptic connection pattern in their brains.

If the genes don't direct the wiring of all the synapses, what does? It appears that for many connections between neurons the architect is experience. (pp. 67–68)

Caine and Caine (1997) presented a holistic perspective: "[N]either inherited characteristics nor the environment can ever be the sole determinant of development and behavior. . . . [because] our biologically growing brain . . . builds new connections based on what we experience" (p. 29).

Gopnik et al. (1999) also maintained a holistic view, believing "nature and nurture are inseparably intertwined" and explained that their "innate endowments enable babies to use their powerful learning mechanisms to take advantage of the information they receive from [their environment]" (p. 131).

Growing Up

Furthermore, by the learner-centered constructivist view, the more opportunities young people have to experience and learn from situations in which they are asked, or need, to make and carry out responsible, realistic decisions and plans (prefrontal cortex activities), the more their prefrontal cortex dendrites and synapses grow, causing their prefrontal cortex to increase in volume and weight. In this view, both their prefrontal cortex growth and their more mature thinking and feeling depend on their having prefrontal cortex-types of learning experiences.

The quality and quantity of these types of experiences affect how quickly young people become able to think and behave more maturely, more responsibly, and more wisely.

This view leads not to "dumbing down" curricula but, instead, to developing curricula that appropriately challenge young students to do prefrontal cortex types of activities, such as solving problems, making decisions, and being responsible. Would young people be more responsible and have good judgment sooner if they had the kinds of experiences from which they could learn to be these ways? Perhaps one day, with cross-age, cross-experiential research, we will have an answer to this question.

PLASTICITY

As a result of our experiences, our brains grow dendrites, form synapses, arrange and rearrange where the axons connect, and eliminate (prune) unused connections. All this happens because of what is commonly called the brain's plasticity.

> The neuron and its thousands of neighbors send out roots and branches—the axons and dendrites—in all directions, which intertwine to form an interconnected tangle with 100 trillion constantly changing connections. . . . The connections guide our bodies and behaviors, even as every thought and action we take physically modifies their patterns. (Ratey, 2001, p. 20)

> "Learning changes the structure of the brain. . . . These structural changes alter the functional organization of the brain; in other words, learning organizes and reorganizes the brain" (Bransford et al., 1999, p. 103).

Some day we might be able to look at people's neural networks and see what experiences they had that produced their particular neural patterns.

Figure 3.14 Neural Networks and Grading

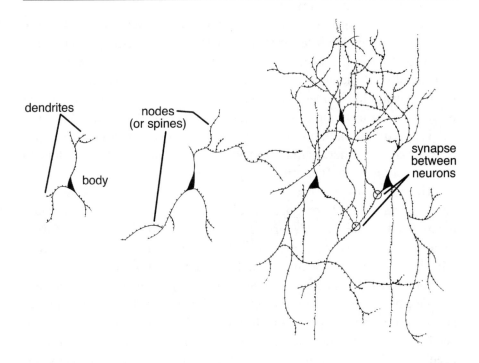

Until then, however, we do know that experience causes the brain to adapt and modify and does have a physical effect on—is physiologically actualized in—the brain, causing us to think, feel, act, and react as we do.

In the next chapter, the sections "Negative and Positive Self-Image Networks" (page 87) and "Our Cultural Experience and Our Eyes" (page 91) take this issue a step further.

NEURAL NETWORKS AND GRADING: NOT JUDGING A BOOK BY ITS COVER

Figure 3.14 shows what happens in school. The neural network at the right of the figure represents the body of knowledge and the skills the teacher has as the goals or objectives for a unit, course, or program. The teacher's curriculum is designed to facilitate students growing those particular networks, that is, learning that body of knowledge and those skills. The neurons at the left and in the middle represent two students coming into the class with different levels of knowledge and skill.

We can see that the relevant neuron of the student in the middle has long enough dendrites from relevant and sufficient prior experiences to be almost "catching on" to the higher level of knowledge and skill (the more complex neural network) that is the curricular goal. With a bit of time and practice, this student literally will physiologically "catch on" (grow the new neural structures at the next and higher level).

The relevant neuron of the student at the left, however, comes into the class with so few dendrites, from insufficient prior learning experiences, that this student will experience the new material as "over my head"— literally, physiologically "over my dendrite level." The goal of the course is too far beyond this student's current neural level for the student to catch on with the same amount of time and practice that the prepared student needs in order to catch on. As a result, the prepared student might get an A in the course, whereas the underprepared student might not be able to do better than a C or D or might simply drop out.

The grade, however, does not necessarily mean one student is less intelligent or less talented or a poorer student than the other student. It could mean that one student is "dendrite disadvantaged" from lack of opportunity to have acquired the prerequisite foundation for this course or subject. The other student, in contrast, might simply be "dendrite advantaged" from having had more germane foundational learning experiences rather than simply being more intelligent or more talented than the underprepared student. See the discussion in Chapter 4 regarding standardized tests and the uneven playing fields from which students arrive at the same classroom. Also, we need to take into account the effect of emotions on a student's behavior, attitude, and performance, as discussed here and in Chapter 4.

With all these variations of influences on students, both internally and externally, we cannot judge students' potential by their products or grades. By developing and delivering curricula that give all of them the opportunity to learn by their brains' natural learning process, we can make it more possible for all students to realize and fulfill their potential.

WHAT ABOUT PIAGET?

Piaget, who focused on children's thinking and learning, has been one of the most influential contributors to the field of educational psychology.

Some of Piaget's Contributions

- He founded the field of cognitive development, specifically the study of children's thinking.
- He made "more important empirical discoveries, on a wide range of topics, than any other developmental psychologist, and he is not likely to be displaced from this lofty seat of honor soon. . . . [He also] asked important questions and drew literally thousands of researchers to the study of cognitive development" (Borklund, 2000, p. 100).

- He believed children are intrinsically active and self-motivated to construct their own knowledge, to think, and to learn: "Children should be able to do their own experimenting and their own research. Teachers, of course, can guide them by providing appropriate materials, but the essential thing is that in order for a child to understand something, he must construct it for himself; he must reinvent it" (Piaget, 1973, p. 27). Piaget observed that although repetitive practice can train children to give correct answers, this kind of teaching does not help the students "form an intellectual instrument, a logic required to [reach the correct answer]" (p. 8).

- He believed cognitive development is stage-based. He posited three major stages of development (the second stage comprised of two sub-stages) related to approximate ages and believed that all children develop by all these same four stages in this same unvarying order of stages–but not necessarily at the same ages because each child might need a different amount of time to acquire enough understanding to move to the next stage of development.

- He was a constructivist who believed development "proceeds gradually, with later developments being based on earlier developments" (Bjorkland, p. 79), specifically that new learning is constructed on or grows cumulatively from previous understanding: "The [conceptual] structures constructed at a given age become an integral part of the structure of the following age" (Piaget, 1973, p. 51). In his description of the construction of understanding, he seemed to anticipate what later research saw as the physiology of learning and development, as the growing, branching, extending of neural networks: "Each of these [periods of mental development] extends the preceding period, reconstructs it on a new level, and later surpasses it to an ever greater degree" (Piaget & Inhelder, 1969, p. 152).

Piaget's Three Stages of Development

Piaget and Inhelder (1969, pp. 6–12) described the following three stages of development:

1. The first stage, the *sensorimotor* stage, is from birth to about 2 years of age. During this period, babies learn from interacting with their environment.

2. Piaget saw the second stage as comprising two substages:

   a. The *preoperational* stage is from about 2 to 7 or 8 years. Children can use language and other symbolic modes to think about objects not in their immediate environment.

b. The *concrete operational* stage is from about 7 or 8 to 11 or 12 years. Children can begin to think logically about concrete objects and phenomena "placed on the table or immediately represented" (Piaget, 1973, p. 60).

3. The third stage, called the *formal operational* stage, takes place from about 11 or 12 to 13 or 14 years. Older children and young adolescents can think abstractly and logically, having "the capacity to study statements and propositions" and not just concrete objects or phenomena (Piaget, 1973, p. 60).

Piaget Today

Piaget believed that even toward the end of the sensorimotor stage, at about 2 years of age, children have the ability to do abstract thinking about what they have experienced. "In this stage the child becomes capable of finding new means not only by external or physical groping but also by internalized combinations that culminate [after prior experiences] in sudden comprehension or *insight*" (Piaget & Inhelder, 1969, p. 12).

Although it might be difficult to prove that infants have "sudden comprehension or *insight*" when they are learning, recent research (Chapter 2) seems to show, even as Piaget believed, that infants are thinking abstractly. For example, when Piaget was asked why it takes about 18 months for infants to learn to speak, he answered,

> Our reply is that speech is bound up with thought and thus supposes a system of interiorized action . . . no longer carried out materially but from within and symbolically. . . . A long practice of pure action is needed to construct the substructure of later speech. (1973, pp. 12–13)

Some curricula, however, might underestimate young children and, in a mistaken attempt to accommodate their assumed low thinking ability, not address their natural ability to do abstract thinking.

Similarly, some educators underestimate the thinking abilities of English-as-a-second-language (ESL) learners and also of developmental (formerly called remedial) or underprepared college or precollege students. This underestimation, again, can lead to "dumbing down" a curriculum (e.g., Martinez & Martinez, 1987; Reynolds, 1986; M. Rose, 1995) and not giving students the opportunity to do the kind of thinking of which they are capable—and would enjoy doing.

Figure 3.15 Convergence of Stages

	PIAGET'S SENSORIMOTOR SUBSTAGES	NATURAL HUMAN LEARNING PROCESS STAGES
	Learning from Birth to Two Years	**Learning Any New Skill or Concept at Any Age**
	Motivation	
1	Reflexive response to external events	Response to stimulus, practice starts at a basic level
	Beginning Practice	
2	Habits formed by repeated cycles of activity	Practice, practice, practice
	Advanced Practice	
3	Beginning of coordination, means-end function clearer	More practice, increase of skill and confidence
	Skillfulness	
4	Purposeful use of means to achieve ends more effectively, combining old means in new ways to get new ends	Doing it one's own way, creativity
	Refinement	
5	Exploration and discovery of new means by groping to achieve ends more effectively	Further improvements, learning new methods, creativity, independence
	Mastery	
6	Comprehension, finding new means by using the mind (not physical groping)	Full understanding, increased creativity

Note: See also Figures 2.5 through 2.9.

Piaget and the NHLP

Piaget further posited six subperiods in the sensorimotor period. These are essentially the same as the six stages of the NHLP as self-reported by almost 5,000 people (Figure 3.15). Specifically, this NHLP research on how people, young and old, learn a specific skill or concept, from starting to learn it, through four to six stages, to mastering it, converges with Piaget's research on how babies learn through those subperiods from birth to 2 years. Both Piaget's and the NHLP's approaches to the development of knowledge and skill propose that learning, up to and including thinking abstractly, progresses through a sequence of stages or levels of development, each new or higher one constructed on the previous or lower one.

A THEORY OF LEARNING

When two epistemological approaches—Piaget's observation of individual children doing specific tasks and the NHLP self-reports of children and adults—arrive at similar descriptions of the stages of the development of knowledge, it seems to justify a degree of confidence in their convergent findings. If we hypothesize that a learning process reported by thousands of learners of different ages and similarly observed by Piaget is actually how the brain naturally learns, then we would have a rational basis for a theory of learning and, based on that, a method for developing curricula and selecting instructional strategies (Chapters 6 and 7).

This book proposes such a brain-based, natural-learning theory and, from that, a method for developing and delivering curricula that give students the opportunity to use their brains' natural learning process. When students have this opportunity, they are the eager, successful, natural learners they were born to be. Later chapters focus on developing and delivering brain-based, natural-learning curricula for any subject at any level.

GLIAL CELLS

New research findings are beginning to surface on the role of glial cells in learning. However, it is too soon yet to tell how valuable this new and forthcoming research will be regarding teaching and learning.

Personal Experience, Individual Differences, and Learning

4

EMOTIONS AND THE BRAIN

Someone is about to step in front of your moving car. Your heart instantly starts pounding faster and your foot slams on the brake. What happened is that your brain, seeing the danger, sent an immediate message to the adrenal gland, which instantaneously shot adrenaline into your brain and caused those emotional–physical reactions. No conscious thinking, just quick and excellent teamwork.

The Fight or Flight Response

These kinds of reactions happen because certain organs in the body, including the brain, produce chemicals in emotional situations. The emotionally produced chemicals instantly flood into just the right synaptic gaps to affect the workings of the brain and also the body, which the brain largely controls.

If we are feeling fear or anxiety because a situation seems too dangerous for us to handle, chemicals will shoot into specific synaptic gaps and stop the flow of the thinking and remembering neurotransmitters. As a result, we stop thinking and focus all our attention and energy on an immediate action, like slamming the brake or running away. Our brain, our survival organ, impelled to see patterns and solve problems, has figured out how to survive in a threatening environment. This is the flight response that no doubt saved some of our ancestors from the saber-toothed cats. Sometimes the fear chemicals might be such that we cannot even move. Perhaps this saved a few ancestors from a predator who suddenly appeared at their cave door while they cowered in the dark immobilized by fear.

Students come into the classroom to take a test. They have studied a great deal, have practiced and worked with the skills and concepts and, thus, have a good neural network for the material. But as soon as they sit down, their brains go blank. They might believe they have bad memories. But if they have grown the dendrites and synapses and have constructed neural networks, then their memories are all there as physiological structures that do not simply disappear this quickly. What has happened is that chemicals produced by anxiety (perhaps about not being able to succeed) have invaded their synaptic spaces and sabotaged their brains' ability to think and remember. They cannot flee from the room; so, instead, they sit immobilized, unable to think and remember.

Alternatively, if students come into the test feeling curious, confident, and up for the challenge, then different chemicals flow into the synaptic spaces, causing their brains to think and remember quickly and easily. This is the so-called fight response: It makes people focus, pay attention, concentrate, marshal their forces, and get down to business to meet the challenge.

Thus, we can identify a fifth rule of the brain:

- *Emotions affect learning.* Emotions produce chemicals that enter the brain and physiologically affect the synapses and, consequently, the brain's ability to think, learn, and remember. Thus, emotions and thinking, learning, and remembering are inextricably bound together.

Safety in the Classroom

Making the classroom an emotionally positive place, particularly a place of respect and safety, is not just being nice or "touchy-feely." It is imperative to do this because emotions powerfully affect how we learn, think, and remember. For example, Mike Rose (1995), after a 4-year journey through America's public school classrooms, reported that students are more motivated and successful in classrooms in which they feel respected and safe (pp. 413–414).

Research by Dean Shibata, MD, at the University of Washington "implies we're [even] drawing on emotions when we're making [decisions,] even fairly trivial decisions" (in Mestel, 2001, p. 2).

It is imperative for educators and students—for everyone—to know about the emotions' physiological effect on the brain and what we can do to mitigate or eliminate fear-based emotions and generate confidence-based ones. For example, an antidote for the flight response is to learn how to do relaxing and breathing exercises. Even more important, though, is the information presented here about how emotions affect the brain. When students have this metacognitive knowledge, they are empowered to turn a flight response into a fight response so they can be successful.

NEGATIVE AND POSITIVE SELF-IMAGE NETWORKS

Threats to the Brain's Plasticity

As mentioned in Chapter 3, if students' brains have constructed a network resulting from negative experiences, then they can be in trouble. For example, a child has a dysfunctional parent who repeatedly tells her she cannot do anything right and constantly criticizes, punishes, and humiliates her. Accordingly, the child learns these things about herself, which means that, because of the constant repetition of these negative words and experiences, her brain has constructed a large, well-developed neural network embodying her understanding that she is a failure.

Students, young or old, without help to change such a pattern, are its victims because a powerful, constantly activated, pervasive network like this can obviate the brain's plasticity. These students might not even be conscious of their internalized negative image. Therefore, when they go to school with this negative network active in their brains, they will be failures—or troublemakers if they prefer to be seen as bad rather than failures—even if their brains are otherwise fully capable of learning. On the other hand, students who are conscious of their negative self-image might practice self-defeating inner talk: "I'm so stupid. I don't belong here. I'll never be able to succeed."

The more a negative network is activated, the stronger this conscious or unconscious self-fulfilling prophecy becomes. According to a rule of the brain, we learn what we practice; the more we practice, the better we get at what we are practicing.

If, to the contrary, a strong, constantly activated network is positive, filling the person with confidence and self-esteem, that person will have a powerful ally against negative experiences and will be more able to rebound, land on his or her feet, and go forward.

The problem, however, is that when a person has become habituated to a self-image network, whether negative or positive, the person is less likely to be sensitive and responsive to and able to learn from new and different experiences. The overconfident as much as the underconfident person is liable to make mistakes about reality because of the blindness caused by these fossilized or "cast-in-concrete" networks.

A Rule of the Brain Can Help

However, there is help in another rule of the brain: use it or lose it. This rule can be used to weaken, or perhaps even eliminate, fossilized neural networks. If students learn how the brain works, they will know that a negative self-image is just a network of dendrites and synapses in their brains. Their negative thoughts are not about reality. The reality is that they are natural-born learners. They will not be able to deny this if their teacher has introduced them to the natural-learning-process activity described in Chapter 2. Then, if they know the "use it or lose it" rule, they can say to themselves every time the negative network starts talking to them, "Shut up. I'm not going to listen to you. You're just a bunch of dendrites and neural networks that someone else put in my brain, and you're not telling me the truth. I *am* smart. I *can* learn. I'm a natural-born learner. If I don't listen to you, you'll go away."

By telling themselves—and believing—they are capable of academic success, they will start growing new dendrites and synapses to form a new neural network of confidence, self-esteem, and self-efficacy. Moreover, the more success they experience (as they will with NHLP curricula), and the more they remind themselves of their positive qualities, the stronger the new positive network will become and the weaker and less persistent the negative network will be, eventually growing weaker and perhaps even disappearing altogether over time.

SELF-IMAGE AND SELF-CONFIDENCE

Being Cared About

The AVID system (Advancement Via Individual Determination) was developed in the early 1980s and is now being used in more than 1,200 schools in 21 states. The AVID system is predicated on a relationship between self-image, self-confidence, and success. AVID teachers focus on person-to-person interaction and give unsuccessful and apparently unmotivated students personal and caring attention, intense tutoring, and support. Through this focus, they help students move from a negative to a positive self-image and, hence, to self-confidence and academic success, with many progressing from failure in public school to graduating from college (Freedman, 2000).

Similarly, James Anderson (1988, 1992), who has researched and written about African American students' personal and academic experiences, has found that if even one adult takes a personal interest in a child, it can have a positive effect on the child's self-image and future success.

On June 24, 1998, ABC network's *Nightline* program aired "Cedric's Journey" about a young African American man from a poorly rated high school who went to Brown University, the only student from his school who had ever been accepted at an Ivy League school. When asked about the difference between himself and his high school classmates, he said, "[M]y fellow classmates . . . had so much potential but didn't have anyone to motivate them or push them" as he had had. His father had been in jail; but his mother had always encouraged, believed in, and treasured him (she called him her "jewel").

One of these former classmates, now working in a menial job, when asked about the difference between himself and Cedric said, "[Y]ou've got to make the right choices and Cedric just made the right choices and a lot of kids either are not strong enough or don't have sense enough to make the right choices." Perhaps Cedric's having had one adult, his mother, who supported and valued him was what helped him have the strength and sense to make the right decisions. (There is more about Cedric in Chapter 5.)

Fear of Success

Knowing about their self-image neural networks empowers students to understand what they can do to help themselves gain self-confidence and succeed. The only students with whom this might not work are those who fear success. These are people whose negative self-identity is so completely embedded that success threatens their sense of self. These are the students who, just as they are about to succeed in class, stop doing their homework, start acting up, stop coming to class. This can break the hearts of teachers who see their students' potential being sabotaged by the students themselves.

These students probably need more help than a classroom teacher is able, or trained, to give. These students might need the help of a professional therapist. Perhaps in some cases, though, as the AVID system proposes and James Anderson asserts, one caring adult can change even such students' lives for the better.

A Fossilized Positive Self-Image

Unfortunately, some people with a fossilized *positive* self-image network might be just as unrealistic about themselves as are people with a negative self-image. Believing they are always correct, they might appear arrogant or know-it-all, not opening their minds to corrective or useful advice, not listening with an open mind and respect to others' views, impatient with those who do not agree with them.

Yet until and unless they experience so much negative feedback that they cannot ignore it, including the failure of their own efforts, they might not feel any need to change. If they do decide they want to change, their having metacognitive knowledge about the "use it or lose it" rule will be helpful: "I know I'm smart, a natural learner, but I'm going to have to stop using the neural network that tells me I know everything. Instead, I'm going to start growing a new network that tells me I can learn some things from others if I stop being so closed-minded and start to open my ears and eyes and mind."

LEARNING FROM EXPERIENCE

Dendrites, Synapses, and Neural Networks Are Our Eyes

Our dendrites, synapses, and neural networks, which grow as a result of our personal experiences, are our knowledge; they are the eyes with which we see. A student brought this home to me. He was in his 50s and, having suffered a debilitating physical injury that had ended his career as a mechanic, was at the community college to retrain for a new career. He was in my basic grammar course because he needed to improve his reading and writing skills. He was an excellent student, mature, motivated, a fast learner, and one of the highest achievers in the class.

About halfway through the term, he had to go to the hospital for surgery and missed a week of school. When he returned, I invited him to my office for tutoring so he could catch up. As he sat next to my desk and I stood by my office chalkboard about to go through the lessons he had missed, I thought to myself, "He's very smart and catches on quickly. I can go through these lessons faster with him by himself than I was able to do with the whole class." So I began writing one of the new grammatical constructions on the board, explaining as I went, not giving him the time he would have had in class to try it on his own, talk about it, practice it, get feedback, assess his work, and try it again. (See "Four Major Instructional Practices" in Chapter 7.)

After I had finished, I asked him to write a sentence using the new construction. He sat silently staring at the board. He was not able to do it. He had not understood. I asked why not, had I talked too fast? Then he said something that taught me a lesson I have never forgotten:

"No. But if you don't have eyes to see it, you can't see it."

I had not given him the opportunity to grow his new eyes. He had not had the opportunity to grow his new dendrites and synapses that would have made it possible for him to see, to understand, to use this new grammar concept. It was not that he was not fully capable of learning this concept; it was that he had not had the time and practice every learner needs in order to grow the specific new dendrites, synapses, and neural networks for seeing, understanding, and having skill for a specific new object of learning.

Our Cultural Experience and Our Eyes

Learning involves information processing: interpreting sensory events, putting new information into familiar categories, and searching one's memory for similar ideas and personal experiences. How people do this is largely determined by the cultural patterns they have learned through personal experience, by the acculturated eyes with which they see (Cole & Scribner, 1974, p. 89).

> Work in social psychology, cognitive psychology, and anthropology is making clear that all learning takes place in settings that have particular sets of cultural and social norms and expectations and that these settings influence learning . . . in powerful ways. (Bransford et al., 1999, p. 4)

Based on their extensive study of education and neuroscience research, Bransford et al. concluded that

> [e]ffective instruction begins with what learners bring to the setting; this includes cultural practices and beliefs. . . . [L]earners use their current knowledge to construct new knowledge[,] and . . . what they know and believe at the moment affects how they interpret new information. (p. xvi)

Bransford et al. viewed this as the "foundational role of learners' prior knowledge in acquiring new information" (p. xix). In other words, as emphasized in Chapter 3, it is only from this personal foundation, from these existing neural networks, that a student's new learning—new dendrites, synapses, and networks—can grow. Therefore, because lifelong, pervasive cultural networks pose a challenge to the brain's plasticity, students need help to learn culturally unfamiliar or different ideas and skills.

When the students have this metacognitive knowledge, they are better able to learn from, and also enjoy, their teachers' helping them add to and enrich what they already know and understand as well as helping them call on their own cultural heritage to add to and enrich what others know and understand.

Discussing the cultural context of school failure, Hull, Rose, Fraser, and Castellano (1991) wrote, "There is a troubling history in American education of perceiving and treating low-achieving children as if they were lesser in character and fundamental ability. . . . [T]he 'problem'—as has been the tendency in our history—shifts from the complex intersection of cognition and culture and continues to be interpreted as a deficiency located within families and students" (pp. 299–300).

Thus, if the knowledge and skills that students of whatever culture bring to school are not compatible with, are not expected by, are not provided for in the curriculum and pedagogy of the classroom, then the students can be at a critical academic, emotional, and social disadvantage in that unfamiliar world (Heath, 1982, 1983; McPhail, 1979, 1982, 1983; McPhail & Morris, 1986). "Until and unless ways are found to make classroom and institutional practices . . . both multicultural and multicognitive, the vision of the learning-centered community college shall remain ephemeral for African Americans and other learners of color" (McPhail & McPhail, 1999, p. 27).

The antidote is brain-based, natural-learning curricula. These curricula are learner-centered in that every new lesson or unit starts with what each student already knows.

> [L]earner centered" [refers] to environments that pay careful attention to the knowledge, skills, attitudes, and beliefs that learners bring to the educational setting. . . . Teachers who are learner-centered recognize the importance of building on the conceptual and cultural knowledge that students bring with them to the classroom. (Ladson-Billings, 1995, pp. 465–491)

Metacognitive knowledge, again, is critical and should be shared with students as, for example, their learning about the following two rules of how the brain learns.

- *We grow neural structures for what we actively, personally, and specifically experience and practice.* If we practice a lot, we get better at what we are practicing. This is what we know; these are our eyes.
- *Dendrites do not grow from nothing. They grow from what is already there.* Thus, to teach or learn something new, we must always start with something familiar and progress from there (Chapter 6 shows how to do this).

INDIVIDUAL LEARNING STYLES, PREFERENCES, AND MULTIPLE INTELLIGENCES

A number of years ago, when learning styles inventories were all the rage, Mt. Hood Community College in Oregon had each of its faculty members do a learning styles inventory to determine his or her learning style. Then the college had every incoming student do the inventory to identify her or his learning style. Students were given a list of the faculty showing what each one's learning style was and were advised to take courses with teachers who had the same learning style as theirs so that compatibility would reign and there would be no frustrating learning-style dissonance.

This did not last long. For one thing, no one expanded his or her repertoire; for another, there was too little variety of styles to enrich class discussions and interactions. Healy (1994) wrote that "[w]e're not sure where people get their unique [learning styles], or how much we can—or should—change them" and suggests educators try "expanding, not altering" them (p. 154). Sternberg and Williams (2002), discussing the different learning preferences of either the "surface-processing" or "deep-processing" approach, suggested that even though "students' preferences for depth of processing are more likely to be stable across situations and subjects . . . teachers can encourage students toward taking a deeper or surface approach" (pp. 143–144). In other words, it seems learning styles or preferences are not unalterable, are not "cast in concrete."

Learning styles or preferences, as defined by Sternberg and Williams, "can range from straightforward preferences for physical surroundings to more fundamental differences that may be rooted in culture or personality" (p. 143). This definition can just as well be applied to eating styles and preferences. Some people prefer to eat alone with a book, some with friends and conversation. Different people prefer spicy food or mild food, crunchy food or soft food. Some people are vegan and some are red-meat eaters. Many of these preferences, as with learning preferences, "may be rooted in culture or personality" or in health requirements, palate, and even "straightforward preferences for physical surroundings."

But no matter what they prefer, once the food is in their mouths, their digestive organs and systems function physiologically the same way, using the same physiological processes unless, of course, the organs or systems are malfunctioning, requiring medical intervention. A doctor who understands how the heart works understands what every heart needs to function properly. In the same way, human beings have brains and cognitive systems that perform physiologically the same functions by the same physiological processes no matter what their personalities or preferences.

An educator who understands how the brain learns understands what every student needs in order to learn.

Learning Similarities

Specifically, the brain learns by growing dendrites and synapses and forms neural networks as and because the person is having experiences.

Successful learning depends on whether, and how well or how much, learning experiences bring into play the brain's inner resources and the rules of how the brain learns (Chapter 3). Chapter 6 introduces a method for developing and delivering curricula that provide these kinds of learning experiences so that all students can grow their neural structures and be the natural, successful learners they were born to be.

Internal Factors

People's brains, across age, gender, race, culture, and individual differences, learn by the same physiological process. However, certain internal factors physiologically affect the learning process. For example, emotions produce chemicals that affect the synapses, and the food people ingest either does or does not provide the nutrients the brain needs to function well. This is not to say that everyone is the same or has the same interests, preferences, aptitudes, and intelligences. It is only to say that no matter what individual differences people have, their brains learn by the same physiological process of growing and connecting neural structures during experiences.

Some people, though, might have an electrical, chemical, or physical brain difference so that the neural structures do not grow and connect as well as they otherwise would. But unless the difference is incapacitating, these people will also learn what they learn by the same physiological process of growing and connecting neural structures. (For learning experiences that are most effective for students with "special needs" brains, see Sousa, 2001.)

Ways of Learning That Seem Cast in Concrete

There are, however, two exceptions to the view of learning styles just described. First, some people are visual learners; for example, they understand a lecture better when they also have the opportunity to see what they are hearing, as with pictures that illustrate the lecture. They miss a lot if they have to learn only by listening to a lecture or explanation. They might say, "Show me a picture of what it looks like or give me something to read about it so I can see what you mean."

Second, some people are auditory learners; they miss a lot if they have to learn only by looking at pictures or reading. They understand better if they can also listen to someone lecturing or explaining. They might say, "Don't draw a picture. Just tell me—let me hear—what the idea is." These ways of learning seem to be hardwired in the brain as physiologically preferred sensory input channels.

Teachers are better able to reach all students when they provide both visual and auditory information. For example, when talking to their students, teachers could, at the same time, be illustrating what they are saying by drawing pictures or diagrams on the board or showing overheads. If these or other visual aids accompany their talking, and if their talking also accompanies any visuals they are presenting, all the students will be more likely to comprehend the material.

Kinesthetic or Hands-On Learning

Some people believe there is a third exception, that some people are hardwired as kinesthetic learners. The perspective I describe here is that everyone is probably a kinesthetic learner, if that means being a hands-on learner. Although it is true that some people say they learn better by watching or listening, they might not actually acquire or internalize—that is, grow their own dendrites, synapses, and neural networks for—a new skill, concept, or body of knowledge until and unless they work on it, experience it, practice it for themselves, going through the stages of the brain's natural learning process. They might be able to start by imitating someone, but they will perhaps not acquire competency or expert skill or understanding (not grow a rich, complex neural network) until they do it or work on it themselves, until they get their hands on it in one way or another to make it their own.

People who say they learn best by observing or listening (or both) and will not try it themselves until they feel well acquainted with the new object of learning, might be people who are fearful of taking risks, of making mistakes. By first becoming familiar in this way with the new object of learning, they might indeed make fewer mistakes. Or, by having some prior personal experience, they might improve by watching those who are more expert (Gallwey, 1974). In either case, they will eventually need to practice, making and correcting their own mistakes, if they are to gain their own true expertise and in-depth understanding.

There are, as well, people who prefer an overview of a new object of learning before beginning to try it themselves. This orientation is important to those who prefer to know where they are going and why and what steps are needed to get there. They will, however, also need to do hands-on work before acquiring their own expert knowledge and skill about an object of learning. Summarizing the research, Healy (1994) wrote that

> emerging from all the data is a clear message. Each [learner] must build individual networks for thinking; this development comes from within, using outside stimuli as material for growth. . . . Explaining things to [learners] won't do the job; they must have a chance to experience, wonder, experiment, and act it out for themselves. (p. 39)

Multiple Intelligences

Howard Gardner (1993), looking at how people learn, proposes "a pluralistic view of mind . . . , acknowledging that people have different cognitive strengths and contrasting cognitive styles" (p. 6). He has identified nine intelligences, defining intelligence as "the ability to solve problems, or to fashion products, that are valued in one or more cultural or community settings" (p. 7): linguistic, logical-mathematical, spatial, musical, bodily-kinesthetic, interpersonal, intrapersonal (pp. 8–9), later adding naturalist intelligence and, after that, existential or spiritual intelligence.

Concerning the intelligences, Gardner "assume[s] that faculties like . . . memory may well differ . . . across intelligences, with memory for spatial information being better or worse than memory for musical information in a particular individual" (p. 45). Gardner while emphasizing that culture defines intelligence, also believes in the plasticity and interactivity of the brain:

> [I]ndividuals may differ in the particular intelligence profiles with which they are born, and . . . certainly they differ in the profiles they end up with. I think of the intelligences as raw, biological potentials, which can be seen in pure form only in individuals who are, in the technical sense, freaks. In almost everybody else the intelligences work together to solve problems. . . . (p. 9)

In contrast, Gardner, like Sternberg and Williams (2002), believes an individual's learning style, as differentiated from an intelligence, can be the same for all contents and subjects across the board: for example, "a person . . . is deliberate with respect to music as well as to mathematics, a person . . . sees the 'big picture' whether he is doing physics or painting" (p. 45).

Serving Every Student

Education ought to be so sculpted that it remains responsive to [the differences between people]. Instead of ignoring them, and pretending that all individuals have (or ought to have) the same kinds of minds, we should instead try to ensure that everyone receives an education that maximizes his or her own intellectual potential. (Gardner, p. 71)

To make the class rewarding for all learners, we need to know how to create curricula that maximize every brain's innate and natural ability to learn, curricula that accommodate different learning styles, preferences, and intelligences, whether hardwired or not, and make it possible for every student to succeed. Chapters 6 and 7 explain how to do this; Chapters 8 and 9 provide classroom-proven examples.

Aptitudes

There are also inherited talents or abilities. For example, some families seem to pass along through the generations an aptitude for a specific skill or activity, such as music, athletics, language, math, or art. Of an aptitude a parent, the parent's siblings, a grandparent, and his or her children have, we say that it is a trait that "runs in the family."

John Carroll (1963) defined an aptitude as the ability to learn something more quickly and easily and to a higher level than others can. It seems that those who are fortunate enough to enjoy an inherited talent, a genetic or DNA advantage, have neurons that grow dendrites, synapses, and neural networks more quickly and easily and to a high level for that special skill or activity. Having an aptitude for one skill or activity, however, does not give that person a DNA advantage for other skills or activities, as noted in Chapter 2 in the case of Einstein (see Figure 3.8).

Students With Special Needs

Some students have special needs because of what has been called a learning problem or because they learn differently. These learning differences might be caused by a chemical, electrical, or structural anomaly in their brain. Such anomalies often have no deleterious effect on the student's intelligence. Students with dyslexia, for example, are well known for their extraordinary range and depth of knowledge about a wide variety of topics.

As noted in Chapter 2, Levine (2002) proposed that every child has a special strength or "wiring" that can be used to help overcome a learning miswiring or weakness. His message is that all children are precious and valuable. All children should be recognized for their special strengths and not be known only for their special needs or weaknesses. Each one has a unique and valuable strength to share with others. Sousa (2001) offered ways to respond to these students' special learning needs.

STANDARDIZED TESTS

With all these personal differences, how can one standardized test fairly assess all individuals? As Gardner (1993) put it,

> All normal human beings have all of these [intelligence] potentials, but for both genetic and environmental reasons, individuals differ remarkably . . . in the particular profiles of intelligence that they happen to exhibit at any give moment of their lives. (p. 71)

Consequently, a major decision must be made about which factors should be taken into account when assessing students. Should students be assessed "normatively," that is, by comparing "each test taker's scores with the performance of all the test takers" (Haynes & O'Brien, quoted in Sternberg & Williams, p. 470)? Or should they be assessed by "reference to criteria," that is, by measuring "a student's performance relative to what the student should know . . . to [see what] the child does and does not understand" (Sternberg & Williams, p. 471).

Factors That Might Explain
Differences in Test Scores

Wanting to see whether small class size affects tests scores, National Assessment of Educational Progress (NAEP) test makers controlled for factors other than class size that affect student performance on a standardized test (Johnson, 2002). To ensure that their results would not be tainted by nonidentical circumstances, they included, along with class size, five factors from background information: race and ethnicity, parents' educational level, availability of reading materials in the home, free or reduced-price lunch program participation, and gender. By factoring in these non-class-size but affecting circumstances, the NAEP was able to measure the results of student progress in small versus large classes.

After controlling for all these factors, researchers found that the difference in reading achievement on the 1998 NAEP reading assessment between students in small classes and students in large classes was statistically insignificant. That is, across the United States, students in small classes did no better on average than those in large classes, assuming otherwise identical circumstances (p. 29).

Because the NAEP did not control for the factors of teachers' pedagogy and curriculum, did the NAEP assume all the teachers were teaching identical curricula with identical pedagogy? This is an unanswered question.

Teaching to the Test

"The brain's capacity to learn is vast. . . . [It] is constructed for much more demanding intellectual activity than it usually experiences" (Caine & Caine, 1997, p. 36), especially when education focuses on teaching to standardized tests. As Kenneth Wesson (2000) wrote,

> Can any meaningful concept be reduced to a bubble response? Can such a reduction then be used as a valid assessment of superior levels of cognition? As Louis Albert, the former vice president of the American Association of Higher Education, has said, "It is deep and long-learning that we are after." . . . Much of what is found on standardized-assessment tools would not suggest such deep understanding. High ideational complexity, inventiveness, applying one's ingenuity and creativity . . . cannot be converted into the "bubblized" property of standardized tests. (p. 3)

Although it is true that not every question is answered with a "bubble response," the way the open-ended or essay questions are evaluated should cause even graver concerns.

> [T]he essays written by students in many states are not evaluated by educators; they are shipped off to a company in North Carolina where low-paid temp workers spend no more than two or three minutes reading each one [and are offered a] two hundred dollar bonus that kick[s] in after eight thousand papers. (Kohn, 2000, p. 12)

This company, Measurement, Inc., says it "has provided such 'educational assessment services' for half the states" (p. 70).

Kohn also wrote that students can do well on standardized tests by having "memorized the process without really understanding the idea" (p. 11). This was true of my own experience as a high school student many years ago in New York state, where Regents exams were—and still are—the standardized tests. For example, I was a top-scoring student on our math Regents year after year. But I did not, until many years later, appreciate the beauty and power of mathematics, as was finally revealed to me by my mathematician friends.

Kohn accurately described my high school experience with those well meaning but misguided teachers who deprived students of meaningful understanding of math. How did we learn math? Old Regents exams were our textbooks, and the teachers spent most of our class time preparing us for the exam by "administering and reviewing practice tests" (p. 29). We learned, as Kohn said, by "memorizing math facts and algorithms [rather than] understanding concepts" (p. 29). Hopefully, some students, most likely those with an aptitude or intelligence for math, have been able to thrive despite the Regents or standardized-test treatment.

Some teachers of English as a Foreign Language (or English as a Second Language) say they have the same reservations about the standardized test (Test of English as a Foreign Language or TOEFL), and preparation for that test, in their field.

Social Implications

That which is quantifiable is sometimes devoid of significant educational, personal, or social value. And the assessment tools currently being used are not capturing the best indicators of the traits, characteristics, and skills we need to encourage in our young people. Although these may defy easy or precise calibration, they may be of far greater educational value for students in the long run. (Wesson, 2000, November, p. 4)

Schools not teaching for meaning and understanding, for richness, depth, and complexity of thought and feeling, are not focusing on the full flowering of the best in students—and, consequently, on the flowering of the best for society.

Just as detrimental to both students and society is the issue of unequal playing fields, as noted in the Introduction:

[T]est scores were more honestly reflections of the economic advantages and disadvantages seen in American society. High scores have had a high correlation to socioeconomic characteristics such as the parents' occupation or level of education, the family's income bracket, and the location of students' elementary and secondary schools (the highly predictable "ZIP Code" factor). . . . It is widely acknowledged by test-development experts that a higher socioeconomic background gives students a positive boost in standardized-test achievement. (Wesson, 2000, November, pp. 1, 3)

Our students are not on a level playing field. How well would students do if they were moved at an early age from their lower- or higher-academic-quality playing field to the opposite playing field? Can standardized tests assess the academic *potential* of students who have not been nurtured academically? What, actually, are standardized tests assessing? We might even ask what democracy means.

If social engineers had set out to invent a virtually perfect inequality machine, designed to perpetuate class and race division[,] . . . those engineers could do no better than the present-day accountability systems already put to use in American schools. (Wellstone, in Kohn, 2000, p. 74)

As James H. Berry put it, "There is nothing more unequal than the equal treatment of 'unequals'" (personal communication, June 9, 2002).

Do we need to hold responsible parties (schools, teachers, government, voters, parents, ourselves) accountable for developing the full critical-thinking and creative potential of every student–that is, of every future responsible member of and contributor to society? If so, how can we do that?

DEVELOPING THE POTENTIAL OF EVERY STUDENT

This chapter has looked at many kinds of differences between people and also at one way in which people are similar: the way the brain naturally, physiologically learns from experience.

What if we give every student the opportunity to learn by the brain's natural learning process? If we do that, every student will have an equal opportunity to grow and connect the neural structures needed to actualize his or her potential to be a successful student in any course or subject and to be successful in life in general.

Then it would be only a question of how long it would take for students who started on a playing field that did not provide the prerequisite academic preparation to catch up. How long would it take them to grow enough relevant prerequisite neural structures to be successful learners in schools that expect a certain level of preparation (see Figure 3.14)?

An Irony

It is ironic that whether people's experiences are emotionally nurturing and supportive or dysfunctional and destructive, the same process of experience-dependent learning takes place. As discussed earlier, people with positive emotional experiences grow positive neural structures and, thus, learn that they are safe, valued, and respected. They have self-esteem and self-confidence and behave accordingly. With negative experiences, people grow negative neural networks and learn they are unsafe, not valued, not respected. They have low self-esteem, lack self-confidence, and behave accordingly.

Because the human brain is the most complex entity known to science, there will certainly be innumerable variations, differences, and combinations of positive and negative not only among individuals but also within a single individual.

BEYOND INDIVIDUAL DIFFERENCES

However, no matter what the individual's unique and idiosyncratic characteristics, emotions, personality, experiences, and level of knowledge and skill are, the physiological process of growing, connecting, constructing, and reconstructing neural networks is how learning happens for anyone and everyone. Even though these individualistic networks *are* each person's own unique knowledge of self, the world, and everything and anything else, these networks, nevertheless, all come into existence by the same physiological process: the growing of neural networks by the brain's rules for learning.

Thus, to help all students learn, since they all learn by the same physiological process, teachers can facilitate their growing, connecting, and constructing their new neural structures—their new knowledge and skill—by making sure the classroom is positive and supportive so that students feel safe and respected.

Can it ever be a mistake, then, to believe absolutely that all students, young and old, would love to learn, and could learn, if only they had the opportunity, both intellectually and emotionally, to do so?

Chapters 6 and 7 introduce a theory and a method for creating and delivering curricula that accomplish this goal. Chapters 8 and 9, then, provide examples of such curricula.

> "When the brain is (1) properly nourished, and (2) allowed to develop in a positive, reassuring and encouraging atmosphere, it responds favorably to that rich supportive environment." (Wesson, 2002, p. 456)

A HANDOUT FOR STUDENTS

Students appreciate receiving a handout of "The Major Points About Learning," in the box below, along with the following advice:

"Put this in your notebook, tape it to your bathroom mirror, and read it at least three times a day."

Major Points About Learning

1. Your brain was born to learn, loves to learn, and knows how to learn.

2. You learn what you practice.
   - Practice is making mistakes, correcting mistakes, learning from them, and trying over, again and again.
   - Making and learning from mistakes is a natural and necessary part of learning.

3. You learn what you practice because when you are practicing your brain is growing new fibers (dendrites) and connecting them (at synapses). This *is* what learning is.

4. Learning takes time because you need time to grow and connect dendrites.

5. If you don't use it, you can lose it. Dendrites and synapses can begin to disappear if you don't use them (if you don't practice or use what you have learned).

6. Your emotions affect your brain's ability to learn, think, and remember.
   - Self-doubt, fear, etc., prevent your brain from learning, thinking, and remembering.
   - Confidence, interest, etc., help your brain learn, think, and remember.

7. Remember, you are a natural-born learner.

The Student's Experience 5

Metacognition, Motivation,
Self-Evaluation, and Achievement

METACOGNITION AND MOTIVATION

Students need a user's guide to the brain so they can know what to do and how to do it to be successful learners. When they find out not only how they learn (Chapter 2) but also how the brain learns (Chapter 3), their self-empowerment and confidence increase, as shown in the following notes from students.

The first is from a student in my Introduction to Learning, Cognition, and Instruction course at Western Washington University's Woodring College of Education. At the end of the term, he wrote to me that he had "received the best GPA of my school career. I believe that has a lot to do with your class and the confidence you enabled me to have in myself" (Breck Ivy). "The confidence you enabled me to have in myself." What more rewarding comment could a teacher hear?

That self-confidence came from his finding out about his brain's natural learning process and from knowing how to have this process work for him in school, making it possible for him to do well in all his classes.

Another student in one of my educational psychology courses wrote this:

The most important idea or concept that I have learned in this class is dendrite growth and the NHLP [natural human learning process]. When we had our first class and we learned about dendrite growth I was truly fascinated by the learning system. I was really under a different impression of how we all learn. So when you then started us in our own NHLP planning model (i.e., first write down what we know about the subject, then discuss in small groups, and then report back to the larger group), I was really excited. I just couldn't wait to hear what you were going to say next. Then when the exercise was done and I then knew that I wasn't born stupid" or "dumb," I really became empowered to keep learning. I think that empowerment is one of the most important tools to motivating and creating an enriched learning environment for my future students. When I then teach them about the NHLP . . . they will begin to understand more about themselves and what is needed for them to feed their dendrites and keep themselves learning. (Christina Lundberg)

In addition, here are some notes written by students at North Seattle Community College who had been introduced to how the brain learns. The first comes from Lynn Sharpe's English as a Second Language (ESL) Oral Communication Class.

The more we use the brain to solve problems, the more dendrites can grow. If we learn with a positive emotion, we can grow our dendrites normally. But if we learn with a negative emotion, [this] will block the dendrites. . . . [P]ractice is so important to get to a high level of learning from a low level. Now I see why learning is so difficult sometimes. I need to encourage myself to relax and keep my [positive] emotion in all my learning. Otherwise, I can't build up the neural network and will ruin the natural learning ability of the brain. (H. C.)

The notes below are from Jane Harradine's English composition class.

You will be happy to know that I am nurturing my dendrites as I write to you! I am thrilled to know they exist, and I am happy to have a new relationship with them! This newfound relationship has reassured me. . . . All of my classes had me a little nervous which, just as you shared, was having an affect on my learning. Just knowing my dendrites know what to do has calmed me. Additionally, . . . I have already had the experience of being stuck, stepping back to fill in the missing dendrites, and then moving forward again. (L. D.)

I appreciate your telling us that we're not stupid. Before, if I didn't understand something, even though I tried my hardest, I would've given up. Now I know that all I need to do is just be persistent, and eventually my dendrites will grow. I have a friend who gets ten times better grades than I do, but I know now that all he does is study harder than I do. If he doesn't understand something, he keeps at it until he does. So after what you said, he's not smarter than me, he just has his dendrites growing faster. (Q. T.)

As long as there is a desire to know, I can learn anything. The encouragement that I get from the previous phrase, nothing can describe. (D. B.)

The information nugget which stuck with me most was that of overcoming fears. To me, this seems like the biggest barrier to most people's achievement and personal growth. . . . [This] shed much light on the how's, what's, and why's which I have about this fear issue. (E. B.)

These students' notes, representative of many more such responses, reveal what some students have been feeling and thinking but not saying about themselves as learners. Even though they are motivated to learn, they have been restricting themselves or giving up too quickly. They say this is because of fear of failure, negative emotions, and lack of self-confidence. In these notes, we can see their confidence—their believing they can succeed—has been strengthened by finding out how the brain learns and that they are natural-born learners. They have also learned what they can do to help the brain learn instead of sabotaging its natural ability to learn and its knowing innately how to learn. They know they are responsible for their own learning and what they must do to become successful.

Even sixth graders can understand and benefit from this metacognitive knowledge. Here are some excerpts from notes sent to me by students after I had visited one of Alex Kroeger's sixth-grade science classes at the Brighton School in Lynnwood, Washington:

I'm glad about the rule use it or lose it, because now I'm prepared to listen and pay attention more in school, I sure don't want to lose dendrites! . . . I'm so interested in this stuff now. (Shannon)

When you came and spoke about the learning process, it was the first time I actually considered the steps it takes to learn. . . . In the time you spent with us I felt I learned again how to learn. (Alex)

I never knew that when I was little and liked to experiment with [and] mix things like flour and vanilla extract together that I was actually trying to find things out, like what would happen. I also had no idea how many dendrites we have, and how important they are. (Katie)

(Even though I did not include comments from every note, I also want to thank Diana, Eliot, Elly, Evan, Ian, John, Kara, and one student who did not include his or her name for their thoughts.)

INTRINSIC REWARDS

We now know that human beings are not only born with a brain that has an innate learning process but also that, when a person is learning successfully, the brain produces the so-called pleasure chemicals, serotonin, dopamine, and endorphins: "These chemicals are key factors in feeling satisfied and rewarded, and therefore in providing motivation" (Ratey, 2001, p. 117). Thus, human beings not only have an inborn impulse to learn, we also have an inborn motivation system that rewards us with a feeling of pleasure when we do so: "[We] don't just compute, learn, reason, and know. [We] are driven to do all these things and are designed to take intense pleasure in doing so" (Gopnik et al., 1999, p. 164).

As noted earlier, if someone seems uninterested in learning, that person is not feeling and behaving naturally. Something has happened to sabotage his or her brain's innate learning and motivation-for-learning systems. As suggested by the students' comments featured here, knowing how the brain learns can make it clear to hesitant learners that they have a natural endowment they have not been enjoying and that they have the power to reclaim it.

Behaviorists, however, generally have believed teaching and learning are no different from training animals to perform desired behaviors and that students need external rewards to motivate them to learn. Jensen (1998), citing work by Deci, Vallerand, Pelletier, and Ryan (1992), Kohn (1993), and Restak (1979), pointed out that even today

> schools often try to reward students for solving challenging cognitive problems, writing creatively, and designing and completing projects. There's an enormous difference in how the human brain responds to rewards for simple and complex problem-solving tasks. Short-term rewards can temporarily stimulate simple physical responses, but more complex behaviors [like creative writing and designing projects] are usually . . . not helped, by [external] rewards. (p. 63)

The intrinsic reward from using their brains' inner resources keep students motivated to work long and hard at solving challenging problems, seeking patterns, using their logic and their creativity to explore, experiment, discover, and create. Extrinsic rewards are no match for the intrinsic reward of personal satisfaction people feel when they are engaged in these natural learning activities. For this reason, extrinsic rewards can be counterproductive, "particularly when the goal is something deeper, more complex, or longer lasting" (Kohn, 2000, p. 23).

According to Sternberg and Williams (2002),

[u]nmotivated students are the greatest challenge for many teachers. A teacher may have prepared a terrific in-class lesson and take-home assignment; however, if her students are not motivated to listen to her, she cannot simply present the lesson and reach them successfully. (p. 344)

They explained that different students are motivated by different rewards but that intrinsic motivation "is increasingly important as students progress through the grades" (p. 348).

Gopnik et al. (1999) reported that even babies experience intrinsic motivation when learning. If you have observed any babies, you have probably seen for yourself that when babies are learning something new, they get excited, laugh, try again and again, enjoying the process immensely. No extrinsic rewards are needed. The intrinsic reward of the brain's own chemistry is enough to keep learners working long and hard to explore, to experiment, to do, to make, to think, to create, to discover patterns, to solve problems, to find out how something works and how to make it work for themselves.

Here is an example of a 1-year-old boy meeting and conquering a novel challenge. This story was sent to me by K. D. Taylor, Associate Dean, School of Learning Resources at Utah Valley State College, who, by the way, is also the boy's grandmother.

My grandson Robert Blake Taylor was about one year old when he learned to walk. He toddled around the apartment, feeling quite independent, now that he had conquered vertical mobility. When he came to visit us for Easter, he discovered a new challenge, the hearth.

Our fireplace has a stone hearth that is two inches higher than the carpet. Blake was immediately intrigued by the challenge of taking his new skill to a higher level, literally. He confidently stepped up onto the hearth, tottered briefly, and fell over onto the carpet. Not at all discouraged, he tried again. This time he fell into a sitting position on the hearth. Obviously, there was more to this than he had thought. But he was undaunted. A third try brought similar results. This time he stood up from the sitting position while still on the hearth and tried stepping down onto the carpet. Alas, gravity won again.

By this time the conversations of the adults all trailed off into silence as we focused our attention on Blake. Oblivious of his audience, he made several more attempts, all coming to similar ends. A moment of tottering gave us hope on the next attempt, but he toppled once more, then gave a heavy sigh.

We all commiserated with "oh's" and "oops." He just sat there for a moment, staring at that hearth. We thought perhaps he was through, but he gathered himself to take on his own little Everest once more. He was plucky, if not yet coordinated.

On his twentieth or so attempt, he stepped from the carpet up to the hearth and stood there for two or three seconds. Finally realizing that he had actually triumphed, he turned around to face the room, extended both arms in a V, and yelled "Aaee!" We all cheered. His dad scooped him up and danced around the room with him, telling him he was a good boy over and over. As soon as Blake's feet met the carpet, he headed straight for the hearth, wanting to verify his victory. He did and we all cheered again.

I don't think any of us will ever forget the day Blake conquered the hearth. It had been one very big step for one very little boy. (Personal communication, April 16, 2002)

We see, then, that the problem is not that students are not motivated to learn. Nor is it that we need to find ways to motivate all these unmotivated students. Nor do we need to offer them external rewards (Blake was clearly on his own mission to learn independent of his father's saying he was a good boy). No, the problem is how to remove the barriers that block students' motivation to learn. If we can remove those barriers, students will feel the natural, innate motivation to learn with which they were born.

REMOVING THE BARRIERS

Bartoszeck (1996), a teacher of neurophysiology, contrasted instruction that raises barriers to instruction without barriers:

In my view, most current teaching of physiology still overburdens students with large quantities of factual information without involving them in the process of integrating this material with their previous knowledge or placing it in a wider context. Students are subjected to countless passive learning experiences (such as lectures or conferences) and laboratory demonstrations in which they participate very little (in part due to lack of equipment, reagents, etc.). Few of these experiences encourage the "active learning" that can lead to the development of thinking skills. It is the instructors' duty to create a learning environment in which they can help the students build their own understanding of the subject matter, organize their own ideas, and reason with their own cognitive models. (pp. 3–4)

SELF-EVALUATION AND METACOGNITION

A powerful way for students to take responsibility for their own success, or lack of it, is the self-evaluation instrument shown in Figure 5.1. This instrument asks students to use their metacognitive knowledge of both their natural learning process and also the brain's physiological learning process.

These evaluations have two parts. The first part is a postevaluation for the chapter or unit just completed. The second is a preevaluation of the chapter or unit to come. Although students invariably score themselves lower on the second part, with metacognitive knowledge they understand that they cannot know what they have not yet had the opportunity to experience and practice. As a result, they have confidence in their ability to learn the material in the next chapter or unit.

Here are some examples of student self-evaluations (Figures 5.2, 5.3).

Notice in these students' comments that they are using their metacognitive knowledge to explain their level of achievement: "I am presently unfamiliar w/pronouns but I have learned them in the past. With some booster info and practice I will once again have better understanding. USE IT OR LOSE IT [sic]"; "I think I have this amount of dendrites *because I have been practicing a lot* [italics added] and my dendrites are still growing, in fact let me draw some more."

The confidence produced by having metacognitive knowledge is also illustrated in this ABC network *Nightline* interview by Michel McQueen with Cedric Jennings (introduced in Chapter 4), the student from a poorly rated high school who was attending an Ivy League college:

McQUEEN: [The question is] whether despite all his talent and drive, kids who start out as far behind as he did even belong at a place like Brown. It is a question Cedric likes to tackle head on.

CEDRIC JENNINGS: I think that in this country we must also mistake lack of exposure for incompetence. At Ballou I wasn't taught everything

Figure 5.1   Student Self-Evaluation Form

Post-Evaluation

a. Where are you now in your knowledge of the skills in the chapter we have just finished?

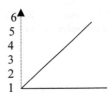

b. Draw on these cell bodies what you think are the length and amount of the dendrites you now have for the skills in this chapter. Why do you think you have this length and amount of dendrites?

Pre-Evaluation

a. Where are you now in your knowledge of the skills in the next chapter?

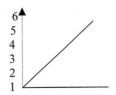

b. Draw on these cell bodies what you think are the length and amount of the dendrites you now have for the skills in the next chapter. Why do you think you have this length and amount of dendrites?

---

that a lot of the students here were taught, you know, prior to coming to Brown. So of course there are going to be things that I don't know. It doesn't mean that I'm not capable of learning these things. It just means I don't know 'em. I wasn't exposed to them. (McQueen, June 24, 1998)

"Of course there are going to be things that I don't know," Cedric said, if "I wasn't exposed to them." Without being exposed to those things, of course a person cannot learn them. Because of this invaluable meta-cognitive awareness, Cedric is able to evaluate himself realistically: He separates his intellectual capacity from his lack of knowledge and has

Figure 5.2   First Student's Self-Evaluation

Post-Evaluation

a. Where are you now in your knowledge of the skills in
the chapter we have just finished?

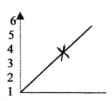

b. Draw on these cell bodies what you think are the length and amount of
the dendrites you now have for the skills in this chapter. Why do you think you
have this length and amount of dendrites?

.I'm not very comfortable
with helper verbs. At
times they are (tenses are) still
unclear.

Pre-Evaluation

a. Where are you now in your knowledge of the skills in
the next chapter?

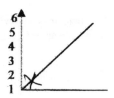

b. Draw on these cell bodies what you think are the length and amount of
the dendrites you now have for the skills in the next chapter. Why do you think
you have this length and amount of dendrites?

I am presently unfamiliar
with pronouns but I have
learned them in the past.
With some booster info and
practice I will once again have
better understanding. "Use it
or lose it" ☺.

confidence in his ability to learn when and if he has the opportunity to
experience—to be exposed to—a particular object of learning.

ANOTHER METACOGNITIVE EXPERIENCE

Students who are academically underprepared (dendrite disadvantaged
from lack of opportunity to grow prerequisite neural structures) but do

Figure 5.3 Second Student's Self-Evaluation

Post-Evaluation

a. Where are you now in your knowledge of the skills in
the chapter we have just finished?

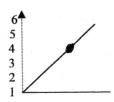

b. Draw on these cell bodies what you think are the length and amount of
the dendrites you now have for the skills in this chapter. Why do you think you
have this length and amount of dendrites?

*I think I have this amount of
dendrites because of the simple
fact that I have been practing
a lot and my dendrites are still
growing, in fact let me draw
some more.*

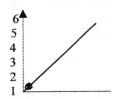

Pre-Evaluation

a. Where are you now in your knowledge of the skills in
the next chapter?

b. Draw on these cell bodies what you think are the length and amount of
the dendrites you now have for the skills in the next chapter. Why do you think
you have this length and amount of dendrites?

*I think I have this amount
of dendrites because of the
simple fact that I thought
abot it so I am growing
some.*

---

not have Cedric's metacognitive knowledge are at a grave disadvantage. If
they fall further and further behind, all too often they give up and their
potential for academic success can be lost.

The students in my ninth-grade English class (Chapter 1) had already
taught me that academically unprepared students are eager and willing to
learn. Another experience several years later showed me again that
students who seem as though they cannot, or do not want to, learn are, in
fact, natural learners.

A friend who was teaching a high school class during summer school
asked me to fill in for her for one session. The class was composed of the
usual group of students who go to summer school. A few had missed

school because of prolonged or recurrent illness or other legitimate reasons (one girl had been out of the country with her family for several months). The others, however, were students who had slacked off, failed, been suspended for part of the year, or who were chronically absent without cause. There was a large group of what could be immediately identified as "bad boys" in the back of the room. They were already acting up, talking, and snickering, advertising their lack of interest and lack of intention to cooperate.

My plan for the session was to conduct the NHLP research activity (Chapter 2). When the students were asked to think of something they had learned outside school that they could do well, the boys in the back increased their disruptive behavior, laughing and talking loudly to each other. One of the boys, with a big smile, said what he and his friends knew how to do would not count.

"What do you know how to do?" I asked. "Drinking," he laughed. "Getting girls," another boy said loudly, also laughing. "That will be okay," I said. "If it's something you learned to do well, it'll work." Their response seemed to show that this neutral acceptance of what had clearly been an antiauthority challenge had been unanticipated; they stopped laughing and looked like they might even pay attention.

"Now think back to before you knew how to do this and write down how you got from there to being really good at your specialty. This isn't to hand in. It's just to help you remember." Everyone, including the boys in the back, began writing. When it was time for them to share what they had written with three or four people around them, the "bad boys" participated as eagerly as the other students.

The next task was for them to debrief together as a whole class. The "bad boys" enthusiastically contributed along with everyone else, for example, "I watched my brother"; "I threw up the first time but then my friends told me to slow down so I got better." At the end, we could see that all the students had learned pretty much the same way. First they observed someone or just jumped in and tried it or knew they wanted to do it. Then they practiced and learned from their mistakes. After that, they kept practicing. Finally they began to see how to do it better and better until they got really good at it and could even teach it to others. I reported that thousands of other people who had done this activity had also learned more or less by this same learning process—the natural human learning process.

At the end of this activity, I can always point out honestly that everyone in the group is a natural-born learner and has an excellent brain that knows how to learn. In this class, I looked directly at the boys in the back

Figure 5.4   Eva Slaughter: April 2

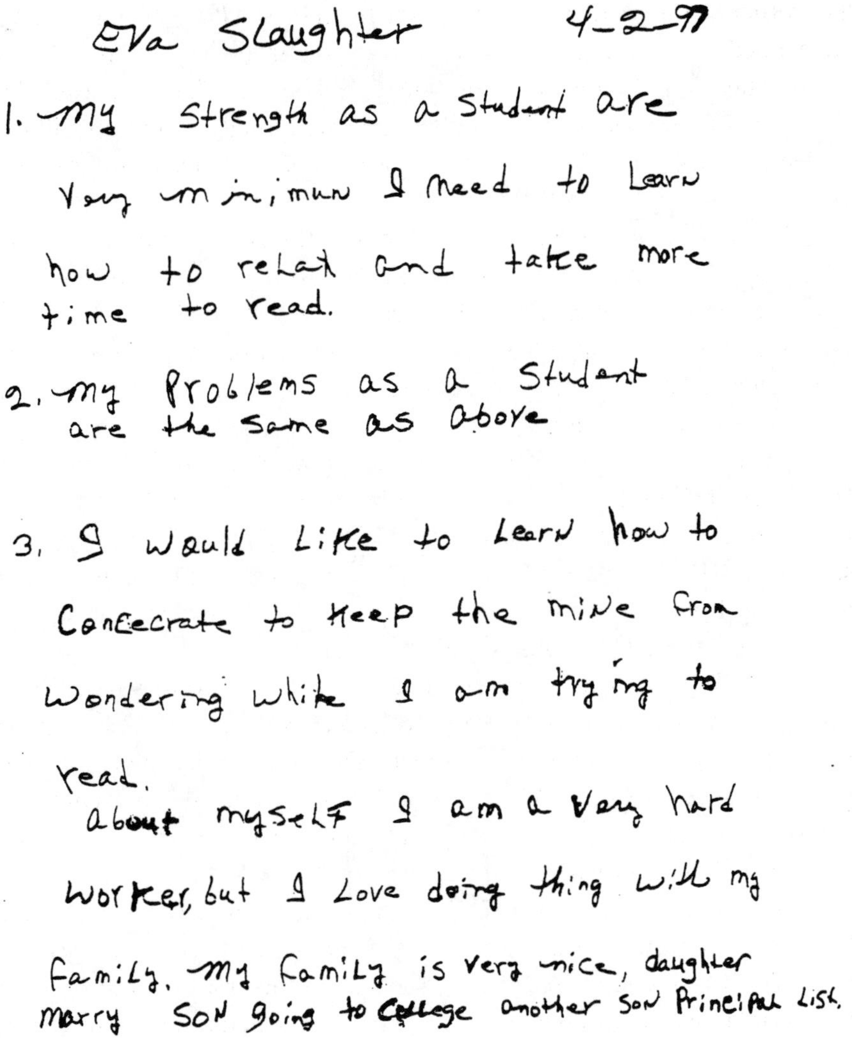

Eva Slaughter   4-2-97

1. my strength as a student are very minimun I need to learn how to relat and take more time to read.

2. my problems as a student are the same as above

3. I would like to learn how to confecrate to keep the mine from wondering while I am trying to read.
  about myself I am a very hard worker, but I love doing thing with my family. my family is very nice, daughter marry son going to college another son principal list.

and sent that message strongly and clearly to them. I ended by saying, "This means you are very smart." They sat silently, their faces unguarded and open. At that moment, they were ready to learn.

The subject for the rest of the period was how the brain learns and the relationship between the brain's natural learning process and how people, including themselves, actually learn. As usual, every student in the class, even the boys in the back, was focused and attentive.

With their new metacognitive knowledge, they were certainly better equipped and, thus, more motivated to succeed in school. A big problem, though, would be teachers who, knowing them as trouble-makers, would

Figure 5.5   Eva Slaughter: May 31

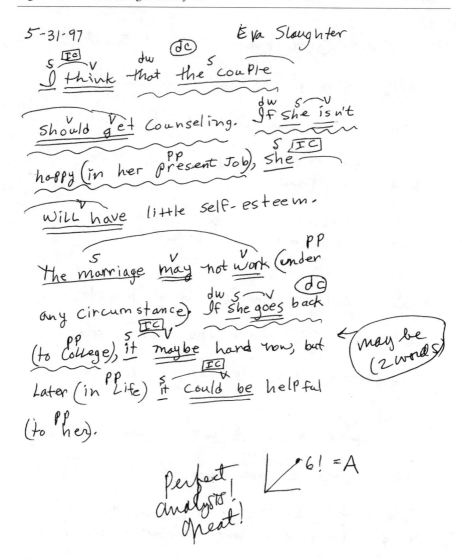

not believe these students had the desire and ability to learn. Or, if they did believe this, they might not know how to help them grow and connect their neural structures so they could progress over time from where they were to where they needed to be to achieve academic success.

ACHIEVEMENT

When students have the opportunity—and *opportunity* is the operative word—to learn via the brain's natural learning process, they become the motivated, successful learners they were born to be. Chapter 6 introduces guidelines and a model for creating brain-based, natural-learning curriculum that gives all students this opportunity.

To demonstrate the kind of success students achieve with such curriculum, Figures 5.4 and 5.5 provide writing samples from a student in my community college developmental grammar course. This grammar course focuses exclusively on sentence-level grammar, and aspiring college students enroll in this class if, as noted earlier, their placement tests show they are reading at the fourth- to sixth-grade level and do not know how to write grammatically correct sentences. After having acquired sentence-level grammar knowledge in this course, students are able to go on to one or more precollege essay-writing courses and then on to college-level English (see Chapter 9, "Planning a Developmental English Program").

Teaching sentence-level grammar in high school has been so unsuccessful that the National Council of Teachers of English has recommended that high school English teachers no longer offer it as an independent subject. As a result, some students have been graduating from high school not knowing how to identify and correct their grammatical errors. But in one term of 11 weeks, a class of 25 to 28 students who are starting below the middle school level of reading and writing can successfully learn by this brain-based, natural-learning curriculum to express their ideas and feelings in grammatically correct sentences and know exactly what they are doing.

WRITING SAMPLES

The samples are by Eva Slaughter, a woman in her mid-40s. The writing prompt for the first sample, the pretest on the first day of class, was to write about their strengths and weaknesses as a writer and also something about themselves (Figure 5.4). All errors have been retained.

The prompt for a test 8 weeks later was a moral dilemma: "A married couple is doing very well financially. Then the wife's company is downsized, and she loses her position. She wants to return to college to retrain for another career. Her husband tells her that, instead, she must go out and find any kind of job because they need the money. You are a marriage counselor. What do you think about this situation?" (Figure 5.5).

Not only was Eva able to express her thoughts in grammatically correct sentences, but she was able to analyze her own writing to show she understood exactly what she was doing. The symbols the students used for the analysis are as follows:

IC Independent Clause

dc dependent clause

dw   dependent word (subordinating conjunction)

S   Subject

V   Verb

PP   Prepositional Phrase

____   underlining for independent clauses

^^^^   underlining for dependent clauses

As noted, this course focuses exclusively on sentence-level grammar. It does not mention spelling or vocabulary. Yet, somehow, Eva's spelling and vocabulary improved as well. It also looks as though her intelligence had increased. No, she had the same intelligence she had had 8 weeks earlier. The difference was that she now had an instrument for expressing her thoughts. Many students halfway through the term say that, for the first time in their lives, they are able to express their thoughts in words. Chapter 9 focuses on the curriculum for this grammar course and shows Eva's progress through it.

AGE AND ACHIEVEMENT

The fact that the majority of the students in this class are older than 18, and that some are in their 40s, 50s, and 60s, means that their dendrites, synapses, and neural networks for writing incorrectly have been practiced for many years and, thus, are very strong; we might even say they are fossilized. However, as these students stop using their incorrect neural networks, by the rule of "use it or lose it," these networks atrophy. At the same time, by the rule "we grow neural networks for what we practice," new networks for knowing and using correct grammar grow—and grow stronger the more they are practiced.

In these developmental grammar courses, there are many ESL students. In one class there was a Korean man in his 50s. His neural networks seemed fossilized because he did not improve no matter how much he practiced or how hard he tried. Nevertheless, I did not think he was hopeless but, rather, assumed his neural networks could and would grow if only I could find the way to help him get started. I did not believe his age in and of itself was the problem because "[t]here is no evidence that learning ability decreases with age" (Greenfield, 1997, p. 119). In fact, it seems that "one's mental potential continues to increase steadily throughout life, only beginning to tail off after about the age of sixty–and even this tailing off may not be necessary" (Russell, 1979, p. 65). Ratey (2001) also wrote that age-related decline is "not inevitable" (p. 360).

Even though the class had done the NHLP activity early in the term and had talked about how the brain learns, I thought some private tutoring might help this student increase, and actively begin to use, his metacognitive knowledge. In our first tutoring session, we reviewed the rules of the brain and how they might apply to him. By the end of the session, he realized that he needed to go back and start growing his English grammar dendrites from the beginning. He knew that he had started the class with strong incorrect neural networks (incorrect English grammar) from many years of speaking and writing English incorrectly. He had been trying as hard as he could, yet failing, to grow correct new dendrites from his old incorrect ones. He said he had not wanted to go back to the beginning of learning English because he did not want to "be like a baby again."

He had not allowed himself to do what was necessary for learning something new because he was afraid he would look and feel like a baby. Once he brought this out in the open and talked dendrite talk rather than self-image talk, a light went on. He looked happy, relieved. It was not that he was stupid and could not learn correct English; it was that he had not been learning by his brain's natural learning process.

After that, with tutoring so he could catch up, he went back to the beginning and began growing his new correct foundation dendrites. Finally, the perseverance and determination he had shown all along, but which had formerly not helped him succeed, began to pay off. He made good progress and, catching up with his classmates, finished the course successfully. Metacognition and self-evaluation had made it possible for this motivated student to achieve success.

With metacognition as a key element in their user's guide to the brain, students have the knowledge to help themselves be successful learners. Tragically, too many students in classes from first grade to graduate school have given up or failed. This is an unnecessary tragedy because all human beings are born with an innate motivation to learn and so all could be successful learners.

Part II

Theory and Application

Sequencing of the Curriculum   **6**

Through steadfastness and right attitude, the blossoming can occur.

Ralph Blum

CHALLENGES

The Association for Supervision and Curriculum Development (ASCD) in their summer 1999 *Curriculum Update* reports that, according to educators, "[k]nowing 'what to teach when' has always been a challenge for those who develop a curriculum. . . . Likewise, knowing 'how to teach what' has always been a challenge for those who deliver that curriculum in the classroom" (Checkley, 1999, p. 1).

Two and a half years later, these challenges were again a focus of *Curriculum Update*:

> Although years of evidence point to certain instruction practices as keys to promoting student achievement, . . . [there is] the difficulty of a wealth of strategies. . . . [Also, teachers] are encouraged to adapt a variety of strategies into a rich combination that meets their specific classroom needs. . . . [However, after learning] all of these strategies in an inservice, . . . it can be easy to "fall back into the old ways of the lecture rut." (Allen, 2002, pp. 2–3, 8)

Moreover, the wealth of strategies that we can select from is continually increasing. For example, *Classroom Instruction That Works: Research-Based Strategies for Increasing Student Achievement* (Marzano, Pickering, &

Pollock, 2001) "presents and exemplifies instructional strategies that [the authors] have extracted from the research base on effective instruction. Teachers can use these strategies to guide classroom practice in such a way as to maximize the possibility of enhancing student achievement" (p. 3). Marzano et al. also looked forward to a day when even more instructional strategies will prove to be effective. They wrote that there are still many questions to answer to "help move teaching from an art to a science" (p. 9). Some of these questions are about which instructional strategies are most effective for specific subject areas and grade levels and for students from different backgrounds and with different aptitudes. Add to this the challenge of developing curricula with a similar "wealth" of curriculum-development methodologies to select from when planning "what to teach when."

The dilemma is that classroom teachers are already working hard and running fast to fulfill all their many duties and responsibilities. How and when are they going to have the time and energy to study this plethora of strategies and methodologies, make informed selections among them, and become skillful at using new or different ones? Thus, unfortunately, this ever-increasing accumulation of riches might only intensify the challenges of "what to teach when" and "how to teach what."

Because "[w]e need a way of selecting the methodologies that will maximize learning and make teaching more effective and fulfilling" (Caine & Caine, 1991, p. 88), it would be good news if, as Marzano et al. (2001) suggested, there were a science, a comprehensive and integrated method, for doing this.

THE MISSING LINK

Educators who know the research on how the brain learns have been able to develop a variety of brain-compatible instructional strategies (e.g., Caine & Caine, 1997; Hart, 1999; Healy, 1994; Jensen, 1998; Kovalik and Olsen, 2001; Marzano et al., 2001; M. Rose, 1995; Sprenger, 1999; Sternberg & Williams, 2002; Sylwester, 1995). Up to now, however, there has been no research- and theory-based method for creating and delivering brain-compatible curriculum to teach a complete unit, course, or sequential program from beginning to end.

Although educators have an understanding of how the brain learns, that alone is not enough to generate a methodology for developing and delivering curricula that trigger and sustain the brain's innate learning process as well as the learner's motivation and attention.

Two Problems

The First Problem

The first problem is the widely held view that all brains learn differently. Yes, all people are unique individuals with different learning preferences and styles, emotions, experiences, strengths, abilities, intelligences, and whatever other categories of individual differences there are (see Chapter 4, especially Gardner, 1993, and Wesson, 2000). These would include both inter- and intrapersonal variations in functioning and performance for different reasons in different situations at different times. Because of this view, many researchers and educators have focused on using an array of instructional strategies to accommodate these many differences.

This view leads to the conclusions that, first, no one strategy works in all situations and, second, that there can be no one type of curriculum or pedagogy that makes it possible for all students to learn successfully. This view obviates the need to seek a viable theory and methodology for developing and delivering whole curricula that will work with all students.

On the other hand, there is a universal process by which human beings, across gender, age, culture, educational level, and all other individual differences, acquire new knowledge and skill. Even though every brain is different from every other brain in many ways, all brains are the same in one fundamental way: when they learn (gain new knowledge and skill), it is because they are growing and connecting neural structures, which is the physiological cause and embodiment of their learning (Chapter 3).

Thus, even when students who, whether by nature or nurture, are different—in their levels of preparedness (neural structure growth) in general or for a specific subject, concept, or skill—begin learning something new, they will all learn by the same constructive, physiological process of neural growth.

Because teaching is facilitating the growing and connecting of students' brain structures, a critical question is, "What kind of curriculum and pedagogy will stimulate every student's brain structures to grow and connect so that every student will learn successfully?" This question is answered here and in Chapter 7.

The Second Problem

The first problem is the view that all brains learn differently and, therefore, teachers should address the innumerable variations in learners. The second problem is that there has been a missing link between knowing how the brain learns and knowing how to translate this physiological

Figure 6.1   The Brain's Innate Resources

- The brain has a natural learning process (NHLP).
- The brain has an innate sense of logic.
- The brain is an innate pattern-seeker.
- The brain is an innate problem-solver.
- The brain is innately motivated to learn.

Figure 6.2   Five Rules of How the Brain Learns

1. Dendrites, synapses, and neural networks grow only from what is already there.

2. Dendrites, synapses, and neural networks grow from stimulating experiences.

3. Dendrites, synapses, and neural networks grow for what is actively, personally, and specifically experienced and practiced.

4. Use it or lose it.

5. Emotions are inextricably bound up with thinking, learning, and remembering.

process into curricula and pedagogy for teaching whole units, courses, or programs. This issue is addressed in Chapters 8 and 9.

CONVERGING RESEARCH

Natural-learning research (Chapter 2) and brain research (Chapter 3) converge, yielding the following observations:

- The brain has innate resources (Figure 6.1)
- The brain has rules for how it learns (Figure 6.2).
- There is a correlation between the quality and quantity of the learner's experiences and the growth of neural structures (Figure 6.3).
- There is a correlation between increase of knowledge and skill and the growth of neural structures (Figure 6.3).

All these actions occur simultaneously:

- The learner is actively, personally, and specifically experiencing, processing, and practicing an object of learning.
- The learner's brain is growing and connecting neural structures.
- The learner is gaining new knowledge and skill; that is, the learner's ceiling level is rising for that object of learning.

The ceiling level, as defined in Chapter 2, is as much as learners know and can do at any moment. To raise their ceiling level, learners need more experience and practice so that their brains can grow and connect more

Figure 6.3   The Correlation Between, and Convergence of, What People Do to Learn (x axis) and the Brain-Based Natural Human Learning Process (y axis)

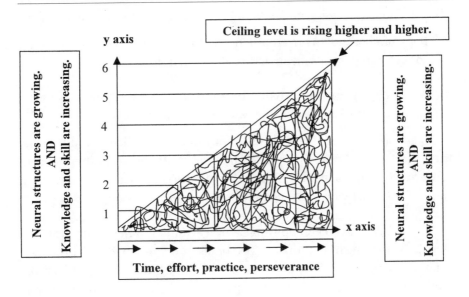

- **The learner is experiencing, practicing, processing.**

- **The neural structures are growing.**

- **Knowledge and skill are increasing, i. e., the ceiling level is rising.**

dendrites and synapses and construct additional, as well as more complex, neural networks. Thus, as noted earlier, a learner gaining knowledge and skill, instead of saying, "I'm catching on" or "I'm getting it," might more accurately say, "I feel my dendrites growing. I feel my synapses connecting."

Six Principles of Learning and Their Implications for Teaching

In this convergence of the research, we also observe the following principles and implications for how human beings learn:

1. *Principle*: Learning is physiological. New structures grow in the learner's brain during learning, and learning is the growing of new brain structures. In other words, learning and growing new brain structures are the same thing.

Implication: Teaching is like gardening; the purpose is to help students grow their own new brain structures.

2. *Principle*: Brain structures grow specifically for what is practiced. Brain structures that grow for one object of learning are only for that one object. (See Chapter 7 for a discussion of transfer of learning from one object to another.)

Implication: Students need practice with the target object of learning so they can grow brain structures for (learn) it.

3. *Principle*: New brain structures grow with practice and processing over time. Usually new brain structures take time to grow.

Implication: Students need sufficient time for practicing and processing to grow their brain structures. The time spent on this authentic work (on growing knowledge structures for the target object of learning) is some of the most well-spent class time.

4. *Principle*: For each new object of learning, it is necessary, as a first step, to help each student make a personal connection with it. This makes it possible for every student to "catch on" and have a foundation from which to then grow higher structures (more knowledge and skill) and start constructing the new network.

Implication: It is critical to give every student the opportunity and time to make a personal connection with a new and unfamiliar concept, skill, or body of information.

5. *Principle*: Students need to have a foundation of personal, basic familiarity with a new object of learning before they can do critical or creative thinking about that object of learning. Learners cannot do higher-level thinking about an object of learning unless and until they first have a foundation of familiarity about it.

Implication: Curricula should give opportunities to students to construct a foundation of new knowledge (new neural structures) through the first stages of the brain's natural learning process before assigning activities at the higher, critical or creative thinking, stages.

6. *Principle*: DNA can affect how quickly brain structures grow for different objects of learning, accounting for aptitudes.

Implication: Some students might have a genetic advantage for a specific subject or skill, making them able to learn (i.e., grow brain structures for) that object of learning more quickly and easily than others can or than they themselves can for an object of learning for which they have no special aptitude.

The result of teaching according to these principles and implications might be that teachers would give students more opportunities and time to grow their knowledge structures through sufficient specific practicing and processing.

THE THEORY AND GUIDE

This convergence of the research (Figure 6.3) supports the theory that there is, in fact, a brain-based natural human learning process (NHLP) and that knowing this process can help educators see better how to develop and deliver curricula that make it possible for every student to be a successful learner.

Putting the Theory Into Practice

The six research-based principles and implications for teaching listed in the previous section suggest a guide for putting the theory into practice. This is a research- and theory-based guide for creating and implementing an effective curriculum for any subject at any level.

Figure 6.4, then, describes the activities learners need to do at each stage. Figure 6.5 is the NHLP model. It shows that, at each stage or level of learning, students need to engage in an activity (task) that gives them the opportunity to grow the foundation of neural/knowledge structures they need to be able to progress to the next higher stage.

This guide has six stages because that is the most stages ever reported in the NHLP research. Interestingly, other developmental theories also identify six stages (e.g., Kohlberg, 1981; Krathwohl and Bloom, 1989, 1999; Piaget and Inhelder, 1969 [see Figure 3.15]).

Thinking at Higher Levels

Even though they are innately capable of high-level thinking, students think at a high level about only those objects of learning for which they have first constructed a foundation of knowledge (neural structures) to think *about* (Figures 6.4 and 6.5, Stages 1–3). In other words, the more experience learners, young or old, have with an object of learning, the more structures their brains grow for it, the more knowledge and skill they have about it, and the more high-level thinking they can naturally do about that particular object of learning (Figures 6.4 and 6.5, Stages 4–6).

Causal Sequences

An administrator at a community college at which I had given a workshop sent me the following message:

[A] computer faculty member said [after your presentation] that he did not believe in "that stuff." However, after thinking about what you had said, he restructured his summer class to find out more

Figure 6.4 The Causal Sequence of Stages of the Natural Human Learning Process (NHLP) for Acquiring the Concepts, Skill, and Knowledge of a New Object of Learning

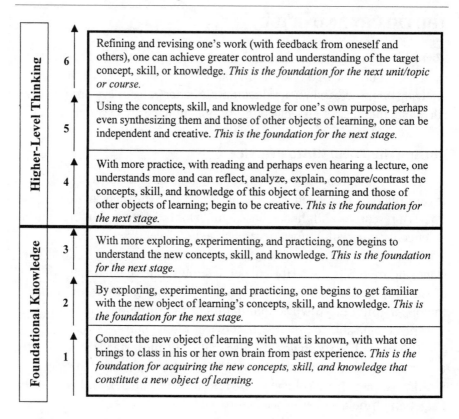

Note: Also see Figure 2.9.

about his students' knowledge and experience base upon entering class, and he simplified the complexity of his assignments letting them build upon one another. . . . He said it worked well beyond his expectations and that he had never gotten better student work or better student creativity. He's now sold on the idea of focusing on the learner. (James Ball, Carroll Community College, Westminster, Maryland, personal communication, August 19, 1999)

The principle for acquiring knowledge and skill about a new object of learning is that at each stage students need to construct a foundation for the next stage so that the complexity of the activities or assignments can "build upon one another," as shown in Figures 6.4 and 6.5. Again, acquiring foundation knowledge is what makes it possible for students to be able to think and perform at a higher level about that object of learning. This is a causal sequence of learning.

Figure 6.5   The Natural Human Learning Process Model for Creating and
Implementing Curricula

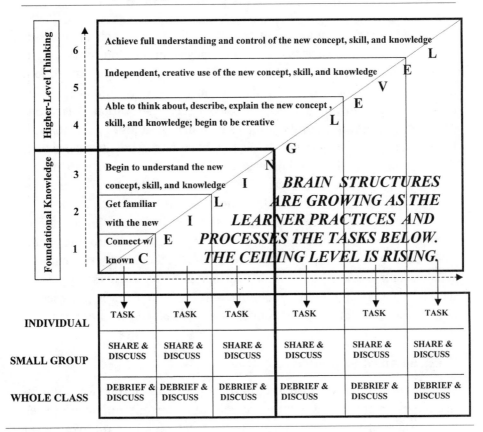

See "Front Loading" in Chapter 8. It discusses the importance of spending enough time at the beginning of a new unit, course, or program for students to construct a foundation for learning the new concepts, skills, and subject.

Constructing New Knowledge

This causal sequence of learning through levels of knowledge must be seamless. That is, following the first rule of how the brain learns (Figure 6.2), new knowledge can be constructed only on knowledge that is already there, just as a twig grows on a branch and not out of nothing (Chapter 3). Therefore, making a connection between the new and the old is imperative at every stage of learning, including at the all-important first stage.

If every new lesson, topic, or course would begin with an activity that asks each student to make a connection with something he or she already knows, every student would start by succeeding. The following section presents a method for determining what that first activity might be for any curriculum.

PLANNING THE SEQUENCE
OF THE UNITS OR TOPICS IN A CURRICULUM

A complete curriculum for a course is typically an ensemble of topics or units. For example, a curriculum for an English composition course might comprise units on different kinds of writing, for example, narration, description, definition. It might also—or instead—have units that focus on concepts or skills, such as audience, evidence, organization. An astronomy course might have units or topics on different kinds of astronomical bodies, for example, gas giants and smaller terrestrial worlds, which themselves might then be composed of subunits or subtopics such as asteroids, meteors, and comets. The question is, "What topics or units should I include and in what order should I teach them?"

Teachers have to determine the best order for presenting the units or topics in a curriculum. They might do it logically, chronologically, intuitively, by following the chapters in the textbook or a department syllabus, or by some other organizing principle. Some teachers might start with a tentative plan and then change it as the course develops as seems most appropriate for the particular students in that course that term.

Using a Causal Sequence

In contrast, the brain-based, natural-learning method for organizing the units and topics is cumulatively, in a causal sequence (Figures 6.6A and 6.6B). To help clarify the concept of a cumulative causal sequence, Figure 6.6A presents this method's planning guidelines verbally. Then Figure 6.6B presents the same guidelines visually. As these figures indicate, the teacher first identifies the goals and objectives of the curriculum, that is, what the students will know and be able to do at the end. Then the teacher deconstructs the goals and objectives of the course to determine which skills and concepts and what knowledge students need at each stage as a foundation to prepare them to understand and do the work at the next higher stage. These planning guidelines address the question of what to teach when.

> The teacher identifies where the students need to start, what basic foundation they need to construct first, then orders the units/topics so that they begin with that basic foundation of knowledge, skill, and concepts. Then, cumulatively, in a seamless causal sequence, presents the units/topics, stage by stage, up the levels of knowledge, skill, and concepts to the ones that are the goals and objectives of the course.

Figure 6.6A   Planning Guidelines for Identifying the Causal Sequence of Units/Topics in a Curriculum: What to Teach When–*Verbal Version*

1. Where do I want my students to be at the end of this unit, course, or program? What do I want them to know and/or be able to do?

2. What constituent concepts and skills do they need in order to know and to be able to do that?

3. In what sequence should I teach these constituent concepts and skills? That is, which ones are the foundation concepts and skills for later ones? (What do they need to know and be able to do before they can know and do what is needed at the next level?)

4. **The key question: Will they be able to see and do *that* if they do not first know and can do *this*?**

5. The curriculum needs to start with the knowledge structures students bring to class with them.

6. How can I find out what they know so I can know where to start? That is, what is the students' level of readiness for this unit, course, or program?
    (a) If I think they do not have knowledge about the subject, I can give them a no-fail task using the knowledge they bring with them and then construct the new knowledge stage by stage until they reach the goal.
    (b) But if I think they know something about the subject, I can ask them to write down everything they know about it, e.g., "Write down everything you know about Egypt."

Learning Activities for Units and Topics

Individual units and topics are taught via learning activities. Learning activities give students the opportunity to acquire the concepts, skills, and knowledge in a unit or topic. For example, one teacher might employ the teacher-centered learning activities of demonstrating and lecturing. Another teacher's student-centered learning activities might be to have students explore, experiment, work together, and do research.

The First Activity

A critical question is what to teach first. If students begin a new unit or topic not knowing the new object of learning (having no neural structures for it), they need to do an activity or task that will let them connect to and use relevant knowledge/ neural structures they already have. Once existing knowledge/structures are stimulated, learners can then connect new knowledge/structures to them and start growing higher ones specific to that curriculum. Thus, from activity to activity, students can seamlessly grow and construct higher and higher levels of knowledge structures, each higher level connected to and constructed on the prior foundation.

Chapters 8 and 9 focus on the development and delivery of complete curricula for courses or multicourse programs, with examples from different

Figure 6.6B   Planning Guidelines for Identifying the Causal Sequence—*Visual Version*

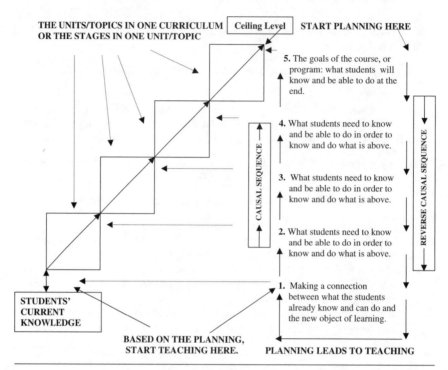

- The learner is experiencing, practicing, processing the objects of learning in each unit/topic.
- Neural structures are growing throughout.
- Knowledge and skill are increasing throughout.
- The ceiling level is rising throughout.

disciplines. In contrast, this chapter focuses on the first unit or topic of a curriculum and, more specifically, on the first learning activity of the first unit.

How can a teacher determine which activity would help students make the all-important initial connection at the beginning of a new unit or topic? Figure 6.7A provides a method for doing this. Then, in the following section, Figures 6.7B and 6.7C give specific examples.

Two Classroom Examples

Here are examples of initial or first-stage activities in two different NHLP lesson plans (sets of learning activities). One introduces Egypt in a social science class (Figure 6.7B), and the other introduces fractions in a math class (Figure 6.7C).

Dave Williams, then a student in the Master in Teaching program at the Evergreen State College, Olympia, Washington, was, as a student teacher, introducing Egypt to a sixth-grade class. He thought they would

Figure 6.7A   The First Activity: Finding Out What Students Know

1. If you think they know anything about the topic, concept, or skill, ask them to write down what they know about it. For example, to find out where they are in their knowledge of Egypt, use the first task in Figure 6.7B:

   - *Individually*: "Write down what you know about Egypt."
   - *Small groups of no more than four*: "Share and discuss what you wrote."
   - *Whole class debriefing and discussion*: "What did you come up with?"

OR

2. If you expect students do not know about the topic, assign a no-fail activity that will let each student start to learn the new topic by making a connection to it from something he or she can do or already knows. Figure 6.7C shows the first activity in an introduction-to-fractions lesson plan; the complete lesson plan is included in Chapter 9.

---

know something about Egypt, so the first task he gave them was to write down what they knew about Egypt (Figure 6.7B), thereby activating their relevant neural/knowledge structures, which now would be the foundation for their new learning. Dave's complete lesson plan is in Chapter 9.

In the next example of a first-stage or initial activity, the math teacher, Joanne Rawley, knew from experience that most or all of the students in her St. Petersburg (Florida) Junior College developmental math class would not know about fractions. Therefore, she could not ask them what they knew about fractions. Instead, she gave them a no-fail task that they could do by calling on related knowledge/neural structures (Figure 6.7C). These activated structures, then, became the foundation on which they could construct their new dendrites and synapses for the concept of fractions and the skill of using them. Her complete introduction-to-fractions unit is also in Chapter 9.

Students and the NHLP

Each new NHLP lesson or unit begins, as in the examples in Figures 6.7A and 6.7B, with what might seem to some students as a "baby step." After students have done the natural-learning activity (Chapter 2) and learned about the brain (Chapter 3), however, they have the metacognitive knowledge (Chapter 5) to know it is necessary to grow their dendrites and synapses from the bottom up for every new object of learning. They accept the fact that if this first step is a baby step, so be it.

They also understand that they are the only ones who can grow their brain's neural structures, so they cannot just listen, observe, take notes, then expect to use the new skill or new knowledge with full understanding and expertise. They know they must be actively involved in their own learning process. There is also, of course, a place for teachers to lecture

Figure 6.7B   No-Fail First Activity in an Introduction to Egypt Unit Lesson Plan
(teacher expects students do know something about this topic)

Stage 1
PREPARING TO LEARN
Using Current Knowledge

Individual	"Write down everything you know about Egypt."
Small Groups	"Tell each other what you wrote." **One student said, "I know only one thing." Another student in the same group said, "I know only two things." The teacher said, "Then between you, you might have three things."**
Whole Group	"What did you write down?" **Teacher writes down all answers verbatim on the board. Note: This is a complete NHLP pedagogical cycle: Individual, Small Groups, Whole Group (I/SG/WG).**

Note: This has been used successfully in 6th grade and could be used in lower or higher grades.

and to assign readings in an NHLP curriculum, as seen in Figure 6.4 (Stage 4) and as discussed in Chapter 8, "Lectures and Textbooks."

Furthermore, when students are aware that everyone is different and everyone might learn at different rates in different subjects, they are able to keep their motivation and self-confidence high even in the face of having to practice more in one subject than in another or more than another student in the same subject (see Figure 3.8). Thus, with their metacognitive understanding, students are empowered to learn; and, when they have the opportunity to learn by NHLP curriculum, learning activities, and pedagogy, they learn naturally and successfully.

The NHLP planning guidelines (Figures 6.8 and 6.9), which are fully explicated and illustrated in Chapters 8 and 9, specify the learning activity (task) and goal for each stage of a unit/topic lesson plan. Although six stages are not an arbitrary number, neither is this number cast in concrete. Not every curriculum or lesson plan needs all six stages (examples in Chapter 8). See also "Front Loading" in Chapter 8.

Sometimes students will even need more than one task at certain stages, as shown in the "1–6" self-assessment method in Figure 6.8 (Whole Group activity, Stages 2 to 6). See "In-Class Assessment" in Chapter 7 for a full discussion of this in-class assessment method.

Figure 6.7C No-Fail First Activity in an Introduction to Fractions Unit Lesson Plan (teacher expects students do not know about this topic)

Stage 1
PREPARE TO LEARN
Using Current Knowledge

Individual	**Teacher gives each student four 8 ×11 sheets of paper, each one a different color (e.g., white, blue, red, green).** "Tear the blue sheet into two equal pieces and place them on the whole white sheet. Write down how you would tell or think about how you would tell or explain to someone how many of the blue pieces *one* of the blue pieces is."
Small Groups	"Tell each other what you wrote or thought. Discuss what you were thinking when you were trying to figure out what to write or say."
Whole Group	"What did you write or say?" **If their answers are too long to write verbatim on the board, this activity can be done only orally.** "What were you thinking when you were trying to figure out what to write or say?" **Note: This is a complete NHLP pedagogical cycle: Individual, Small Groups, Whole Group (I/SG/WG).**

Note: This plan has been used successfully from 2nd grade to college.

Figure 6.9 introduces the instructional strategy ("Pedagogy Guidelines") used in an NHLP Curriculum.

Before reading about the details of this pedagogy in Chapter 7 ("The Pedagogical Model") and the rationale for it ("Why Only This Pedagogy?"), here is an example of how one community college teacher used the planning and pedagogy guidelines to help him design and implement a unit for an anthropology course.

DEVELOPING A CURRICULUM

An Anthropology Unit and Its Learning Activities

James Bannen, an anthropology instructor at Seattle Central Community College, planned a unit on a sub-Saharan desert tribe

Figure 6.8   Planning Guidelines for NHLP Learning Activities

	Stage 1 PREPARING TO LEARN *Using current knowledge*	Stage 2 STARTING TO LEARN *Experimental practice*	Stage 3 CONSOLIDATING NEW BASE *Further practice*
Individual	**TASK:** Making a connection with something already known and familiar to the learner. **GOAL:** To alert existing relevant neurons to get ready for learning/ growing new dendrites/networks.	**TASK:** Hands-on practice or experience with the new concept/skill at a low level of understanding/skill. **GOAL:** To gain superficial familiarity with the overt characteristics/nature of the new concept/skill.	**TASK:** More concrete practice or experience at a slightly higher level of understanding/skill. **GOAL:** To make the basic foundation of understanding/skill clearer and stronger.
Small Groups	**TASK:** Share/discuss as actively and fully as possible: listen carefully, think seriously, respond sincerely, reconsider own work. **GOAL:** To activate neurons so they will grow.	**TASK:** Share/discuss as actively and fully as possible: listen carefully, think seriously, respond sincerely, reconsider own work. **GOAL:** To activate neurons so they will grow.	**TASK:** Share/discuss as actively and fully as possible: listen carefully, think seriously, respond sincerely, reconsider own work. **GOAL:** To activate neurons so they will grow.
Whole Group	**TASK:** Share the questions/ideas/problems/experiences/knowledge students came up with in the SG session. **GOAL:** To increase skill/understanding/confidence. Teacher can write all points verbatim on the board.	**TASK and GOAL:** Same as before. Writing a 1----6 scale on the board, the teacher can ask who is totally confused (0-1), who gets it (4-5), who is starting to get it (2-3). If most are low, repeat work at this stage. If most are high, go on. Help lower ones outside class.	**TASK and GOAL:** Same as before, including the 1----6 scale for student self-assessment to see whether to go on or do more tasks at this stage. It is counterproductive for the teacher to add anything before students are ready, as they will be after Stage 4.

(Figure 6.10). This unit's learning activities can be used at any level from elementary school to college because students will bring to it the amount of knowledge and experience they have and will construct their new neural/knowledge structures on that foundation. The adult students in the community college course for which this lesson was developed were at a high level of knowledge about society in general but at a low level of knowledge about anthropology and, particularly, about the sub-Saharan tribe that was the subject of this unit. Younger students could also understand the life of this tribe, but not as completely as the older, more experienced students.

Even though from childhood the brain is capable of high-level thinking, it can learn only as much as its foundation neural/knowledge structures has available from experience and previous learning on which to construct further growth.

Figure 6.8 *(Continued)*

	Stage 4 BRANCHING OUT *Knowing in more detail*	Stage 5 GAINING FLUENCY *Using it, doing it*	Stage 6 CONTINUED IMPROVEMENT *Wider application*
Individual	**TASK:** More in-depth and challenging practice/thinking/ experience. **GOAL:** To see connections, to see more clearly and in finer detail.	**TASK:** An assignment in which learners use their new concept/skill on their own. **GOAL:** To produce work that shows understanding of the new concept and competence with the new skill.	**TASK:** A similar assignment (or a revision of the previous one) in which learners improve their work. **GOAL:** To reinforce/confirm the skills/concepts learned in this unit.
Small Groups	**TASK:** Share/discuss as actively and fully as possible: listen carefully, think seriously, respond sincerely, reconsider own work. **GOAL:** To activate neurons so they will grow.	**TASK:** Share/discuss as actively and fully as possible: listen carefully, think seriously, respond sincerely, reconsider own work. **GOAL:** To activate neurons so they will grow.	**TASK:** Share/discuss as actively and fully as possible: listen carefully, think seriously, respond sincerely, reconsider own work. **GOAL:** To activate neurons so they will grow.
Whole Group	**TASK and GOAL:** Same as before, including the 1----6 scale for student self-assessment. Now that students have a basic foundation of skill/knowledge, they are ready/eager for the teacher to add/clarify/correct, if necessary, with a lecture or reading assignment.	**TASK and GOAL:** Same as before, including the 1----6 scale for student self-assessment.	**TASK and GOAL:** Same as before, including the 1----6 scale for student self-assessment. Stage 6 knowledge/skill will be the basis for--and what is recalled/ reviewed--in Stage 1 of the next unit.

Planning the Unit

Jim developed this anthropology unit while participating in an NHLP curriculum development workshop. First, the participants were to identify in one of their courses an upcoming unit or topic that they had not taught before or that had not been completely successful in previous terms. Then they developed an initial NHLP learning activity for the unit, tried it out on colleagues in the workshop, got feedback, revised the activity, used it in class with students, and then reported on and discussed the results at a subsequent workshop session. This cycle was repeated several times so that participants had the opportunity to learn from their experience and then do further practice with other learning activities or units/topics.

Jim said he had a wonderful film about a sub-Saharan tribe to introduce this tribe's culture to his class. Unfortunately, however, to his surprise, students were bored and inattentive when he showed the film. He wanted to find a more effective way to introduce this tribe.

Figure 6.9   Pedagogy Guidelines for the Natural Human Learning Process

Individual	For the first stage in learning something new, learners first must recall/activate/stimulate/review what they already know that is in some way related to the new concept/knowledge/skill. This prepares the brain to be able to acquire new knowledge and skill (grow and connect new neural structures). **The very first task must be a no-fail activity, a task that everyone will be able to do:** "Take out a piece of paper and write down what you know about . . . (whatever the new topic is)." If the students are too young to write, they can be asked just to think about it. **OR** **If you cannot assume students know much about the topic,** assign an activity which asks them to use prior knowledge and experience. (See sample lesson plans.)
Small Groups	Small group activity is not for the purpose of coming to a single solution or consensus. It is to 1) heighten the level of activity and inter-activity to stimulate the brain and 2) have all students interact with their different perspectives and express and re/consider their own ideas and experiences. Students come to this activity with something that they have just written (or done or thought) individually. **"Get into a group with 2 or 3 students around you. Share and discuss what you wrote (or did or thought). If you disagree or did it differently, explain your point and reasons. Ask others questions if you don't understand why they did what they did. You don't need to agree or make a group report."**
Whole Group	The teacher then debriefs the students. They respond and participate as individuals rather than as group members whose group has come up with one unified idea. Since each student's individual brain must do the learning for that student, each student must return to consulting, questioning, exploring his or her own brain about the work. **"What did you come up with? What ideas, questions, problems? You can give your own idea or an idea you liked from someone else in your group."** It is essential that the teacher writes students' ideas/points/ contributions *verbatim* on the board. Otherwise, students feel co-opted and get the message their ideas aren't good enough. The goal here is not to tell students the "right answer" or have them come up with a "right answer." The point here is for students to be exploring, practicing, thinking, and also feeling positive about their own attempt to participate. This *student-centered approach* helps them trust and depend on their own learning process, their ability to learn from their own and each other's work, and their own intelligence. Learners need self-confidence and self-esteem in order to learn because emotions affect the brain's ability to learn. It is not harmful for the teacher to write students' mistakes on the board because any mistakes or deficiencies will be corrected later *by the students themselves* as the teacher provides appropriate learning tasks in an appropriate sequence. When students have the opportunity to practice appropriate learning tasks in an appropriate sequence, they learn from their own mistakes. Because human beings learn what they practice, students need the opportunity to practice, practice, practice, i.e., to make and correct mistakes and try again.

Note: These steps are further discussed in Chapter 7.

The Causal Sequence and the First Learning Activity

According to the NHLP planning guidelines for identifying the causal sequence of a unit (Figures 6.6A and 6.6B), the first step is that the teacher identifies the goal for the unit. Jim's goal for this unit was that his students would gain an understanding of the relationship between the tribe's social, political, and economic structures and the tribe's ability to survive. He had previously started the unit with the film, followed by a lecture and then a reading assignment. Despite all this information, students' curiosity and interest were not sparked; they were not engaged in thinking or caring about the tribe's survival and its structures. How could he do it differently?

Following the reverse causal sequence (Figure 6.6B), he asked himself what students would need to understand in order to be able to understand that goal. He decided they would need to understand why the tribe had created those specific structures. Then, continuing back down the causal sequence, he asked what the students would need to understand in order to understand why people would even want or need to create any such structures. From there, he worked backward until he determined that the first thing the students would need to understand is what surviving is all about.

Because the goal was for students to understand that those structures helped the tribe survive, Jim started with a no-fail task critically related to that goal (Figure 6.7A, Question 2): "Write down what you need to survive" (Figure 6.10, Stage 1). Every student could do that.

After this individual work, the students discussed their lists of survival needs with each other in small groups for a few minutes and then debriefed as a whole class, with Jim writing all their items verbatim and neutrally on the chalkboard. Their lists for this Stage 1 assignment included items such as food, a home, a car, a phone.

The Causal Sequence and the Next Learning Activities

Then they were ready to proceed with the next learning activity (Figure 6.10, Stage 2). For the Stage 2 assignment, Jim gave them the opportunity to connect with the ideas already stimulated by the Stage 1 activity. He showed on the overhead a picture of a desert, told the students that they live in this desert, and asked them what they would now need to survive. Students bent eagerly to the task, then shared their lists with each other in small groups, and finally debriefed together again as a whole class. This time their lists included items such as water, camels, a map, sunscreen.

The Stage 3 task, again connecting to—growing structures on—the ideas that had been stimulated, was to write down what people who had lived there for thousands of years needed for their survival. Again, after

Figure 6.10 Introduction to Sub-Saharan Tribe Unit: A Six-Stage Lesson Plan

	Stage 1 PREPARING TO LEARN *Using current knowledge*	Stage 2 STARTING TO LEARN *Experimental practice*	Stage 3 CONSOLIDATING NEW BASE *Further practice*
Individual	"Make a list of everything you need to survive."	"You live here. Now make a list of what you need to survive."	"People have lived here for thousands of years. What do you think they need in order to survive?"
Small Groups	"Share your lists and discuss your survival needs."	"Share your lists and discuss your survival needs."	"Share your lists and discuss what they need to survive."
Whole Group	"What did you come up with?" **The teacher transcribes on the board verbatim whatever the students contribute.**	The teacher asks, "What did you come up with?" **The teacher transcribes on the board verbatim whatever the students contribute.**	The teacher asks, "What did you come up with?" **The teacher transcribes on the board verbatim whatever the students contribute.**

Note: See pp. 141-143 for a description of Stages 4-6.

their individual writing and small-group sharing, they came back and reported to the whole group as Jim once more wrote their points verbatim on the board. This time they listed such things as making a living, having health care, educating children.

Each new learning activity gave them the opportunity to use their previous idea as the foundation for a new idea. They were making connections. Their understanding was growing stage by stage. The students, with interest and pleasure, were using their brain's inner resources and were experiencing their brain's natural learning process. After this, at Stage 4, they saw the film and were to write down what they saw the tribe doing to survive.

Jim reported back at the next workshop session that he had been amazed at how interested and attentive the students were at each stage, including at Stage 4 when they finally watched the film. He said they were excitedly pointing out features of the tribe, calling out, "Oh, I knew that!" or "Oh no, I never thought of that!" whereas formerly they had been unresponsive and passive during the film.

After the film and their small- and whole-group discussions on what the tribe does to survive and, later, on whether what the film shows is similar to or different from what they thought the tribe would be doing, his plan called for him to give a lecture if any important points had been left out or corrections were needed. He said he had not needed to give a lecture because the students had seen and figured out everything he would have said at that point. (This reminded me, as reported in Chapter 1, of my being glad not to have given my poetry lecture after the students had gone further and deeper than I would have gone in the lecture.)

At the fifth stage, instead of giving them a reading assignment, he asked them to write down everything they now knew about this tribe—in effect, to write their own textbook.

They then discussed in small groups what they had written and, finally, shared their writing and ideas as a whole class. Alternatively, at Stage 5 they could have written formal papers individually or as small groups, discussed their papers in their groups, and at Stage 6 they could have revised their papers. Jim, however, preferred to give them a test at Stage 6, which everyone passed.

They could also, as a second activity at Stage 6, have corrected their tests together, using them as a review, referring to their notes and perhaps their official textbook as well, and then retaken the test. They would probably all have passed the new test with even more insight and understanding than before. Jim, however, ended the unit with the one test at Stage 6.

Teachers using the planning guidelines find that all sorts of inventive and interesting variations in activities are possible.

Participating in brain-based, natural-learning activities in an NHLP curriculum is a pleasure for students; seeing the students learning with keen attention and interest is a pleasure for teachers.

YOUNG STUDENTS THINKING AT A HIGH LEVEL

When I was working with high school students in an after-school program for students who had failed one or more of their day-school courses, I used Jim's college-level anthropology unit as a stimulating and challenging experience for them. The students gave the following responses to the first learning-activity task, "Make a list of what you need to survive": "food, air, water, shelter, interaction, money, love."

After seeing the picture of a desert, they responded to the second learning-activity task, "You live here. Now make a list of what you need to survive," with this list: "food, water, air conditioning, shade, sunscreen."

Then, for the third task, "People have lived here for thousands of years. What do you think they need to survive?" They responded with these points: "all of the other things, knowledge of the land, how to use it to make it work for you, natural resources."

Unfortunately, we did not have the film, so the unit ended here. The students were involved and attentive throughout—and eager to learn more. I believe that if their high school courses were taught with NHLP curricula and pedagogy, these students would not have failed. There is more about these students in Chapter 8.

SOME MORE WORDS ABOUT THE NHLP

A Success Story

NHLP curriculum and pedagogy have been used in the developmental grammar course mentioned in Chapter 5. The average retention—and success—rate has been 80 to 90% for this course. In contrast, the national average retention rate for such a course is 50% (Boylan & Bonham, 1992; Waycaster, 2002). Chapter 9 describes the curriculum and pedagogy of this course and includes samples of one student's progress.

I also teach a course at Western Washington University's Woodring College of Education on this brain-based, natural-learning approach to teaching, and an education major sent me this unsolicited message:

> As I am now student teaching, I feel it is time to let you know that you are still the professor who had the greatest impact on my studies to become a teacher. The . . . philosophies that you imparted to us have carried me through the best and worst of times. . . . When I start teaching, I will be teaching the NHLP with my students and coworkers. Students will have the opportunity to learn from one another and will be given more chances to be successful than on just one try—thank you for this gift of a learning lifetime. (Deborah Cuevas)

Finally, research- and theory-based NHLP curricula and pedagogy invite the brain to use its innate resources (Figure 6.1) as well as incorporate the five rules of how the brain learns (Figure 6.2). As a result, the brain naturally grows new neural structures, and students successfully acquire new knowledge and skill. Moreover, with NHLP curricula and pedagogy, students are naturally motivated and attentive.

This NHLP approach to teaching works because it is based on how, from birth throughout life, the human brain actually learns. The more that learners are invited to use their innate resources, and the more that the curricula and learning activities employ the rules of the brain, the more motivated and successful learners will be.

A Joy for Teachers

All this thinking, analyzing, and lesson-planning might seem like a lot of laborious, unnecessary work, perhaps even daunting, to a teacher. However, the good news is that it helps a teacher fall in love with his or her subject all over again.

When we teachers contemplate our subjects or disciplines, we see the complex elements all richly interwoven as a whole picture while our students might not be able to see it clearly—or at all. We can tell our students what we know in lectures that are well-prepared and well-delivered, that are entertaining and even inspiring. Or, instead, we can help our students begin by learning it for themselves. If we choose this natural learning process approach, we need to deconstruct our subject (Figure 6.6A and 6.6B) by first asking ourselves, "What do I need to know to have this full understanding of my subject? What is the foundational knowledge I have that makes it possible for me to have this high-level understanding?" Then, after figuring that out—it is not easy, but it is challenging and invigorating—asking, "And what do I need to know to know *that?*" As we work our way back down the levels of the causal sequence, we are seeing our subject in a new way. We are appreciating it in a new way and, very likely, falling in love with it again.

This joy is compounded when our students become personally interested in, and even excited about, our subject, just as we were when we started exploring it, because they are starting where we started and are following our path up the causal sequence to more and more knowledge and understanding. They are thinking, working, wondering—and becoming empowered with new knowledge and skill. As Julie Noble, a teacher who has used this approach at both the community college and university levels, said, "There is no better way to experience the joy of teaching than to see students' joy of learning blossom. There is no greater motivator than success, and that's what all of us—students and teachers alike—experience is an NHLP learning environment" (personal communication, April 4, 2002).

The Pedagogical Model and Guidelines   *7*

The pleasures arising from thinking and learning will make us think and learn all the more.

Aristotle

Before we look at the pedagogical guidelines, let us first look at our expectations for our curricula and pedagogy. Do we expect that students who earn good grades in our classes will be able to use their new skills and knowledge in—will be able to transfer them to—other classes or even their lives outside school? Let us start with a discussion of transfer, which has been and remains one of the most vexing issues in education: "Precisely what it is that transfers, and why it transfers, are far from understood, though these are essential questions for education" (Gregory, 1987, pp. 780–781). I hope this discussion will help us understand why students are able to apply or transfer what they learn and, if they cannot, why not.

TRANSFER

An educator of corporate sales and management personnel had this to say about the brain-based Natural Human Learning Process:

You have this . . . concept of graduated learning that is truly helpful. The chart you supply to outline the development of a concept is very useful. The concept of "connective thought" not becoming applicable until the neural paths can connect is a huge help to me. It explains why it is useless to assume understanding on the part of the listeners when the relationship I am trying to teach is "basic" to me but foreign to some of the listeners. To understand that each step of the learning process is unique and not transferable until the networks interconnect is critical. (Ed Weinberg, President, Targeted Results, Inc., personal communication, July 14, 1999)

The Problem

Students' inability to transfer what they have learned from one situation or task to another is a common problem. For example, students in an English class correctly identify and correct errors in the sentences on grammar worksheets or in a workbook. The expectation is that they will also be able to identify, avoid, or correct similar errors in their own sentences. However, typically—and disappointingly—they are unable to do so. Is it the students' fault? Are they cognitively deficient or just incompetent students? The answer to this question is not that students are incapable. It is, rather, that the transfer of learning is problematic.

Positive and Negative Transfer

Bransford et al. (1999) defined positive transfer as "the ability to use what was learned in one setting to deal with new problems and events" (p. 15); however, "Psychologists [who] have studied the conditions under which transfer takes place [find it] surprisingly hard to get positive transfer" (Sternberg & Williams, 2002, p. 330). "Negative transfer," on the other hand, is more likely to occur because people typically apply in a new situation the knowledge, skills, and behaviors that are familiar to them. For example, "Many aspects of school failure can be explained as a mismatch between what students have learned in their home cultures and what is required of them in the school culture" (Bransford et al., 1999, p. 225).

Sternberg and Williams (2002), focusing on both positive and negative transfer, wrote that "transfer of knowledge gained from earlier problems can either help solve new problems or hinder their solution" (p. 329), as when learning a new language: "[T]he skill of learning Latin is generally supposed to transfer positively to the learning of other languages, although it may transfer negatively [when learning] differently constructed languages" (Gregory, 1987, p. 781).

The difficulty of positive transfer and the ease of negative transfer are frustrating and disappointing both for us and for our students.

A Brain-Based Solution

As discussed in Chapter 3, neural structures (knowledge and skill) grow for what is personally and specifically experienced and practiced (Figure 6.2, Rule 3). To avoid negative transfer and promote positive transfer, different new neural/knowledge structures are needed for each different new concept or skill. Yes, learners can certainly use relevant prior knowledge when learning similar new concepts and skills. In fact, when learners use—transfer—prior knowledge, it "can greatly increase the speed of new learning" (Hart, 1999, p. 165). The problem here is that learners cannot do this as readily for objects of learning that are somewhat different. It is even more difficult for ones that are significantly different.

Transfering Learning

Learning Is Specific

As discussed in Chapter 3, learning is the producing of specific new physiological structures in the brain as and because we are processing a specific object of learning (Figure 6.2, Rule 3). As we do this, knowledge- and skill-specific dendrites and synapses grow, creating an increasingly complex neural network (higher and higher levels of knowledge and skill) for that specific object of learning.

Learning Is Constructive

Learners naturally construct new knowledge (new neural structures) from preexisting knowledge structures (Figure 6.2, Rule 1). This is why negative transfer happens naturally. That is, students beginning to learn something new and different will naturally use their current knowledge structures as the foundation for the new and different learning. The result is that they will see only what they already know and will not see what is new and different. Thus, whatever new learning they do will be off the mark, sabotaged by their brain's natural attempt to grow the new structures off the old.

What they need to do, instead, is start with a new foundation. Remember the Korean student, highlighted in Chapter 5, who did not want to go back to the beginning of learning English and make the crucial initial and correct connection at a baby level. Consequently, having begun with a connection to his own highly developed Korean language structures, he was practicing negative transfer and so was not successful in his sincere attempts to learn English.

Positive transfer is a more complicated matter because it requires intervening in the natural constructive process of learning (connecting new knowledge structures to what is already in the brain). What students need is to begin the learning of a new and different concept, skill, or body of knowledge by making a new and different first connection to something they already know—but it must be to something intrinsically relevant to the new and different object of learning. The planning models (Figures 6.6A and 6.6B) can help teachers identify what that first relevant activity might be.

Bransford et al. (1999) list effective ways to help students positively transfer what they have learned to new problems and situations, including spending a lot of time on task, practicing the skill in different contexts, and learning with understanding rather than merely by rote (pp. 223–225). It is critical as well to help students start learning a new and different concept, skill, or body of knowledge by helping them first make a connection to something relevant that they already know and then giving them opportunities to construct their new knowledge and skill, stage by stage, from that relevant foundation. This provides students with the power of positive transfer.

Unequal Transfer Does Not Work

It might seem counterintuitive that people with a high level of knowledge and skill about one object of learning cannot easily understand and be skillful with a new object of learning. But they typically cannot because neural networks (knowledge and skill) grow with tailor-made precision for what the learner is actively processing (Figure 6.2, Rule 3). The neural structures they grow *are* their knowledge and skill. Therefore, when someone has learned a task, skill, concept, procedure, or body of knowledge to a high degree, it means that the learner has grown a highly complex neural network for that specific object of learning but not necessarily for any other.

That complex neural network can then make contact with—can literally catch onto—the neural network of a different learned object; this will happen only if both networks are more or less equally well grown. The learner then "catches on," has an "aha" experience, and can say, "Oh, now I see how these areas relate!" The learner sees this because the two previously separate neural networks are now, in fact, physiologically connected, making it possible for the learner to transfer—to apply what is already known separately to this new interrelated situation—and, thus, to compare, contrast, and synthesize the two areas of knowledge. For example, an art history major takes a history course and during a class about halfway through the term has an "aha" experience—the student is suddenly able to see and appreciate the relationship between the historical context of an era and the subject matter of that era's artwork. The student has finally grown enough new history knowledge structures for there to be a connection between them and the well-grown art history structures.

Examples of Transfer Problems

As noted above, it might seem that if people have a high level of knowledge and skill about an object of learning, they should be able to understand and skillfully use that knowledge and skill to learn a new one. But, again, this is not feasible with highly complex objects of learning and unequal networks.

An example of lack of transfer between unequal networks is an experience I had in graduate school. Many years after getting a bachelor's degree in English and a master's in speech, and after teaching for almost 20 years, I entered a doctoral program in educational psychology. This research-based program requires that candidates take a number of math-based statistics courses. Unfortunately, I hadn't taken a math class for 30 years. Also, most of the students come to these doctoral-level statistics courses from their master's-level statistics courses; however, because I had always been a successful student and had excellent study skills—I had even written a study skills textbook (Smilkstein, 1983)—I believed I would be able to do well even in this very different subject, even at this high level.

I was completely wrong. None of my excellent study skills did me any good because I did not understand the terminology, nor did I know the concepts the teacher and textbook assumed the students knew. The lectures and textbook were over my head. I was dendrite-disadvantaged. I just did not get it. That great a cognitive gap is terribly painful, causing the sufferer to think, "I don't understand anything he's talking about. I'm stupid." A number of students dropped out, but I did not. Having the advantage of knowing that a teacher should start a new subject by going to where the students are, I had a plan for surviving.

I would be my own teacher and start where I was, at the beginning. I went to the university bookstore and bought a freshman statistics book. I was the student and also, for now, my own teacher as well. I studied that first-level book, teaching myself the basics, beginning to construct a foundation of knowledge. After a month, because my dendrites had been growing and connecting to form my new neural network for statistics, I was starting to catch on. My dendrites could even begin to grow at a higher level because there were now statistics-specific lower-level ones from which they could grow.

By the end of the term, I had caught up enough to pass the course; and, because I now had foundation knowledge, my dendrites and I were ready to advance to the next statistics course.

At first I had not been able to transfer my high-level knowledge of study skills to graduate-level statistics because I had no statistics structures with which my study skills structures could connect. However, I could use my study skills knowledge in the second statistics course because I now had a statistics network to which I could connect. I could now read the textbook and take notes in lectures with appreciable understanding. Being able to transfer both my new statistics knowledge and my prior study skills to learning the material in the second statistics course, I was able to learn it better than I had the material in the first course.

I was never a great statistics student. I could not compete with the students who were math and science majors, who had much richer and more complex knowledge networks than I had about this highly complicated, math-based subject. But I passed every course, sometimes sitting in on the same course a second time to fine-tune my new network. As discussed in Chapter 3, it takes a long time to grow a complex network for a complex object of learning.

Teach to the Target

Learning must focus on the target skill or concept, because we learn by growing neural networks for what we specifically and actively practice or process (Figure 6.2, Rule 3). Thus, if students are to acquire knowledge about a complex object of learning, such as how to use correct grammar in their own writing, how to solve word problems in math, or the nature of social structures in a sub-Saharan tribe, this is exactly what they specifically need to practice and process. This is necessary because neural structures are specific. Each different concept or skill is a specific physical structure grown as a result of specific active practice and processing. To learn each new concept, skill, or body of information, learners must construct a new neural network— a new physiological incarnation that will *be* the new knowledge.

The natural human learning process (NHLP) planning guidelines (Figure 6.8) focus on helping students do on-target learning. It also has students begin each new topic by making a relevant personal connection with what they already know so they can transfer this prior or current knowledge to their new learning. Moreover, this approach gives students the opportunity to correct themselves if they are making a negative rather than positive transfer; and, again, if information about learning is shared with students, they will have the metacognitive knowledge they need to be empowered as successful learners. First, however, we will look at several effective instructional or pedagogical practices.

FOUR MAJOR INSTRUCTIONAL PRACTICES

Hunter Boylan (2002) summarized the research on the effectiveness of instructional practices and how best to provide instruction. He described a number of different practices, one of which is feedback from instructors: "Learning theorists have consistently emphasized [that instructor] feedback [is] one of the most important stimuli to learning" (p. 84). Another practice he highlighted is active learning, reporting that it seems to be "the most effective teaching technique available to college instructors" (p. 101) and that

> the basic concept of active learning is that students are directly involved in creating their own learning rather than being passive recipients of instruction (Friere [1970]). In active learning, students are not required to spend all of their time sitting through lectures but, instead, are required to take actions and explore knowledge for themselves. (p. 101)

Boylan also discussed the teaching of learning strategies, including "comprehension monitoring and self-regulating behaviors" (p. 97). *We're Born to Learn* emphasizes comprehension monitoring and self-regulation via frequent self-evaluations (Figures 5.1–5.3). Students do these self-evaluations with metacognitive understanding of their learning process and with an understanding of what they need to do to learn successfully (Chapter 5).

A fourth instructional practice Boylan presented is classroom assessment, which he cites as "probably one of the most successful higher education innovations in the decade of the 1990s. It is also a technique used widely by best-practice institutions in the [Continuous Quality Improvement Network/American Productivity and Quality Center] (2000) study" (p. 104).

Four of the major instructional practices in this book's brain-based, natural-learning pedagogical approach are the instructional practices Boylan identified: feedback (both instructor and peer), active learning, self-monitoring, and assessment (see sections that follow on formative and summative assessment processes and the Small Group Instructional Feedback process).

THE NHLP PEDAGOGICAL GUIDELINES

The NHLP pedagogy is delivered via a three-step process:

1. Individual Work

2. Small-Group Activity/Interactivity

3. Whole-Group Feedback.

For every assignment in every lesson plan, this pedagogical model uses the same three steps to facilitate an active and interactive, feedback-rich, learner- and learning-centered constructive pedagogy. It is also a pedagogy that focuses on positive transfer. A later section addresses the question "why this pedagogy?" The following describes these three steps (Figure 6.9).

Individual Work

The teacher asks a relevant subject-based question, as in the first activity in Figures 6.7–6.11. Students then write (or in some other way express) their answer. This is not to hand in or to be evaluated; it is only to give students the opportunity to do their own thinking. Because all people are different, with different neural structures (different stores of knowledge) from different internal and external factors and experiences, the students need to make their own connections with their own unique brain stores of knowledge.

Small-Group Work

The students then join two or three others in a small group to share, discuss, debate, and get and give feedback on their individual work and ideas. Some of the best learning occurs in this stimulating active and interactive small-group environment because discussion, especially feedback, is essential for seeing how to improve one's own and others' ideas and work—and "[p]eers can serve as excellent sources of feedback" (Bransford et al., 1999, p. 207; also see Caine & Caine, 1997; Hart, 1999; Jensen, 1998; Treisman, 1992).

As a result, students' knowledge structures grow—they learn. Moreover, students are also improving their social and communication skills, which are invaluable assets in school and beyond.

Figure 7.1 is a set of guidelines to help students know how to carry on productive small-group discussions. Students benefit from following and practicing these guidelines.

Guidelines for Small-Group Work

- The ideal number in a small group is three, four at the most. With this number, there are enough people for a rich exchange, and yet all members of the group can share and discuss their work and ideas in a reasonable time. Shy students are also more comfortable in a group of this size. Moreover, students who have difficulty focusing on large amounts of information will have less trouble in a small group of three—or might even do better in a two-person partnership.

Figure 7.1   Guidelines for Class Discussion

---

1. Be a close listener to others.

2. Ask for more information if you are not clear about what someone said.

3. As much as possible, support or illustrate your points with specific examples or quotes.

4. Relate your points to previous ones—or clearly say that you are moving to a new point. Make sure everyone who wants to has had a chance to comment on the point under discussion before you move to a new point.

5. Questions are as important as comments.

6. Everyone should contribute to the discussion. All different perspectives are needed and wanted—and each contribution (comment or question) makes the discussion richer.

7. Everyone is responsible for everyone's participating. Don't blame the talkers. Don't blame the non-talkers. Invite non-talkers to participate.

8. You will learn how to participate in discussions by practicing. If you are shy or insecure about joining the discussion, know that you will improve just by trying or practicing. The rest of us will support you. All of us will support each other.

• The first time students get into small groups, they can join with two or three people sitting near them. If they are in movable chairs, they can simply make a circle. If they are at long tables, they can work either with those beside them or with the people at the table behind or in front of them. If they do not remember each others' names, they should introduce themselves. After being in different groups with different people (see points later in the chapter), and after several whole-group activities, they will be well acquainted with each other.

• As research shows (e.g., Triesman, 1992), peer tutoring is one of the most powerful learning strategies—for both the tutor and those being tutored—and small groups are ideal for peer tutoring. Nonetheless, two caveats are necessary. First, small-group work should always be preceded by individual work so that all members come to the group with their work in hand and their own ideas in mind so they have something to share and work on. Second, students who might have more knowledge and, thus, are doing more to help others in the group, are perhaps getting the most benefit from the interaction: They are problem solving, practicing giving productive feedback, and doing clear communicating, which are essential skills in school and in life. Students need to know this, especially students who are in the position of doing more of the tutoring. They might feel put upon if they are not aware of the benefit they will derive from it. The teacher, after becoming familiar with the strengths of the students, can organize the groups so there is a combination of those who can do the tutoring and those who need tutoring—as long as the students know that everyone benefits, tutors and those tutored. This can help ensure that the peer tutoring will be effective.

- The groups that are the most heterogeneous have the opportunity for the richest and most varied interaction. When students come to the groups with different learning styles and preferences, backgrounds, knowledge, beliefs, perceptions, they will have a profound experience learning from and teaching each other—if they can understand each other. Figure 7.2 depicts students with different ideas about a common topic. Two are trying to express their views, but another does not understand either of them or even what they are trying to do. What will it take for the members of this group to understand each other well enough to compare and contrast and even perhaps to synthesize or further develop their ideas? With their metacognitive knowledge and with a classroom atmosphere of respect and safety, their efforts to understand each other will also challenge and strengthen their social and communication skills—and they will enjoy the interaction immensely.

- If students seem to be gravitating toward creating homogeneous groups, a neutral way to reorganize the groups to ensure heterogeneity and effective peer tutoring is to say something like, "Tomorrow, everyone sitting in rows two and four are going to change seats. Then you will be able to get to know and work with different people."

- When students are starting to work in their small groups, the teacher can say, "If you need help, raise your hands and I'll come over to help." What I have learned is that once I answer their specific question, they want me to go away so they can do their own thinking and problem solving. And as I walk away, I can look back and see them bent intently over their task. It does a teacher's heart good.

- When some groups finish their discussions earlier than others, they welcome the teacher's coming over to hear what they have discovered. While this is going on, other groups have a chance to finish. When at least half of the groups are finished, the class can proceed to the whole-group phase.

- Sometimes a student will say, "I don't like working in a small group." The answer to that can be, "Then just sit next to a group and listen; you don't need to say anything if you don't want to." In my experience, it

Figure 7.2 The Challenge of Small-Group Discussions

has never yet failed that such a student will soon be joining the small-group discussion.

- Some say that students from certain cultures are used to the teacher as the authority and are not used to doing their own thinking or working together to explore their own ideas. In my experience with students from all over the world, after they do the NHLP activity (Chapter 2), learn about the brain (Chapter 3), and experience NHLP curriculum and pedagogy, they enthusiastically participate in small-group discussions.

The main purpose of the small-group work is that each student will grow his or her own knowledge structures, not collaborate or come up with a group answer or decision. After the first foundation stages (Figures 6.4 and 6.5, Stages 1–3), though, students might benefit from collaborating on a project. Nonetheless, before students collaborate, each student's brain needs the opportunity to grow its own individual foundation of structures.

In all the years I have used small groups as described here, only once has a student challenged me. "Hey," he said, "we do all the work but you're the one who's getting paid." I responded, "But those who do the work are the ones who do the learning and grow the dendrites." He looked thoughtfully at me for a moment, then nodded and smiled. "Besides," I added, "I do a lot of work before class figuring out which assignments to give you so that you'll be able to grow your dendrites—and don't forget about all your papers that I read after class." Yes, he agreed, I did deserve to get paid.

Another aspect of the small-group work is that it gets students engaged in discussing topics that normally are noninvolving. How gratifying for an English teacher to hear students eagerly discussing prepositions, for example. Small-group work can be gratifying for students and teachers in any subject at any level.

Whole-Group Work

Guidelines for Whole-Group Work

- Finally, the students reconvene as a whole group, and the teacher asks, "What did you come up with?" They answer as individuals, not as representatives of a group because, again, the students are growing their own neural networks. For this reason, students must be stimulated and do their own thinking, participating, contributing. Even if, at later stages of a lesson plan or curriculum, students are collaborating on a project, they will still be well advised to make their own best-considered contributions to their group's work.

• During the debriefing session, the teacher writes verbatim what the students say on the chalkboard—or on whatever equipment is available—so that everyone can see it. This will show the teacher what the students know. Moreover, all the students will have at least an idea of what everyone else knows. This will put the whole class more or less on the same page. It is essential for the teacher to write verbatim what students contribute; otherwise, when teachers change their words, students get the destructive message from the teacher that "I am smart and you are not."

• The teacher also writes the students' contributions on the board without rejecting or praising any contribution. This is effective for two reasons. First, if the teacher responds to a student's contribution by saying, "That's a great point!" the students see that the teacher is judging their contributions. Students lacking confidence might say to themselves, "No, I'd better not say anything because it won't be great." Second, when the teacher writes each comment on the board in the students' own words and without comment, students feel encouraged just by having their ideas accepted and put on the board in their own words for all to see. The result is that the brain produces feel-good chemicals (Chapter 3) so that students are motivated to keep working, trying—and learning. But what if they make mistakes? See the following section, "Correcting Their Mistakes."

• The whole-group activity builds community and also maximizes learning because the students are listening to, thinking about, responding to, and learning from what others are saying.

• The whole-group debriefing is typically done on a volunteer basis. To avoid having only a few students contributing all the ideas, however, the teacher might call on silent students and say, "Was there anything you heard in your group that you thought was interesting or useful?" It has usually been the case that students called on in this way do have an idea to contribute from the group—and because it is not their own idea, they are less afraid of speaking up. Also, such students, after their contributions are written on the board (which is a positive stroke), often will then raise their hands later to make other contributions.

Correcting Their Mistakes

If there are mistakes in the contributions the teacher has written on the board—and if other students do not correct them, which they are invited to do at the beginning of the activity—they will disappear as the lesson plan progresses from stage to stage and the students subsequently become able to see and correct their errors. A mistake written on the board for a short time—and not reinforced by practice—will not grow dendrites in the students' brains. In fact, having the errors exposed in this way gives the teacher invaluable information. It shows what the students' misconceptions are and, consequently, what activities the teacher might assign to help them discover and correct their mistakes for themselves.

For example, my NHLP unit curriculum for teaching students how to write a narrative essay (Figure 7.3) starts with asking the students to write down, individually, what they did for the previous 30 minutes. Then, when they get into their small groups, I tell them they have all written a narrative, ask them to read their work to each other, and come up with a definition of a narrative.

"What is a narrative?" a student typically asks. "You all just wrote one," I reply. "What did you all do that is similar?" Then they read, ponder, discuss, debate, take notes. Then, back together as a whole group, they call out their answers, all of which I write without comment on the board. One common mistake is their saying a narrative tells a story from beginning to end. Rather than lecturing about this or pointing out their error, I leave the mistake on the board and then assign an activity that will give them the opportunity to figure it out themselves, as described in the following.

"Now write about those same 30 minutes, but this time go backward in time using words such as 'before that' or '5 minutes earlier.'" When they have done this individually, I tell them they have written another narrative. Their small-group task, again, is to read their narratives to each other and see whether they want to change their definition. Of course they do. Now their definition is corrected to say a narrative can go forward or backward in time. In this way, by giving them tasks to do that invite them to use their brains' inner resources (Figure 6.1), they are motivated and attentive—and they learn.

By the way, it took a number of repeated attempts before I could determine for this unit what task to assign when. At first I would walk around the room and listen to their small-group discussions, trying to see where they were so I could see where to go next. When I could not see it clearly, I would go back to my default, non-NHLP unit on writing narratives. Then I would go home and cudgel my brain to try to figure out what to do next.

Fear of Being Perceived as Stupid

The fear of being labeled stupid can have a pernicious effect, as it had on the ninth-grade students whose story is in Chapter 1; they would not participate or behave because, as it turned out, they were aware that they lacked the knowledge and skills of "smart" students.

Figure 7.3   Unit Curriculum for Writing a Narrative

	Stage 1 **PREPARING TO LEARN** *Using current knowledge*	Stage 2 **STARTING TO LEARN** *Experimental practice*	Stage 3 **CONSOLIDATING NEW BASIS** *Skillful practice*
Individual	Teacher says, "Write down what you did during the 30 minutes before class. You will have five minutes to do this."	"Go back in time from when class started to 30 minutes before, e.g., 'I sat down in my seat. Just before that I came into the room. A few minutes earlier I had been hurrying down the hall . . . .'"	"Now start at 15 minutes before class, go up to when class started, then jump back to 30 minutes before class started and work up to where you started (at 15 minutes before class). Write as another person watching you: 'Jo walked up the stairs. . . .'"
Small Groups	"You have all written narratives, whether you know what narratives are or not! Read your narratives to each other and then, by looking at the similarities, come up with your definition of what a narrative is." (c.10 minutes)	"1) Read your new narratives to each other and amend your definition, if necessary. 2) What words/methods did you use now and in the 1st narrative to show the movement in time going forward or backward?"	"1) Read and amend definition as before. 2) What transitions did you use to go back and forth in time? 3) Discuss the differences between writing about yourself and writing as someone else writing about you."
Whole Group	"What is your definition of a narrative?" (The teacher writes ALL points, verbatim, on the board and without comment. Any needed corrections will be made by the students themselves in the following stages. (c. 10 minutes)	1) "Any changes that you want to make to the definition of a narrative?" (Teacher writes on board as before.) 2) "What words/methods did you use to show movement in time?" (On board.) These are called 'transitions.'" (Discussion)	1) "Changes to your definition? 2) "Transitions?" 3) "Differences between writing as 'I' and writing about 'Jo'?" (Discussion of 1st and 3rd person points of view. Teacher asks some students to read their narratives.)

Figure 7.3 (*Continued*)

	Stage 4 BRANCHING OUT *Knowing in more detail*	Stage 5 GAINING FLUENCY *Using it, doing it*	Stage 6 CONTINUED IMPROVEMENT *Wider application*
Individual	(Teacher assigns reading of a narrative in text.) "Write notes about the author's time sequence and use of transitions. What is the point of view? Is it a narrative? Use your definition to answer this question."	"Write a narrative of your own choice on one of your own experiences. Write in your choice of 1st or 3rd person. Use transitions to help your readers follow your movement through time backwards and/or forwards." (Probably as homework.)	"Revise your narrative or write another one. You might want to try a different point of view and/or different time sequence." (Probably as homework.)
Small Groups	"Share and discuss your notes. Point to specific places in the text to show what you have seen."	1) "Read your narratives to each other. Listeners tell what you heard and understood. Discuss transitions and point of view. Give ideas for improvements." 2) "Did you have any problems or questions when writing?" 3) "What makes a good narrative?"	1) "Read and give feedback." 2) "Discuss problems/questions you had when writing." 3) "Discuss ways to improve writing narratives."
Whole Group	"What did you come up with?" (Teacher writes answers on the board as before.) Stage 4 can be repeated so that students can see the range of narratives. Teacher can now lecture if necessary.	1) "What did you learn from the group feedback?" 2) "What are your problems and questions?" 3) "What do you know about writing narratives and what makes a good narrative?" 4) "What can you do to improve your writing of a narrative?"	"What did you come up with?" (Group discussion; teacher writes their points verbatim on the board.) Students hand in for teacher evaluation and, when returned, do further revisions.

Fear of being perceived as stupid is perhaps one of the major reasons a student does not participate. A teacher can counteract this and other negative, self-sabotaging feelings by educating students about their being natural-born learners (Chapter 2) and about how the brain learns and how emotions can either sabotage or bolster their brain's natural ability and desire to learn (Chapter 3). This metacognitive knowledge and self-awareness (Chapter 5) are empowering for students.

Here is an example of fear-driven behavior. When my granddaughter Laurel went to first grade, we were sure she would be an excellent reader. Both her parents are ardent readers, and Laurel could read her own books. As it turned out, she had, as many children do, memorized the books her parents had been reading to her. Her teacher said she had attention-deficit/hyperactivity disorder (ADHD) because she would not stay in her seat or participate and, instead of doing her work, would constantly act up. Why not act up to divert attention from one's humiliating lack of an expected skill? Certainly, having the reputation of being a trouble-maker is far better than the reputation of being stupid. What was the problem? Laurel had a secret. She could not read.

The teacher thought Laurel should take Ritalin. I said that would happen only over my dead body. Instead, she and her parents attended an ongoing program for families with children who have attention-deficit disorder or ADHD. At the end of the first grade, because Laurel had not learned to read, I tutored her. When she could not recognize the word "that" from one minute to the next, this 7-year-old child hit herself in the head and cried out, "Why am I so stupid!" It was clear in 10 minutes that she had a reading problem, later diagnosed by a specialist as dyslexia. The teacher had not caught on—perhaps because Laurel would never sit still long enough for this problem to be detected. After the diagnosis, we were able to provide her with appropriate intervention. (Laurel's successful intervention treatment was brain-repatterning therapy provided by the Developmental Therapy and Education Institute in Seattle, Washington.)

Today Laurel is a successful college student and, like others with brains that learn differently, has an extraordinary memory and a wealth of knowledge about many subjects. She is also a talented artist and writer. Is this just grandmother talk? I do not think so.

Students benefit from—and enjoy—the opportunity to learn by their own natural learning process, as they were born to learn, as their brains want, need, and love to learn. Brain-based NHLP curricula and pedagogy naturally and immediately engage their interest, motivate them, energize them, and keep their attention.

Why Only This Pedagogy?

This is the only pedagogy used with this NHLP approach to developing curricula for teaching any subject, concept, or skill, including applying, modifying, or extending a skill (see examples in Chapters 8 and 9). This is because the pedagogy includes just about every activity that educators and researchers have recommended to help students learn, for example active learning, independent work, feedback, self-evaluation, communication skills, respectful interaction, community building, collaboration (as in learning communities, Chapter 9), and holding students to high standards (see the section on assessment that follows). This pedagogy also includes the nine elements proposed by Kovalik and Olsen (2001): "Absence of Threat/Nurturing Reflecting Thinking [sic], Meaningful Content, Adequate Time, Enriched Environment, Immediate Feedback, Movement, Choices, Collaboration, Mastery/Application" (p. xiii). This NHLP pedagogy not only accommodates different learning styles and preferences but also often results in students expanding their repertoires (Chapter 4).

Also, the motivational strategies some people advocate for gaining and keeping students' attention and interest—for example, background music, physical activities, visual imagery, dramatics—are not needed. All that is needed is to invite the innate resources of the students' brains into the classroom and provide students with the opportunity to experience curricula based on the brain's innate rules of learning (Figures 6.1 and 6.2).

The NHLP approach works well even with students afraid of failure because, from the start, they are succeeding: every first activity is a no-fail activity (Figures 6.7–6.9 and Chapter 8). Also, they have discovered in the initial NHLP activity and the brain presentation that they are natural-born learners.

Learning From Students

Course after course, year after year, I saw more and more clearly how to create curricula that incorporate the rules of the brain's natural learning process and that are designed to call on the brain's inner resources. I would know I had assigned the appropriate activity when the students bent eagerly to the task rather than looking confused as though the task was above their heads—above their knowledge structures—which, of course, it would be if they could not do the task. As always, the students guided me and I learned from them how to help them learn. The following section on Student Group Instructional Feedback, sometimes called Small-Group Instructional Diagnosis, describes a way for teachers to gain invaluable information about their teaching.

ASSESSMENT

Student Group Instructional Feedback (SGIF)

Students Evaluate Their Teachers and How They Are Teaching

The SGIF is a method of evaluation of teachers by their students. It is the most instructive and enlightening form of evaluation that I know. It is thanks to the SGIF that many of us have been able to improve our teaching.

How SGIF Works

Teachers conduct this evaluation, which might take 40 to 45 minutes, by the following steps:

1. Two teachers agree to do an SGIF for each other at some time after the first 3 weeks and before the midterm so that there will be time for them to make improvements in their teaching.

2. In the class session before the evaluation, the teacher to be evaluated says to the students, in effect, "I asked my friend to come to our next class to do an evaluation of my teaching. She is doing this as a favor to me because I want to know how I'm doing and, if necessary, how I can improve so I can help you better."

3. When the evaluator shows up at the beginning of the next class, the teachers shake hands or embrace, demonstrating that they are friends. Then the teacher says, in effect, "I'm going to leave now. After class, my friend is going to tell me what you said. But he won't tell me who said what, and he won't report anything you say to my department head. What you say will be just between him and me. Then, next class, after my friend has told me what you said, I'll tell you the things I can do to help you better. So it is absolutely essential that you tell him the truth, no matter what it is, because that is what will help me the most to help you." The teachers again display friendly feelings, and the teacher leaves the room.

4. The evaluator then says to the students: "There are three issues for you to consider: (1) what works, what helps you learn; (2) what doesn't work, what doesn't help you learn; and (3) any specific suggestions for improvement."

5. The students are instructed to write their answers to the three questions individually.

6. Then the students get together in small groups and share their lists, adding any more items that might come up during their discussion.

7. The evaluator then makes three columns on the board for the answers to the three questions and asks, "What do you have for the first question, what works, what helps you learn?" and transcribes verbatim what the students say.

8. The evaluator asks for a volunteer with good handwriting to copy down verbatim everything that is on the board as the report for the evaluator to give to the teacher.

9. When they have finished, the evaluator asks, "Does everyone agree? If you don't, you can vote on it. I'll record how many are for or against an item." If necessary, voting then ensues.

10. This procedure is repeated for the second and third questions while the volunteer copies everything verbatim, including any voting scores.

11. The evaluator thanks the students, takes the transcribed notes, and dismisses the class. Alternatively, the teacher returns for the remainder of the period.

12. The teachers meet before the next class and go over the report. The evaluator must be honest and not pull any punches. The teacher must be receptive and not defensive. Then they discuss what the teacher can or cannot do about the students' suggestions.

13. Before the next class, the teacher thinks long and hard about what the students have said, trying to see how she can make as many improvements as possible.

14. At the next class, the teacher goes through the list of suggestions and says what she can or cannot do and thanks the students for their help.

15. The teacher then makes all possible improvements.

16. The teacher becomes a better teacher.

At my college, my colleagues have done many SGIFs for me in different classes, and I have done many for my colleagues as well. Every time I am awed by how observant and insightful the students are. The SGIF reveals that they know they would learn more and better if they could, for example, have the opportunity to discuss the ideas or information, ask questions, try to work with or apply the ideas themselves; if, for example, the teacher would talk more slowly, give more examples, go over the exams and not just hand them back with a grade. Why have they not said these things in class to their teacher? Perhaps it is because they know how to be "good" students and what schooling is all about: teachers impart, students takes notes and tell it back.

An interview William Glasser had with a panel of high school students gives another example of students' perceptiveness. Glasser, the author of *The Quality School* (1992), asked the students what they thought about a certain teacher. They said the teacher was strict, like a general in the army, and that was fine. Then Glasser asked about another teacher. They said he was a fool because he acted like a general but he really was not that kind of person.

Perhaps the students are somehow wrong; however, wrong or not, while students are sitting quietly in class, they are observing and making judgments about their teachers, about how they could better help their students learn.

SGIFs Have Helped Me

An evaluator for one of my English 101 composition courses reported to me that students had almost come to blows over one point. A student had listed in the "what doesn't help" category that when it came time for them to write their own essay (at Stage 5), he wanted to select his own topic and not have me assign it. Another student had disagreed, saying they should do what I said. At this point, many students had jumped in to support the first student. The evaluator said he had had a difficult time restoring order.

They were talking about the assignment at Stage 5, "Gaining Fluency: Using it, doing it." From their feedback, I realized that students are ready to be independent at Stage 5, to use what they now know and do it for themselves; I had been wrong not to give them that opportunity at this stage in their learning process. From that time on, all Stage 5 tasks in my writing classes give students the freedom to choose their topic rather than write on a subject I have chosen for them.

Formative Assessment Process

Unlike summative assessment (discussed below), such as a grade, formative assessment describes where the students are, whether and how much they are learning during a class period. For this purpose, the following in-class formative assessment procedure is invaluable.

In any unit curriculum, at any stage after Stage 1, the teacher writes on the board at the end of the whole-group activity the numbers 1 and 6 with a line equivalent to four numbers between them (1 – – – – 6). The teacher then points to the 1 and says, "Raise your hand if you don't get it or are totally confused." Because the students are metacognitively astute, they know there is no shame in being confused and not understanding. They know that if they do not understand something it simply means they have not yet had the opportunity to grow their dendrites and synapses for it. They will eagerly raise their hands if this is true for them, saying they need—and want—another activity at that same stage before going on to a higher stage and getting even more lost.

Then the teacher points to the 6 and says, "Raise your hand if you totally understand." After that, the teacher can point to the middle of the line between the 1 and 6 and ask, "Who is sort of, but not completely, getting it?" When students raise their hands here, they often wave it in the sign for "sorta-kinda." Then the teacher can point to the section of the line between the midpoint and the 6 and ask, "Who is here? Who almost has it?" The last question is about the section of the line between the mid-point and the 1: "Who is just beginning to get it?"

Now the teacher knows where the class is. If most of the students are at the midpoint and below, the teacher will help the students progress by assigning another activity, for more practice, at that same stage. If, however, most of the students are at the midpoint and above, the teacher can proceed to the next stage and invite the students below the midpoint to come to the office for personal tutoring. In this way, the teacher knows how to target the work and when to assign the next higher activity. This formative assessment can be done as often as seems necessary to know whether to proceed or do more practicing at the current stage.

Students say they appreciate their teacher's doing this because it shows that the teacher cares about them, accepts their reality, and wants to teach them where they are so that they can succeed.

Some educators wonder whether taking extra time to do these formative assessments will prevent completing the curriculum. Chapter 8 points out that "front loading"—that is, spending whatever time it takes to help students construct a foundation—pays off in quicker and easier progress later in the unit or course.

Summative Assessment Process

This summative assessment process was created by James Harnish, a colleague at North Seattle Community College. It puts all the students on a more equal playing field, removes the stress that unfairly taxes some students more than others, and makes testing a powerful review and learning experience. Figure 7.4 is an example of a handout that announces and describes the exam to students.

Figure 7.4   The Summative Exam

Exams: There will be two take-home exams, a midterm and a final exam. You will write the questions and then have an opportunity to study all the questions before the exams. The midterm may be rewritten to improve your understanding and grade (old and new grades will be averaged if you rewrite the same questions).

Exam Process and Preparation

- On the designated day, bring in two to three questions for each section of questions that will be on the exam; the three sections are shown below. You will collaborate on the questions in class and hand in the questions at the end of class. You will receive a copy of the questions the following class period and will have a week to study the questions before the exam.
- There will be an opportunity in class during the pre-exam week to practice writing answers so you can see what constitutes a good answer.
- Study with a group or partner during the pre-exam week. Since only some of the study questions will be on the exam, be sure to study all the questions.
- The exams will be emailed to you or can be picked up at the secretary's desk on the designated date.

1. **Identification/definition questions** (out of a list of c. 8-10 questions, you will select four for 10 points each = 40 points). Done from memory (closed book), on your honor.

2. **Short answer questions** *based on texts and lectures* (one paragraph). Open-book. You should use quotes or references (include page numbers) to support your answers. Out of a list of about 5-6 questions, you will select two for 15 points each = 30 points. Though you should study together, your answers should be your own ideas in your own words.

3. **Essay questions** based on *your own ideas* (a few paragraphs). Open-book. You may use quotes or references (include page numbers) to support or clarify your answers (out of about 4-5 questions, you will select one for 30 points). Follow the same directions as for the short-answer questions.

Note: To be adapted by the instructor according to his or her own judgment.
SOURCE: Based on a process developed by James Harnish, North Seattle Community College.

Some Procedural Suggestions

1. To first introduce students to the process, the teacher writes on the board an example of each kind of a question and asks students to come up with another example of the same kind of question.

2. During a later class session in which students bring in their prepared questions, they work in small groups to synthesize any duplicated questions in their group and give the teacher their unduplicated and synthesized questions.

3. Subsequently, the teacher synthesizes and compiles the questions from all the groups, adds other questions if necessary, and then provides the students with the list to be used as study questions.

The students have up to a week to study the questions outside class, preferably in study groups.

4. In the next class session, during which the students practice writing answers to sample questions, they individually answer a designated definition or identification question from the list of study questions. Then they share their answers in small groups and decide what makes a good answer. This is followed by a whole-group debriefing and discussion of both the answers and also what makes a good answer. This process is repeated with one short-answer question. If time allows, the teacher might have students do the same with one essay question.

With this kind of exam and exam preparation, all students can learn and succeed. Their grades are given fairly for what the students know and understand; but they will all know and understand more and better as a result of this exam process. A teacher once said, "Well, then, everyone will get an A or B," as though that were a bad thing. My reply was, "Right." The brain is born to learn; every person is born a natural learner. Why not make it possible for every student to succeed?

What about the grading curve? It unfairly rates students for how dendrite advantaged or dendrite disadvantaged they are, through no fault of their own (Figure 3.14). Again, if we see people who do not want to learn or cannot learn, we are seeing people who have been abused out of their natural birthright, or we are seeing people who are different learners who have not had the good fortune to have been provided with appropriate assistance.

EDUCATION COURSES AND FACULTY DEVELOPMENT PROGRAMS

Themes and Objectives

Figure 7.5 is an example of a description of the themes and an objective that might be included in a syllabus for a course in a college of education, in a program for education majors, or in a faculty development program. The teacher or faculty development leader might adapt these for his or her own purposes.

Seminars and Seminar Papers

Figure 7.6 describes an assignment that invites participants in any course, including education courses, or participants in faculty development programs to do their own exploring and thinking, to be independent learners, to use—or develop—their communication and group leadership skills.

Figure 7.5   Themes and Objective for Education Courses or Faculty Development
Programs (to be included in the syllabus or adapted by teachers and
faculty development leaders according to their own judgment)

Course or Program Themes and Objective

There are four major themes which we will explore:

1. The brain has a natural learning process. It is an active, constructive process in
   which the learner first connects new knowledge and skills to his or her existing
   knowledge and skills and then, through experience and practice over time,
   becomes increasingly more knowledgeable, skillful, and creative.
2. Every human being is born with a brain that knows how to learn, wants and
   needs to learn, and loves to learn.
3. Intellectual, emotional, and physical experiences—including cultural and family
   experiences—are inextricably bound together in the brain's natural learning
   process. All these kinds of experiences must be taken into account for successful
   teaching, i.e., for successful learning.
4. When the natural human learning process (NHLP) is used in the classroom,
   students become the enthusiastic and successful learners they were born to be.
   Thus, teaching involves developing curriculum and using pedagogy compatible
   with the brain's natural learning process.

The major objective is to see how you might apply these themes in your own
teaching practices.

Figure 7.6   Seminars for any course or faculty development program: description
to be included in the syllabus (to be adapted by teachers or faculty
development leaders according to their own judgment)

Seminars and Seminar Papers

Each week there will be a seminar (a participant-led discussion of the assigned
reading). To prepare for each seminar, write a one-page (maximum) seminar paper to be
handed in at the end of the seminar for feedback. Unless otherwise stated, address one or
two of the following topics in each paper or a relevant topic of your own:

- One or more ideas you find interesting/important/relevant and why.
- One or more *specific* applications you might make in your own teaching; explain
  the connection between the reading and the application(s).
- At least one question about the reading or at least one topic you would like
  included in a future class discussion and why.
- A synthesis of something in the reading and a previous reading, video,
  lecture/presentation, or discussion.

Sections 1 and 2 of Figure 7.7 provide a method for participants to self-assess their work in seminars. (For more information about seminars, see "Seminars: A Collection of Materials on Seminar Approaches and Evaluation Strategies (1998), available from the Washington Center for Improving the Quality of Undergraduate Education at the Evergreen State College, Olympia, WA 98505; to order, call 360-867-5611.)

Course Evaluation Procedures

Periodically, participants in any course or program, especially education courses and faculty development programs, might be asked to evaluate that course or program. See the section above on "Student Group Instructional Feedback." This process helps teachers and teachers-to-be experience the teaching-learning process from both the teacher's and the student's perspective.

Student Summative Self-Assessment Process

Once or twice during any course, especially those in which teachers-to-be are enrolled, students might be asked to assess themselves in a summative fashion for the work thus far accomplished. Figure 7.7 presents such a summative self-assessment form, which the teacher might adapt for his or her own purposes.

Study Groups

As noted earlier, research shows that students who study together do better than students who do not (e.g., Bransford et al., 1999; Caine & Caine, 1997; Hart, 1999; Jensen, 1998; Treisman, 1992). Thus, study groups might be considered an important part of any course, including courses in colleges of education or in a school's or college's faculty development program. Participants, whether students or faculty, might form study groups or join at least one other person in a study partnership. An e-mail or phone sign-up sheet might be developed and distributed for participants' convenience.

Sections 3 and 4 in Figure 7.7 show how participants might assess themselves for their participation in study groups.

Figure 7.7   Summative Self-Assessment (to be included in the syllabus or adapted by teachers according to their own judgment)

Self-Assessment

Participants will hand in a self-assessment form at mid-program as well as at the end of the program.

Name _____   Date _____

    For your own progress and learning, evaluate yourself as honestly as you can from 4.0 to 0.0 on the activities listed below.

1. Participation in seminars:
    a. Was I reflective and thoughtful in coming up with my seminar papers?
       (always = 4.0) (most of the time = 3.0) (about half the time = 1.0) (no = 0.0)
       Grade: _____
    b. Did I participate wholeheartedly (listening, thinking, discussing)?
       (always = 4.0) (most of the time = 3.0) (about half the time = 1.0) (no = 0.0)
       Grade: _____

AVERAGED GRADE FOR 1a + 1b: _____

2. Participation in non-seminar class discussions:
    a. Did I share my ideas/reactions/questions in the ***small group*** discussions?
       (always = 4.0) (most of the time = 3.0) (about half the time = 1.0) (no = 0.0)
       Grade: _____
    b. Did I listen to others thoughtfully and respectfully, having my own ideas/ reactions/questions, whether or not I shared them in the ***whole group*** discussions?
       (always = 4.0) (most of the time = 3.0) (about half the time = 1.0) (no = 0.0)
       Grade: _____

AVERAGED GRADE FOR 2a + 2b: _____

3. Participation in study group or with a study partner:
    a. Did I meet or talk on the phone or by email with my study group/partner, discussing the works, sharing ideas, questioning, reflecting? (at least once a week = 4.0) (at least once every two weeks = 3.0) (about half the weeks = 2.0) (a few times = 1.0) (no = 0.0)
       Grade: _____
    b. Did I meet or talk on the phone with my study group/partner for one or more substantial study session(s) to prepare for the midterm exam? (yes = 4.0) (no = 0.0)
       Grade: _____

AVERAGED GRADE FOR 3a + 3b: _____

4. Attendance:
    a. Did I attend regularly? (no unexcused absences = 4.0) (1-2 unexcused absences = 2.0) (2 or more unexcused absences = 0.0)
       Grade: _____
    b. Was I late or on time? (always on time = 4.0) (more often late than on time = 1.0) (always late = 0.0)
       Grade: _____

AVERAGED GRADE FOR 4a + 4b: _____

SELF-EVALUATION GRADE = AVERAGE OF THE FOUR GRADES: _____

Good News

The good news is that the missing link between the brain research and classroom application has perhaps now been found and might be the basis for a science of teaching. Nonetheless, because a science cannot be established as such without evidence, preferably quantitative evidence, to prove the validity of its claims, such research is needed.

Until then, however, classroom experience seems to indicate that teachers find it enjoyable, creative, and practical to use this natural-learning, brain-based NHLP theory and its curriculum-development, pedagogical, and assessment methodologies. It is enjoyable because then students are the motivated, eager, successful learners they were born to be. For a teacher, what could be better?

Part III

Using the Brain's Natural Learning Process to Create Curriculum

Brain-Based, Natural Learning Across the Curriculum

8

THE MAGIC WORDS

One evening I was a guest speaker in a high school junior and senior math class introducing the 16 students to their natural learning process and to the brain's natural way of learning. These students, introduced in Chapter 6, were in an after-school program for "grade retrieval." They had failed one or more day-school courses, and the school system was giving these "at-risk" students the opportunity to retake them and replace the failing grades with passing grades. As the session progressed, however, it seemed that whatever had caused them to fail in the first place was primed to make them fail again.

After they, with interest, reported how they had learned to be good at something outside school for the initial natural human learning process (NHLP) activity (Figure 2.5, "Evening High School Students") and attentively heard about the brain, it was time to teach them a concept via an NHLP lesson plan. As soon as I said, "Okay, now we're going to do a lesson," several of the students started talking to each other. One student put on earphones to listen to his radio. Others put their heads down as though going to sleep. A few opened their math textbooks. Less than half the students seemed ready and willing to proceed with the lesson.

Considering the situation, I scrapped the lesson I had prepared and, instead, went to my emergency plan. I put a transparency of a puzzle on

Figure 8.1   Three Puzzles

he	rec	om	est	hera	in

(here comes the rain)

ho	meo	nth	era	nge

(home on the range)

IR	SJF	KFB	IC	IA

(IRS JFK FBI CIA)

the overhead projector (Figure 8.1) and said the seven magic words: "See if you can figure this out."

Immediately, every student looked up and silently considered the puzzle, only the first line of which they could see (I had covered the other lines). They seemed completely absorbed in . . . thinking. People might assume this was an unusual or unexpected response. The reason this is my emergency plan is because it always works this way.

After a few moments, a student said, "rain." Then another student said, "here," and another said, "comes the rain." Then I uncovered the line that read, "here comes the rain." There was a murmuring through the room.

Then I uncovered the next line, the second puzzle. Their attention was fixed on the screen. In a moment, two students at the same time said, "Home on . . ."; then some of the others excitedly called out, "the range."

They seemed to be thinking and responding as one. Yet these students were different from each other. They were of different races, from different cultures—African Americans, Asians, Hispanics, Whites. Nevertheless, all their brains were doing the same things at the same time; they were all pattern seeking and problem solving; and all the students seemed motivated to perform these same natural functions and seemed to find pleasure in it.

Then I uncovered the "home on the range" line and, after that, the next puzzle. Again, complete silence as everyone studied the line. After a few moments, a student said, "There's JFK." One of the girls asked, "Are these all acronyms?" I nodded. I do not know whether anyone heard her or whether anyone else knew what an acronym is—but at least one student in this class of failed students did. At the same time, other students were solving the rest of the puzzle: "IRS . . . JFK . . . FBI . . . CIA." They were captivated by the task—and not because it was merely a diversion. It was because of the invitation and challenge of those seven magic words: "See if you can figure this out."

What Students Want and
Need From Their Teachers

What if students' brains were invited to figure things out in their classrooms? What if students were given the opportunity in all their classes to grow their own dendrites and synapses as a result of their own creative and critical thinking?

For example, when my grandson Rome was in the sixth grade, his school transferred him from the regular program to the advanced placement (AP) program. He had enjoyed school up until then, but he hated the AP program. I asked him why. He said it was because "it isn't really that advanced. They just make you do about five times as much work and they talk out of the textbook most of the time. The writing is mostly answering questions out of the textbook." Seeing how unhappy he was, his mother scoured the school district for a learner- and learning-centered middle school for Rome and finally enrolled him in one of the district's alternative schools for the next year.

When he was in his second year there, I asked whether he liked this school. Yes, he did. Why? "They have us be interactive and we do projects," he said immediately and enthusiastically. "Learning is more based on finding it out and researching it than looking into a boring textbook." Some of the high school students in the private school for rich, high-IQ dropouts (Chapter 1) referred to textbooks as "stupid" and said they were the reason they had dropped out of school.

What Teachers Teach

Rome is learning what his teachers are teaching, that learning is challenging and rewarding. This is a far cry from what Smith (1986) described as the lessons being taught in all too many public schools:

> To see what students learn in school, look at how they leave school. If they leave thinking that reading and writing are difficult and pointless, that mathematics is confusing, that history is irrelevant, and that art is a bore, then that is what they have been taught. (p. ix)

Unfortunately, this seems to be what those at-risk students in the after-school "grade retrieval" program might have learned in school. Consequently, we cannot look at how students are performing and what kind of work they are producing to know their potential for learning because this potential might have been thwarted in school or outside school. For instance, they might be dendrite disadvantaged from lack of opportunity (Figure 3.14) or, possibly, from a "learned lack of interest" (Smith, 1986, pp. 3, 72–73) or a lack of self-confidence—all serious barriers to their being the eager, successful students they were born to be.

Safety

Another barrier to students' ability to learn is that some students' brains might have experienced being in a classroom as a threat to their safety because the demands in that environment have been beyond their ability to cope. Their brains solve this survival problem by going into flight mode and prepare to flee, shutting down their higher-level thinking processes (Chapter 4). Not able to flee physically, students who experience this sit in class intellectually immobilized, not thinking, not learning— and not passing. As M. Rose (1995) found, both a sense of safety in the classroom and respect are essential for student success (pp. 413–414).

Respect

To see what they wanted and needed from their teachers, using the NHLP three-step pedagogy, I asked these students to think about their best and worst teachers and what made them the best or worst. When they described their best teachers in the whole-class debriefing, the first word out of their mouths was "respect" (Figure 8.2), just as M. Rose (1995) discovered (Chapter 4)—and as Smith (1986) proposed:

> Sensitive and imaginative teachers inspire learning of lasting depth and complexity—a love of learning itself—in students with all kinds of interests and abilities. But success like this is achieved only when teacher and students have the mutual respect and trust that is the basis of all effective learning. (p. x)

Some students who feel disrespected by a teacher know of no other way to respond than to be rude, disobedient, or disruptive—that is, disrespectful. However, when these students feel they are respected, listened to, and cared about, typically their behavior improves, sometimes quickly and dramatically.

The Opportunity to Learn Naturally

Again, the problem is not that students are not motivated to learn. They are born innately motivated to learn. This powerful, innate drive does not just go away on its own. It can go away, though, when the environment or situation sets up a barrier to this natural motivation. If we can

Figure 8.2   Students' Views of Their Best and Worst Teachers (Transcribed Verbatim)

Best Teachers	Worst Teachers
Respect Interactive Listen to what students have to say Interested in students Care about students They don't assume Learn about their students and what would be exciting for them	Don't listen to students Scared of students Not intriguing or engaging Boring

remove this barrier (Chapter 5), students will feel the same natural, innate motivation to learn with which they were born.

Providing Students With What They Want and Need

In the following sections are classroom-proven learning activities for individual units in a curriculum. These activities give students, young and old and in different subjects, the opportunity to learn by their brains' natural learning process, to be treated with respect, and to feel safe. The result is that students are successful learners and take pleasure in learning.

The following learning activities could be used as given because all of them have been successful in the classroom. Alternatively, you could view these activities more as a source of ideas that you might want to consider for creating your own.

**Planning Guidelines for a Unit
(Also see Figure 6.6A and 6.6B)**

What skill and knowledge must the students have as the prerequisite foundation for each next higher level? What do they need to know and be able to do in order to understand and be able to do what is needed at the next level?

The key question: Will they be able to see and do *that* if they do not first know and can do *this*?

The teacher needs to know this in order to plan how to help students go from where they are at the start to where they need to be at the end.

THE CRITICAL FIRST STAGES

As discussed in Chapter 6, it is imperative that students learning a new concept or skill begin by making a connection with something they already know. Students who are not able to make that connection will be at a disadvantage as the lesson progresses. For them it will be rote learning at best because the work will be over their heads, that is, over their ceiling levels.

In the sections below are examples of units with different kinds of initial learning activities. Some assume students have background knowledge or experience and can make a personal connection (as in Figure 6.7B). Others assume students do not have that knowledge or experience (as in Figure 6.7C).

THE INTRODUCTION-TO-POETRY UNIT

Look at what happened when I taught the students in the high-school credit-retrieval program about poetry. They not only knew little or nothing about the subject but also started the lesson without the vocabulary needed for fully comprehending the poems.

The students in this class might have been suffering from any or all of the problems discussed earlier: having dendrite disadvantage, feeling disrespected, not feeling safe, not being invited to use their brains' inner resources and rules, having a learned lack of interest, lacking confidence about being capable of academic success. After the students had participated energetically and thoughtfully in the earlier activities (Figures 8.1 and 8.2), however, I took a bold step and asked whether they wanted to learn about poetry. This was not the lesson I had planned to teach them, but the material for the poetry lesson was in my briefcase. Seeing how alert and eager they were, I thought the powerful emotional content of the poems would appeal to them. Most of the students immediately nodded. They were ready to learn.

The First Poem at the First Stage

I put a transparency of the first poem on the overhead projector. Then I read the poem aloud to them (Figure 8.3).

After reading the poem, I was about to assign the first individual activity at the first stage of this lesson plan (see Figure 8.4): "Write down one thing you like about this poem and why you like it." I thought, however, that I should first check to see whether they understood all the words in the poem.

Figure 8.3   Introduction-to-Poetry Unit Lesson Plan: First Poem

Traveling Through the Dark

William Stafford
1962

Traveling through the dark I found a deer

dead on the edge of the Wilson River road.

It is usually best to roll them into the canyon:

that road is narrow; to swerve might make more dead.

By glow of the tail-light I stumbled back of the car

and stood by the heap, a doe, a recent killing;

she had stiffened already, almost cold.

I dragged her off; she was large in the belly.

My fingers touching her side brought me the reason—

her side was warm; her fawn lay there waiting

alive, still, never to be born.

Beside that mountain road I hesitated.

The car aimed ahead its lowered parking lights;

under the hood purred the steady engine.

I stood in the glare of the warm exhaust turning red;

around our group I could hear the wilderness listen.

I thought hard for us all——my only swerving—

Then pushed her over the edge into the river.

I asked what they thought the poet was talking about in the first two lines. Although everyone was looking at the screen as intently as they had earlier looked at the puzzle, there was no response. I paraphrased the lines, pointing to the words: "He was driving in the dark and found a deer dead—a dead deer—on the edge of the narrow road." Still no response. I realized then that this was the same situation as I had experienced with the beginning-level college students and with my cousin's daughter (Chapter 1). They were not comprehending or picturing in their minds what the words denoted.

I then asked them what they thought the poet was saying in the next line. They were attentive and quiet—no one seemed to move a muscle. I

Figure 8.4   Introduction to Poetry: A Six-Stage Unit

	Stage 1 PREPARING TO LEARN *Using current knowledge*	Stage 2 STARTING TO LEARN *Experimental practice*	Stage 3 CONSOLIDATING NEW BASIS *Skillful practice*
Individual	Teacher reads a poem as students read along or just listen. Then says, "Write down one thing you like about this poem and why you like it."	Repeat with a second poem while students can see on the board a list of things students said they like about the first poem. Now they all know many more things one can possibly like about a poem. They have taught each other.	"Write down what you now know about poetry."
Small Groups	"Share and discuss what you like and why you like it."	"Share and discuss what you like and why you like it."	"Share and discuss."
Whole Group	"What did you like about this poem and why?" Teacher records verbatim on board. General discussion.	"What did you like about this poem and why?" Teacher records verbatim on board. General discussion.	"What do you now know about poetry?" Teacher records verbatim on board. General discussion.

asked whether they knew what a canyon is. No one volunteered knowledge of this word. Did they know what "swerve" means? Some shook their heads; a few looked at me and said, "No." I reviewed the scene—a narrow road, a car parked to the side next to a dead deer—and made a swerving gesture with my arm to show what would happen if another car drove by in the dark. Then I left it to them to figure it out.

"There could be a car crash," one student said.

They stared at the screen but no one spoke. After waiting another few moments, I read part of the line again: "to swerve would make more dead" and waited.

"People would die," someone finally said.

In the second stanza, they did not know what a doe or a fawn is. When we got to the third stanza, I asked them what was happening. No response as they sat seemingly mesmerized by the words on the screen.

Figure 8.4 (*Continued*)

	Stage 4 **BRANCHING OUT** *Knowing in more detail*	Stage 5 **GAINING FLUENCY** *Using it, doing it*	Stage 6 **CONTINUED IMPROVEMENT** *Wider application*
Individual	Teacher hands out two poems. "Write down what you think is different and what is similar about them. Use what you now know about poetry."	Teacher assigns a collection of poems. "Pick any poem you want and write for about 30 minutes about it. Use what you know about poetry." This could be for homework.	"Rewrite your last assignment or write on another poem in the collection or from any source."
Small Groups	"Share and discuss what you wrote."	"Share and discuss what you wrote."	"Share and discuss what you wrote. Also discuss any learning and improvements during your writing or rewriting."
Whole Group	"What is similar and different about these poems?" Teacher writes verbatim on board. General discussion.	General discussion. They are all learning from each other about different poems.	General discussion.

"Why was he hesitating?" I asked.

Someone finally answered, "He didn't know what to do."

"What sort of person wouldn't know what to do and would just stand there trying to figure it out?" I inquired.

"He was kind," answered a boy, slowly and quietly.

"What would you have done in that situation?" I asked the class. The same student said, "I would have driven away." No one laughed or even smiled.

After another moment or two of silence, I asked, "Why was the exhaust turning red?" When no one answered, I asked whether they knew what "exhaust" means. I waited until someone said it was the smoke coming out of the tailpipe.

Many students had the answer then: the tail-lights were on and tail-lights are red.

"And what do you think of what he did at the end?"

After another few moments of silence, a student said, "He could have cut the deer and taken the baby out." Then ensued a quiet and serious discussion among the students about his doing that: Did he have a knife, did he know how to do it without hurting the fawn, what would he do with the fawn, what if he couldn't get it into his car?

On that note of thoughtful irresolution, I put the second poem on the overhead.

Deep Understanding

Some reading theorists say prior exposure to or background knowledge of the content of a text, sometimes called a "conceptual framework" or a "schema," is essential for people to understand deeply what they are reading (e.g., Caverly & Orlando, 1991, pp. 94–98; Nist & Mealey, 1991, pp. 47–48).

Other literary theorists believe readers respond in light of, or see through the eyes of, their ideologies, the "deep-seated beliefs, assumptions, customs, and practices of [their] society" as well as their assumptions about literature (Waller, McCormick, & Fowler, 1987, p. 5). According to this "reader-response" theory, when readers' ideologies and experiences are different from an author's, it is difficult, if not impossible, for them to understand accurately and deeply—or even to picture or imagine in detail—the society and experiences depicted in a text. (Chapter 9 applies the reader-response theory to the development of a unit.)

According to both schema and reader-response theories, then, unless or until readers have background knowledge about the content of a text, including its vocabulary, they cannot fully—and definitely not immediately—understand it.

Keeping this in mind, I continued the lesson.

The Second Poem at The Second Stage

Now that they had new neural structures about reading poetry starting to grow at the basic level, they needed more practice close to this level so they could connect higher structures to those lower ones and go further in their understanding and skill. From our experience with the first poem, I had also grown a few new structures. Mine were about how I could better help the students grow their new ones. Thus, this time I kept stopping as I read the poem (Figure 8.5) to ask them whether they knew what certain words mean and what the poet is talking about—not afterward, as before, which had been a waste of time. The vocabulary in the first poem had

Figure 8.5   Introduction-to-Poetry Unit Lesson Plan: Second Poem

Gift for My Mother's 90th Birthday

Burcham Hospital

Maude Meehan

1991

We watched the rain sluice down
against the window of your sterile room
and listened as you told of childhood's
summer showers at the farm; how you ran out
a colt unpenned, into their sudden soaking bliss.

Now you, aged changeling mother,
emptied and clean as a cracked china cup
on the wrong shelf, whisper, "What I would give
to feel that rain pelt hard against my face."

But you had nothing left, so we
conspirators of love, locked the white door
and your granddaughter wheeled you to the bath
where we unclothed your little sack of bones
And lifted you beneath the shower.

She held you up, your legs pale stalks a-dangle
and clasped your wasted body, bracing her taut
young flesh to your slack folds.
And you clung laughing, joyous as a child
to feel the clear fresh rivulets
course down your upturned face.

been so far above their knowledge level that they had not been able to connect with it on either the first or second reading (Figure 3.14). This time,
however, they could connect with the poem on the second reading.

They did not know what "sluice" and "bliss" mean. They did not
understand what "colt unpenned" means. Perhaps this was because of
the syntax, the vocabulary, and the fact that they had never been on a
farm and so could not picture in their minds what life would be like for a
child growing up on a farm.

"A colt is a baby horse and on a farm colts are kept in a pen or behind a fence. What would 'unpenned' mean?"

After a moment of silence in the room, a student said, "Someone opened the gate of the pen and the colt ran out free."

"What would 'sudden soaking bliss' mean?" was my next question. No answer.

We reread the title and the first stanza to review what was happening: the 90-year-old mother is in the hospital on her birthday, it is raining outside, the poem mentions "summer showers" and "sudden soaking bliss."

Still no answer.

"Remember," I said, " 'bliss' means great happiness." No answer, but everyone was still looking at the poem with intense concentration.

Leaving that question hanging, we went on to the next stanza and talked about the meaning of other words: "Why is she talking about her mother as an empty, clean, cracked cup on the wrong shelf?"

After a short silence, someone ventured, "She's out of commission"; and others nodded.

So we continued through the images, lines, and stanzas. The students were gaining knowledge about this strange new form of communication and these strange worlds of a farm and a 90-year-old woman in a hospital. In the third stanza, again, we had to stop and picture what was happening and interpret the metaphors—but not using that terminology because this unit was about orientation, introduction, and their growing basic foundation structures. This unit was not about terminology, theory, or even the art of poetry. That would come in later units, after they had constructed a rich-enough foundation of personal experience with and understanding of poetry on which to then attach higher-level abstract knowledge structures about poetry.

Right now what they needed was the opportunity to use their brains' innate resources and rules to grow basic knowledge structures about poetry and about the worlds of these two poems.

"They 'unclothed' . . . what are they doing?" I queried.

"Taking her clothes off."

"And her 'little sack of bones' is what?" No answer.

"Picture it," I said, "a 90-year-old woman in a hospital. What would it mean to take the clothes off her 'little sack of bones'?"

A stirring and murmuring. They were getting it. Their dendrites were sprouting. They were seeing that they could see it. Students called out, "She was very skinny!" "A bag of bones!" "Her skin was loose!"

After that, the rest went more quickly. One of the problems had been a lack of schemas for reading poetry with poetic syntax, imagery, and metaphoric language. Another problem had been their unfamiliarity with the experiences represented in these poems, such as someone having to decide what to do with a pregnant dead deer and someone wanting to run out like a baby animal into the rain and stand there happily letting the rain smack her hard in the face or someone holding a skinny little naked grandmother under a shower. After we read the poem the second time, though, the students concluded, some of them tearfully, that it was a poem about real love.

Once they began to use their brains' natural abilities in the classroom to see patterns, solve problems, use logic, and be imaginative, they caught on. Their knowledge structures grew, their ceiling level rose. Outside their experience? Then no neural structures, no schema, no understanding. Not their fault. Nothing wrong with them. But given the opportunity to learn by their brains' natural learning process they did wonderfully well in this unfamiliar verbal, conceptual, and experiential environment.

Like those college students mentioned in Chapter 1, these students, too, had apparently not learned to use their imaginations when reading or had not been invited to try to figure out by themselves the meaning in what they were reading.

Throughout this lesson, those seven magic words had been continually in the air: "See if you can figure this out." Their efforts to figure it out themselves was more effective for their learning about poetry—and, perhaps even more important, for feeling confident about themselves as learners—than listening to someone tell them about it or reading a "boring" textbook and then having only rote knowledge rather than their own internalized, personal understanding.

After a few more stages of this unit (Figure 8.4) and, after that, higher-level units, they would have been able to understand abstract concepts and terminology about poetry with their higher, richer network of knowledge structures. At that point, they would have been able to read a poem, interpret it, and appreciate it. But, unfortunately, that was the last time we were able to work together.

Making Amends

One day after a poetry class at the community college, a student came up to me with tears in her eyes. She said, "Do you mean I can have my own personal relationship with poetry?" Apparently her English teachers had done as I had done in the past to too many students, telling them what each poem means—and driving them away from poetry. "Yes, you can," I said, grateful for every opportunity to make amends for past harm done.

FRONT LOADING

The night-school students did not go through the six-stage poetry unit (Figure 8.4) because we spent all our allotted time on the preunit preliminaries, that is, just on their learning how to read and comprehend poems. For these students, then, this unit would have had at least eight stages instead of six because these students needed those first two additional prestages as an orientation or introduction to the poetry unit. As noted in Chapter 6, the NHLP curriculum-development model is not cast in concrete. If students need extra stages or activities, they can have them.

Spending this much time on preparing to learn a new concept or skill—in fact, some might think it an inordinate amount of time—will make sure students are experiencing enough foundation-growing activities so they can proceed with understanding and skill. As noted in Chapter 6, this is called "front loading." Front loading is essential because, otherwise, students might not be able to catch on. They will fail if they lack the relevant schemas, ideology, or basic knowledge structures the teacher assumes they have. However, with front loading—in a typical NHLP lesson plan, this is usually the first, second, and, sometimes, even the third stage—all students in every class at every level can be confident and successful learners.

Yes, front loading can take a long time. But once the foundation has been constructed, the rest of the unit will proceed more quickly and easily. Moreover, students who start the unit with knowledge of the subject are invaluable resources during the first stages as peer tutors in the small-group sessions (Chapter 7). Then, in the later stages, the whole class moves ahead on a more equal playing field.

Front Loading and the Poetry Lesson Plan

The learning activity in the first stage of the poetry unit is that students identify one thing they like about the poem (Figure 8.4). Then they do this activity again in the second stage with the second poem. How could these night-school students have identified at the start what they like about the poems if they could not even comprehend the poems' literal meanings and had little or no background or relevant prior knowledge about the content of these poems or even about the nature of poetry itself? The front- loading activities gave them the opportunity to begin catching on. As a result, their confidence in themselves as learners rose along with their ceiling level.

Without these front-loading activities, what would the result have been? Fear. Flight. Failure.

A SCIENCE LEARNING ACTIVITY
ABOUT THE CONCEPT OF BUOYANCY

Alex Koerger, a former student who is now teaching sixth-grade science, wrote to me about his experience teaching an NHLP science lesson to his students:

> My two 6th-grade science classes have been doing a lot of hands-on learning, exploring buoyancy in terms of mass and volume. The curriculum is challenging because it doesn't give them answers; it forces them to come up with explanations, compare those explanations with others, and test them against new information. It is an advanced curriculum for this age group, and many kids struggle with the more abstract material. (Personal communication, February 22, 2001)

Because his students had a background of knowledge about the subject, Alex started the new lesson with their making a connection to their prior knowledge.

> Last Thursday I was looking at the day's lesson and was noting that it called for a discussion of their "universal" definition of buoyancy. I knew the kids weren't ready to make the leap between mass and volume (density) and the inverse relationship it has with buoyancy, and I was puzzling over how I was going to get them to make the leap.

> I started off the lesson by reviewing the graphs they had in their science journals, getting them refamiliarized with the material and the topic. I then had them spend a few minutes writing what they felt a definition of buoyancy was, encouraging them to use the terms "mass" and "volume" in their definition. It was fascinating to watch as they spent nearly ten minutes writing and rewriting.

> [They] then got together in groups of three or four and discussed everyone's definitions. A secretary from each group took notes and wrote down the group's final choice. Then, reassembled as a whole class, [they] heard and discussed the various definitions; and I wrote what each group contributed on the board. I was having so much fun watching them put the bits and pieces together that I lost track of time. Before I knew it, the entire block period (95 minutes)

Figure 8.6   Library Orientation: A Three-Stage Unit (this lesson plan can be used in classes from elementary school to college)

	Stage 1 **PREPARING TO LEARN** *Using current knowledge*	Stage 2 **STARTING TO LEARN** *Experimental knowledge*
Individual	In preparation for students to do research in the school, campus, or neighborhood library, the teacher gives them this assignment: "Go to the library and, on your own, look for anything there that can help students learn or find information. Write a list of what you find. Also list anything you don't understand and anything you want to know more about."	A librarian (from the library the students will be using) has read the list from Stage 1 as preparation for meeting with the class. After the teacher introduces the librarian and the class to each other: "Tell the librarian what you found in the library and ask your questions about what you didn't understand and what you want to know more about." At the end of the session: "For homework write down 1) what you now know about libraries, 2) why you might want to use the library, and 3) how you might use the library."
Small Groups	At the next class session: "Share and discuss your lists. Also discuss what you didn't understand and what you want to know more about. A librarian will come to our next class to discuss your observations and questions with you."	At the next class session: "Share and discuss."
Whole Group	"What did you find and what do you want to ask the librarian?" Teacher writes their contributions verbatim on the board–then makes a copy to give to the librarian in preparation for the next class session. General discussion.	Teacher writes their contributions verbatim on the board. General discussion.

Figure 8.6 *(Continued)*

Stage 3
CONSOLIDATING THE NEW BASE
Further practice

Individual	Teacher gives students a research assignment to do as a team of three or four in the library. "Using what you now know about how to find information and do research in the library, think about how to do your research assignment in the library."
Small Groups	"Discuss your individual plans and, as a team, work out a plan for how your group will do the research assignment."
Whole Group	General discussion of the groups' plans. Groups revise their plans before proceeding to do the research. Groups proceed to do the research.

had passed. I was forced to extend the lesson beyond the class time so they could spend a few minutes writing about the connections they'd just made. It was so cool! This was probably one of the best lessons we'd had in my class, and my educational assistant, who has seen this material taught for several years in a row, was also impressed with how it went. I walked away from that lesson feeling like they really made a leap in their understanding. I never thought that their learning would be so much fun for me!

I actually did this lesson with both of my 6th-grade classes using the same technique, and it went equally well for both of them.

When learners, young or old, are given the opportunity to do their own thinking and use their brains' inner resources and rules, they are motivated to make the effort to work long and hard to figure things out. This was true for both the at-risk high-school students doing the poetry lesson and the sixth graders doing the science lesson.

A UNIT FOR LIBRARY ORIENTATION

Just as some units might have more than six stages, others might have fewer. The three-stage unit illustrated in Figure 8.6 is to introduce students to the library in their school, on their campus, or in their neighborhood. Because it is for students who have not previously done in-depth library research, its three stages are all front-loading activities. Also, it begins with a no-fail activity.

After this front-loading, orientation activity, the teacher might begin a new unit in which students do research about a topic related to the subject of the course.

Lectures and Textbooks: "The Readiness Is All"

In this brain-based, natural-learning approach, is there any place for lectures and textbook assignments? Yes, after the front-loading or introductory stage(s), after students have made a connection to their prior knowledge and have constructed their foundation knowledge structures up to perhaps Stage 4 ("Branching Out: Knowing in more detail"), students appreciate a lecture or reading assignment because by then they will want to go deeper and "know in more detail" (Figure 6.8—see the "Whole-Group" activity at Stage 4).

For example, in Jim Bannen's anthropology/desert tribe unit in Chapter 6 (Figure 6.10), he showed a film at Stage 4. Previously, when he had not first provided an opportunity for the students to make a connection to their relevant prior knowledge, they had been bored and uninvolved during the film. With the NHLP unit, to the contrary, the students, after several stages, had constructed a high-enough level of knowledge structures to catch on to the content in the film. The result is that they were excited and responsive when they saw it. As Schwartz and Bransford (2000) put it,

> [W]e conjecture that telling [lecturing] is not the optimal way to help students construct new knowledge. When telling occurs without readiness, the primary recourse for students is to treat the new information as ends to be memorized rather than as tools to help them perceive and think. (p. 477)

As Hamlet said, "The readiness is all."

Also see Dave Williams's complete Introduction-to-Egypt unit in Chapter 9. In Stage 3 of that plan, after two front-loading stages, students eagerly began reading the resource book so they could find out more about Egypt. As had happened with James Bannen's college students, when Dave had previously started the unit with a lecture and a reading assignment, his sixth-grade students had, like the college students, been uninvolved and uninterested.

A UNIT FOR INTRODUCTION TO SAFETY PROCEDURES

Because this unit is about students being safe in a potentially dangerous learning environment, the teacher needs to be sure they do learn how to be safe. In this plan, students go through six stages of front-loading and foundation-building activities so they will completely understand—and obey—the safety rules.

This unit was developed for a community college welding program. The teacher, John Guevarra, was attending a curriculum development workshop and, as in the workshop mentioned in Chapter 6, was asked to bring in a unit that was not working well. John said the unit that was not working well was perhaps the most important unit in the whole program. It was the safety unit that students encountered when first entering the program.

The standard safety curriculum began with a lecture, film, demonstration, and state safety handbook. But John said his heart was in his mouth much of the students' first term because they did not always, or rigorously, follow the safety rules and precautions, often putting themselves and others in danger. He said he had nightmares about students losing fingers and suffering other serious injuries.

John developed an NHLP safety unit for his students (Figure 8.7 on page 196) that, as he later reported, solved the problem—to his great relief. This safety lesson is also useful in science laboratory courses or in any course in which safe procedures and practices are issues.

A SCIENCE LEARNING ACTIVITY ABOUT WATER

As noted above, the NHLP approach to curriculum and pedagogy is successful with both old and young students. For example, a former student, Lael Erickson, when she was a teaching assistant in a third-grade classroom, introduced her students to the subject of water for their science lesson. This is her report:

> I taught the lesson Monday with great results! There are 22 kids in the class. The class is quite diverse with several Mexican children, one boy from Bosnia, two children from the Ukraine, one boy from Fiji (although he is East Indian).

> I asked the kids [individually] to write down anything that they knew about water. They already knew that this was a preliminary

Figure 8.7   Introduction to Safety in the Welding Shop: A Six-Stage Unit

	Stage 1 PREPARING TO LEARN *Using new knowledge*	Stage 2 STARTING TO LEARN *Experimental practice*	Stage 3 CONSOLIDATING NEW BASE *Further practice*
Individual	"Think of a dangerous tool you have used and write down what is dangerous about it and how to use it safely (could be a knife, a hammer, etc.)"	The teacher has the students approach an unused machine or piece of equipment they will be working with. "Identify what is dangerous about this and how could you use it safely?"	"Write a list of safety rules to use with this machine or piece of equipment."
Small Groups	"Share your lists and discuss your tool, why it is dangerous and how to use it safely."	"Share and discuss."	"Share and discuss. Write one list of rules together in your group."
Whole Group	Teacher writes students' contributions verbatim on the board. General discussion.	Teacher writes students' contributions verbatim on the board. General discussion. Repeat with the machine turned on or the teacher using the equipment.	Teacher writes students' contributions verbatim on the board and adds any rules students might have missed. General discussion.

to the science lesson about water. Two children told me they didn't know anything about water, but then they ended up writing down suggestions that other kids had mentioned.

Next, kids talked in [small] groups about their suggestions. When it came time to [get together as a whole group to] write them on the board, the children came up with over 40 things that they knew about water! We ran out of time and board space—and they still had more suggestions! Some "things they knew" were the following:

Water is cold and crystal clear

There is salt water

Figure 8.7 *(Continued)*

	Stage 4 **BRANCHING OUT** *Knowing in more detail*	Stage 5 **GAINING FLUENCY** *Using it, doing it*	Stage 6 **CONTINUED IMPROVEMENT** *Wider application*
Individual	Teacher assigns students to plan how they will do a task with this machine or equipment using their safety rules.	Teacher assigns students to do an introductory task on the machine or with the equipment using their rules. Afterwards, "Write down what you learned about being safe doing this."	Teacher shows the state safety film and then has students read the state safely manual. "Write down anything you see in the film and manual that is similar to, different from, or not included in your rules."
Small Group	"Share and discuss."	"Share and discuss."	"Share and discuss."
Whole Group	Teacher writes students' contributions verbatim on the board and then adds more rules if necessary. Students copy the rules in their notebooks.	Teacher writes students' contributions verbatim on the board. General discussion.	Teacher writes students' contributions verbatim on the board. General discussion. Teacher now begins teaching the first unit.

People can drink water

Water has been here for a long time

Fish live in salt and fresh water

Water helps flowers, vegetables, and plants

If we didn't have water we would be dead, or else the whole universe would be dry

Water makes sounds

Animals need water

You can swim in water

Figure 8.8   Introduction to Taking Lecture Notes: A Six-Stage Unit

	Stage 1 PREPARING TO LEARN *Using new knowledge*	Stage 2 STARTING TO LEARN *Experimental practice*	Stage 3 CONSOLIDATING NEW BASE *Further practice*
Individual	Teacher lectures for 10 minutes on a topic of substance related to the course while students take notes.	Teacher continues to lecture for 10 more minutes while students take notes.	Teacher continues lecture for 10 minutes while students take notes.
Small Groups	Students share their notes. Teacher says, "Looking at everyone's notes, decide what makes good notes. Then you discuss what problems you had taking notes and what you can do to improve."	Students share notes. "Evaluate your own and each other's notes, discuss the problems you had taking notes, and discuss what you can do to further improve."	As before.
Whole Group	Teacher asks students what makes good notes and how they will improve their note-taking, writes their ideas verbatim on the board.	Teacher asks students what they came up with and asks how they will further improve their note-taking, writing their ideas on the board verbatim.	As before.

Whales live in it

Water can wash your clothes

You can't write with it, you can't burn it, you can't step on it

Lael ended by writing, "I had a lot of fun with this!" (Personal communication, April 4, 2002)

The theory, again, is that the brain learns the same way from birth throughout life. The only difference between younger and older learners and between beginning and advanced learners is the amount of experience they have had, which leads to the amount of knowledge structures in their brains upon which to construct higher levels of knowledge and skill. But the process is the same.

Figure 8.8 (*Continued*)

	Stage 4 BRANCHING OUT *Knowing in more detail*	Stage 5 GAINING FLUENCY *Using it, doing it*	Stage 6 CONTINUED IMPROVEMENT *Wider application*
Individual	Students are assigned to write instructions on how to take good lecture notes.	Teacher lectures while students take notes.	Students take notes when teacher lectures in the course.
Small Groups	"Share and discuss."	As before.	Students study in study groups throughout the term, sharing notes and improving their notes and their note-taking skill.
Whole Group	Teacher has groups write their own instructions on the board. General discussion.	As before.	Periodically, teacher has a general discussion on any further thoughts students have about note taking, any problems, insights, suggestions for improvement.

A UNIT FOR LEARNING HOW TO TAKE LECTURE NOTES

Figure 8.8 contains another lesson plan that can be used across levels. On the *We're Born to Learn* Web site (www.borntolearn.net), there are more units and lessons that have also been used successfully in classrooms across subjects and levels and have been a pleasure for both teachers and students.

THE PLANNING GUIDELINES

Curricula and pedagogy that incorporate, either explicitly or implicitly, the magic words "see if you can figure this out" and that provide respect, safety, any necessary front loading, and the opportunity to learn naturally will make it possible for all students to fulfill their potential to be motivated and successful learners. This opportunity is provided by the curriculum's learning activities, such as the ones in this book, all of which were designed using the NHLP planning guidelines (Figures 6.6A and 6.6B).

Curriculum Development for Units, Courses, and Programs

9

This chapter addresses the question of what to teach when—in a unit, in a whole course, or in a sequence of courses in a program. The main problem, as noted in Chapter 6, will be the fact that, for teachers, the subject and its constituent topics, concepts, and skills are in their brains in highly complex neural networks. The principles, theories, elements, actions, interactions, relations, interrelations, facts, and terminology of their subjects are all of a piece, fully integrated, and second nature to them—but not so for their students. They might have few, if any, knowledge structures for the subjects; if they have any, they might be incomplete, misunderstood, or just plain wrong.

The problem? How do teachers duplicate their own neural networks in their students' brains (Figure 9.1)?

The solution? The students have to grow their own knowledge structures (Figure 3.5), and the way people grow these structures is by having the opportunity to use their brains' innate resources and rules (Figures 6.1 and 6.2). The lesson plans in Chapter 8 provide this opportunity, but only for individual units. This chapter continues the discussion of unit learning activities but also provides a guideline for sequencing units into coherent, complete curricula for whole courses and multicourse programs.

Figure 9.1   How to Duplicate Our Own Dendrites in Our students' Brains

WHERE TO START

The Goals and Objectives

The first task is to determine what exactly you want your students to know and be able to do at the end of a specific unit, course, or program. For example, choose one of your units, courses, or programs and complete the following information:

At the end of this unit, course, or program
I want my students to know
I want my students to be able to

The Foundations

Planning What to Teach When

As discussed in Chapters 6 to 8, we then step back down from the goals and objectives to what the students must know and be able to do so they will be able to achieve those goals and objectives (Figures 6.6A and 6.6B). Because higher-level knowledge structures can grow only from what is already there (Figure 6.2, Rule 1), we continue stepping down in this reverse causal sequence until we reach where the students are so that we can give them the opportunity to make that essential first connection.

Then we retrace our steps, this time going back up the causal sequence. Now, as we go, we plan a learning activity, a unit, or a course for each level that will make it possible for students to progress naturally and seamlessly from level to level until they have finally constructed the networks they need for achieving the goals of the curriculum.

Figures 6.6A and 6.6B provide guidelines and key questions to help teachers see how best to sequence their learning activities, units, courses, and multicourse programs. Analyzing a lesson plan or curriculum this way can be invigorating and gratifying, especially when a teacher sees how well it works. This chapter suggests ways to develop such lessons or curricula, which can be even more stimulating when done with colleagues.

Even if there is an official curriculum with goals dictated by a standardized or department test, you might still want to plan how to start where the students are. This chapter will also help you create lesson plans for any other goals that you might want to add to the official curriculum.

THE NATURAL HUMAN LEARNING PROCESS (NHLP) CURRICULUM DEVELOPMENT GUIDELINES

The guidelines for developing a brain-based, natural-learning curriculum for a unit, course, or program comprise three elements:

- *The brain's natural learning process*: The brain learns by using its innate resources (Figure 6.1) and its rules for learning (Figure 6.2), which converge with how people naturally experience learning (Figure 6.3).
- *The theoretical model* (Figures 6.3-6.5): As people practice and process an object of learning, their brain structures grow and their ceiling level (knowledge and skill level) rises.
- *The curriculum development guidelines* (Figures 6.6A, 6.6B): Every new level of learning begins when learners make a connection with something they already know. Teachers need to know what they know and what they need to know next.

1. First, identify the goals for the unit, course, or program.

2. Then identify the prerequisite knowledge and skills via the reverse causal sequence.

3. Finally, after thinking about where the students will be at the start (this might need to be adjusted for different classes), develop lessons or learning activities via the causal sequence so that students can, connection by connection, construct their goal-related knowledge and skills.

When I was starting to learn how to develop NHLP curricula, I was at Stage 1, without a guideline, not knowing what I was doing. Then I progressed to higher stages after much practice, trial and error, and perseverance in many classes over many terms with the help of many students. Eventually, I discovered the elements of these NHLP guidelines.

A UNIT ON LITERAL AND INFERENTIAL MEANING

In reading, it is important that students are able to differentiate between what the author is saying and what they, the readers, are reading into the text. According to the reader-response theory (Chapter 8), when readers are unfamiliar with an author's ideology and experiences, they can miss what the author is saying. Instead, seeing through the eyes of their own ideology and experiences, they perceive only what they already know, making it difficult, if not impossible, for them to understand accurately what is in a text.

Perhaps this is not a critical problem when reading for pleasure. But it is a critical problem when reading for knowledge, as in primary source materials and textbooks, and when doing word problems in math. In these cases, it is imperative that readers perceive exactly what is in the text rather than interjecting their own meaning—and often not even being aware that this is what they are doing.

Planning the Curriculum for a Unit

I had long been troubled by my inability to fully eradicate this problem in my literature classes. Then it occurred to me that I could develop an NHLP unit to do this. Using the planning guidelines (Figures 6.6A and 6.6B), and after some brain cudgeling, which is always revitalizing, I identified the goals for this unit: Students will know the difference between literal and inferential meaning and will be able to see whether they are reading something literally or inferentially. Then, taking the first step down the causal sequence, I asked myself what they would need to know and be able to do to know and do that. However, I did not have to travel far down because the only prerequisite foundation of knowledge and skill for these goals that I could figure out was their being competent readers, which they generally are in a literature course.

Then, although I did a great deal of thinking about it, I was unable to see this unit as having any more than two stages: the first one was making the first connection with where they were (competent readers), and the second was making the connection to the unit goals. As it turned out, though, the learning activity at the first stage needed to be repeated a number of times, during which it was obvious that they were increasing their understanding and skill about the target goals.

Later I realized their repetitions could actually be seen as constituting the second and third stages, with the students achieving the goals of the unit at the fourth stage. These goals, which had previously been difficult to achieve, were now achieved in one class session and one homework assignment.

Following are the learning activities for this unit on the difference between literal and inferential reading. By the way, it works every time— and students are invariably attentive and involved.

The Learning Activities

Using an overhead projector, I display the first sentence from Ernest Hemingway's *The Old Man and the Sea*: "He was an old man who had fished alone in a skiff in the Gulf Stream and he had gone eighty-four days now without taking a fish." Then I draw a picture of a skiff and show them on a map (when a map is not available, I draw on the board) where the Gulf Stream is.

Individual Work: "Write down everything you know just from reading this one sentence."

Small Group Work: "Share and discuss what you wrote."

Whole Group Debriefing: "Okay, what did you come up with?" Then I write everything they say verbatim on the board without comment. Here is a typical list:

he's old

a man

alone

lonely

likes to be alone

hungry

a bad fisherman

in a skiff

been there 84 days

there aren't any fish there

Then the question to them is, "Which of these items are written in words in the text?" As they identify the items, I check them on the board.

✓ he's old

✓ a man

✓ alone

lonely

likes to be alone

hungry

a bad fisherman

✓ in a skiff

✓ been there 84 days

there aren't any fish there

Then the terminology is introduced, as always after the students have had the opportunity to experience and think about (process) the experience. This is critical because students need to have relevant new dendrites to which the new and abstract terminology can be connected. Otherwise, the terminology is hanging out there in isolation, only to be memorized by rote, without personal, internalized, connected understanding.

"When something is written in actual words in a text it is called 'literal.' (I write this word on the board.) The checked words give the literal meaning." This word is written on the board for the students to copy in their notebooks. This combined ear-eye-hand activity further stimulates the students' brains to grow and connect their new knowledge structures.

"And where did the other ideas come from?" I ask.

Typically, their answers include the following: "from my imagination," "experience," "figuring it out."

"This is called the 'inferential' meaning. You are 'making an inference' or 'inferring.' This is also called 'reading between the lines.' You are reading your own meaning, not the author's." Again, they copy these words from the board.

Now we are ready for the next learning activity, which is to display the second sentence and ask them to identify what is literal and to make one inference. They do this, as always, individually, then share and discuss in small groups. With excitement and focus, they are actively seeking patterns, solving problems, using their logic, and constructing a higher level of knowledge and skill from the lower level they created in the first activity. Finally, reconvening as a whole group to debrief, they show they are beginning to understand; there are only a few mistakes this time, which, typically, the students correct for each other.

Then we go to the third sentence and repeat the activity. This time, in most classes, students now clearly see what is literal and what is inferential. There are usually no mistakes. The connections have been made. They have new knowledge and skill.

When, however, a class is still making some mistakes after the third repetition, we go to the fourth sentence and do it again. Doing a formative assessment (Chapter 7) after the third or fourth sentence shows whether the class needs more practice.

For homework they read several pages of the book and write down what they think are three important literal meanings and one important inferential meaning. (They will later test the accuracy of their inferences in upcoming pages of the book.) In the next class session, as usual, they share and discuss in small groups and then debrief as a whole class. At this point, they have achieved the goals of this unit, and we can proceed to the next unit.

Where to Go Next

Many years ago, when I first began using the NHLP approach in my Introduction to Literature course and was planning the sequence of units for the whole course, I sometimes was not sure what the next unit should be. For example, after the first unit on literal and inferential reading, I was not sure whether the next connection would be more naturally made to learning about the setting (the time and place) or to descriptions of the characters.

Rather than making the decision myself, which I was finding difficult—I was giving myself arguments on both sides—I asked the class. After I explained what the options were, they almost unanimously voted for the characters. So that was where we went next. Their brains knew what would be the better connection for them. I knew too much: For me everything was so interconnected and interdependent that it was difficult, at that point in my learning how to create NHLP curricula, to see how to proceed so that students could construct their knowledge connection by connection. Formerly, I had lectured, starting with my all-encompassing overview, while they took notes and probably hoped they would eventually be able to understand what I was talking about.

The students, as always, helped me to see what to do,

Figure 9.2   Introduction-to-Egypt Unit Lesson Plan

	Stage 1 PREPARING TO LEARN *Using new knowledge*	Stage 2 STARTING TO LEARN *Experimental practice*	Stage 3 CONSOLIDATING NEW BASE *Further practice*
Individual	"Write down everything you know about Egypt."	"Look at what you came up with and think about what kind of people the Egyptians were and what their society was like. Write down your ideas."	"Here are copies of the *National Geographic* with articles about Egypt. Each group will have a copy to read and then to write a group report on for next week."
Small Groups	"Get together with 3 or 4 other students and share your lists."	"Get together with your group and share your ideas."	NOTE: When this NHLP lesson plan was used in a 6th grade classroom, students grabbed the magazines and eagerly examined them. (I was there and saw it happen!)
Whole Group	"What did you come up with/" Teacher writes their contributions verbatim on the chalkboard.	"What did you come up with?" Teacher writes their contributions verbatim on the chalkboard.	Groups then are given some time during class each day to work on the report. A new lesson plan is also started at Stage 1 for how to write a report.

Note: See also Figure 6.7B.

A UNIT ON AN INTRODUCTION TO EGYPT

Introduced in Chapter 6, the following unit developed by Dave Williams (Figure 6.7B) has only three stages (Figure 9.2).

A UNIT ON AN INTRODUCTION TO FRACTIONS

Also introduced in Chapter 6 (Figure 6.7C), here is Joanne Rawley's complete unit to introduce fractions to beginning math students (Figure 9.3).

Figure 9.2 *(Continued)*

	Stage 4 **BRANCHING OUT** *Knowing in* *more detail*	Stage 5 **GAINING** **FLUENCY** *Using it, doing it*	Stage 6 **CONTINUED** **INFLUENCE** *Wider application*
Individual	However, other related topics might be added to take the students to a higher level of understanding and skill. For example, at Stage 4, connecting to (constructed on) their original study of Egypt, might be a related study of some aspect of Egyptian culture or society that can be best understood only when there is first a basic knowledge of and familiarity with Egypt.		
Small Groups	Then, at Stage 5, after learning more about Egypt at Stage 4, the assignment might be for each student, or a pair, to choose a topic related to Egypt to research and report on to the class. Each student, or pair, would do research, then get feedback in small groups, revise if necessary, and then make a report to the class. It is important at Stage 5 for students to have the opportunity to make their own choices, to be creative. They *want* to do this and do well with it.		
Whole Group	The stages are flexible in that some might need to be repeated for fuller development of skill and understanding at the same stage of development. Sometimes students might need to go back and forth between Individual (in this case perhaps pair) and Small Group work for repeated feedback sessions and revision work.		

By going through these learning activities, students at any level can construct a concept of fractions; that is, acquire the basic knowledge and skill needed to begin to understand and use fractions.

Older students, younger students—their brains all work the same way with the same functions and processes. Again, the major differences between their brains are the quantity and kinds of knowledge structures they have. Older students know more about the world and, thus, have more knowledge structures than younger students. Therefore, older students might be able to go further with fractions than the younger students. The younger students will also be able to use fractions adeptly and with understanding; they will be limited only by the extent of the knowledge structures they have constructed so far in their young lives.

Students with an aptitude for math or for perceiving spatial relations might, of course, progress more quickly and to a higher level than other students. On the other hand, students with special needs might progress more slowly; but, with enough time and support, they, too, will make progress (also see Smilkstein, 1993).

Figure 9.3   Introduction-to-Fractions Unit Lesson Plan

	Stage 1 PREPARING TO LEARN *Using new knowledge*	Stage 2 STARTING TO LEARN *Experimental practice*	Stage 3 CONSOLIDATING NEW BASE *Further practice*
Individual	Teacher gives each student four 8 × 11 sheets of paper, each one a different color, e.g., white, blue, red, green: "Tear the blue sheet into two equal pieces and place them on the whole white sheet. Write down how you would tell or explain to someone how many of the blue pieces *one* of the blue pieces is."	"Now tear the red sheet into four equal pieces and place them on the white sheet. Write down how you would tell someone how many of the red pieces *one* of the red pieces is, then how many *two* of them are."	"Write down how you would tell someone how many of the red pieces *three* of the red pieces are, then how many *four* pieces are."
Small Groups	"Tell each other what you wrote down. Discuss what you were thinking when you were trying to figure out what to write."	As before.	As before.
Whole Group	"What did you write down? (Teacher writes all answers verbatim on the board.) What were you thinking when you were trying to figure out what to write?" (General discussion.)	"What did you write down?" (Teacher writes on board as before.) After the SG discussion at Stage 2, teacher writes 1—6 on the board and points to 1: "How many feel confused about what we're doing?" Then points to 6: "How many feel you understand what we're doing?" Repeats with 2-3 then 4-5. If most students are at 4-6, the Stage 3 cycle can be processed more quickly.	"What did you write down?" Teacher writes all answers verbatim on the board as before. Then the teacher explains that these pieces are called **fractions, which are parts of a whole (from the Latin word meaning "to break")** and they are written as 1/4, 2/4, 3/4, 4/4 (and that 4/4 = 1).

Figure 9.3 *(Continued)*

	Stage 4 BRANCHING OUT *Knowing in more detail*	Stage 5 GAINING FLUENCY *Using it, doing it*	Stage 6 CONTINUED IMPROVEMENT *Wider application*
Individual	"Now tear the green sheet into eight equal pieces and place them on the white sheet. Write the fraction for *one* green piece. Then write a fraction for *two* green pieces, then for *three* pieces, then *four, five, six, seven,* and *eight* green pieces."	"Write down everything you know about fractions, including what the denominator and numerator tell us."	"Write six fractions for any different numbers of white, blue, red, and/or green pieces. You decide what different color pieces you will use and how many pieces you will have in each of your fractions."
Small Groups	As before.	As before.	"Show your fractions to each other. Discuss what your fractions, including the numerator and denominator, are telling other people."
Whole Group	"What did you write down?" Teacher writes all answers verbatim on the board as before—then gives the terminology: the top number is called the "numerator" and the bottom is called the "denominator." If there are any errors, teacher asks the class to correct them.	"What did you write down?" Teacher writes answers verbatim on the board as before. General discussion with teacher later correcting any errors students have not been able to correct themselves.	Some students write their fractions on the board. They discuss what these fractions mean. General discussion. If many students are still uncertain, do another Stage 6 cycle: "Write fractions for other numbers of pieces of different colors" (I, SG, WG). Do another Stage 6 cycle: "What do you know about fractions now?"

Note: See also Figure 6.7C.

Figure 9.4A Khiet's Pretest

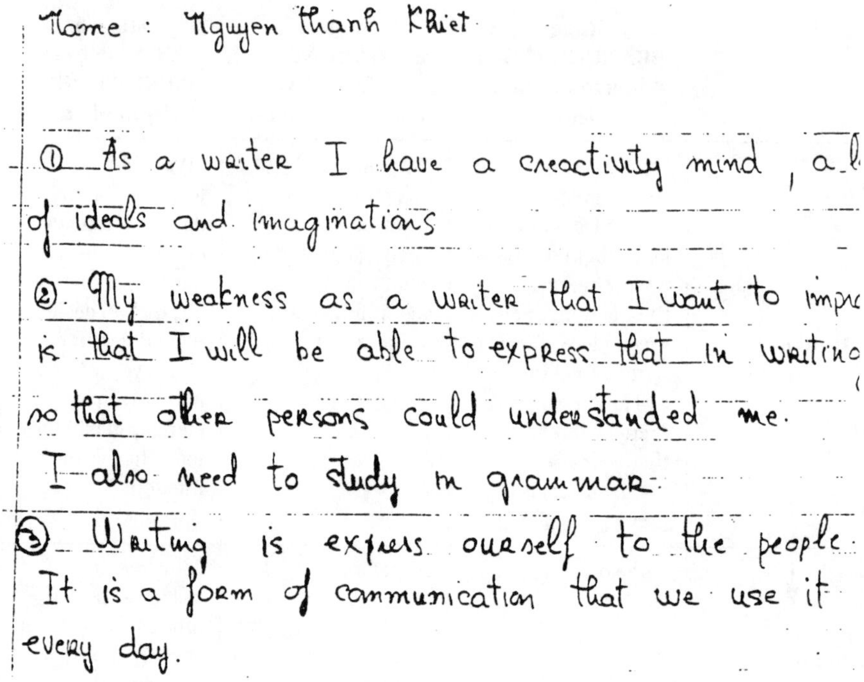

Name : Nguyen Thanh Khiet

① As a writer I have a creactivity mind , a l
of ideals and imaginations

② My weakness as a writer that I want to impr
is that I will be able to express that in writing
so that other persons could understanded me.
I also need to study in grammar.

③ Writing is express ourself to the people.
It is a form of communication that we use it
every day.

A BASIC GRAMMAR CURRICULUM:
A SEQUENCE OF UNITS FOR A WHOLE COURSE

A teacher has a class of students who do not know what a sentence is and
who cannot identify subjects and verbs. How does that teacher help her
students, in one term, to become knowledgeable and skillful in writing
grammatically correct sentences? This is the situation I faced with both
the ninth-grade class and the community college grammar class described
in Chapter 1. It was only after many years and much practicing and
processing that I was able to develop a curriculum that helps students
progress from where they start to the goal level of the course.

Chapter Five gives examples of Eva Slaughter's writing (Figures 5.4,
5.5). Here are pre- and posttests from another student, Nguyen Thanh
Khiet, a man in his 30s, an English-as-a-Second-Language student from
Vietnam (Figures 9.4A, 9.4B).

The prompt for Khiet's pretest had three parts:

1. What are your strengths as a writer?

2. What are your problems as a writer?

3. Why do you think people write?

Figure 9.4B Khiet's Posttest

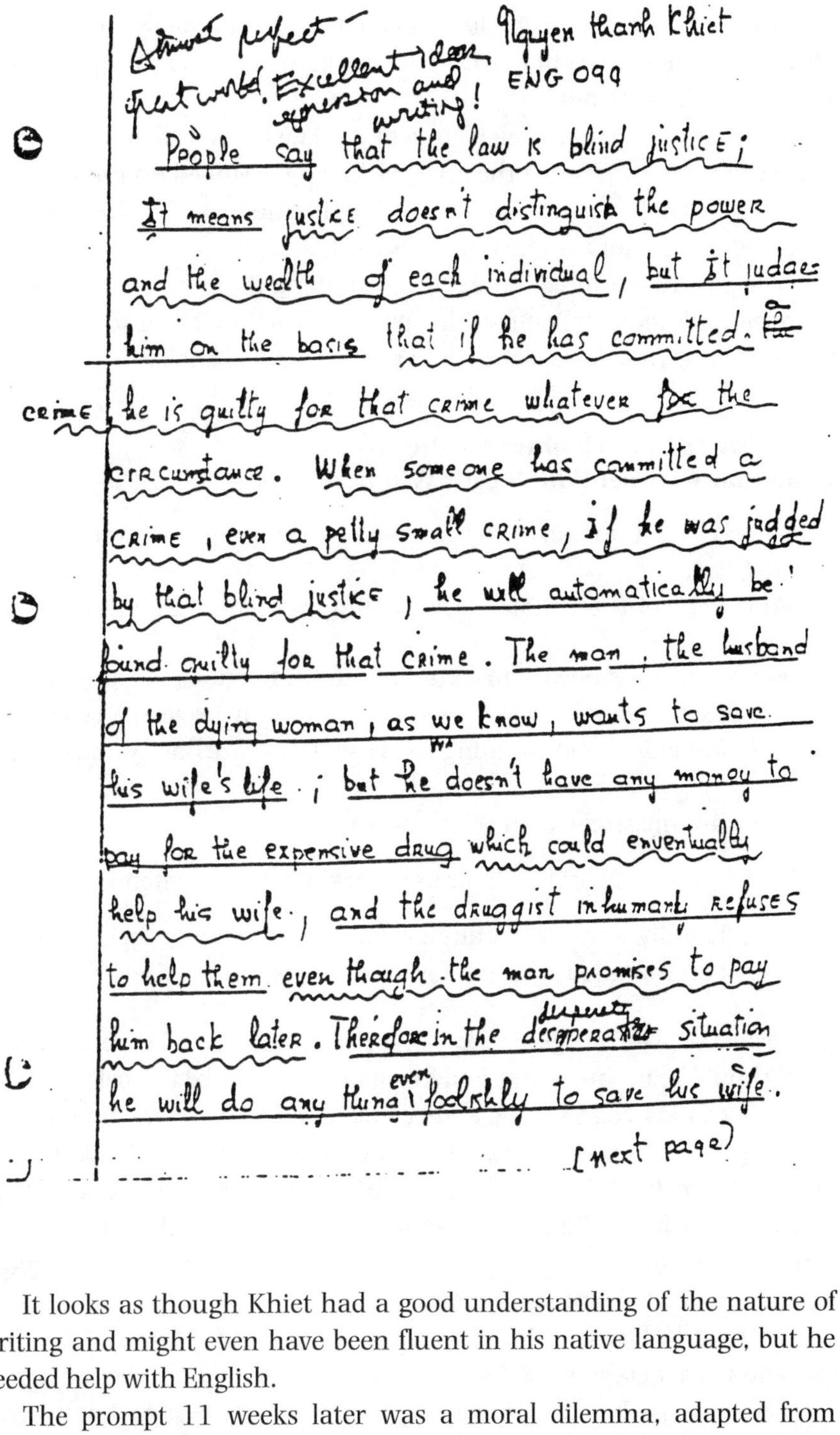

Almost perfect - great work. Excellent ideas, expression and writing!

Nguyen Thanh Khiet
ENG 099

People say that the law is blind justice; it means justice doesn't distinguish the power and the wealth of each individual, but it judges him on the basis that if he has committed the crime, he is guilty for that crime whatever the circumstance. When someone has committed a crime, even a petty small crime, if he was judged by that blind justice, he will automatically be found guilty for that crime. The man, the husband of the dying woman, as we know, wants to save his wife's life; but he doesn't have any money to pay for the expensive drug which could eventually help his wife, and the druggist inhumanly refuses to help them even though the man promises to pay him back later. Therefore in the desperate situation he will do anything even foolishly to save his wife.

[next page]

It looks as though Khiet had a good understanding of the nature of writing and might even have been fluent in his native language, but he needed help with English.

The prompt 11 weeks later was a moral dilemma, adapted from Kohlberg's "The Heinz Dilemma" (1981, p. 12): "An old woman is dying from cancer. A scientist has discovered the cure for her cancer. Her husband, a poor retired janitor, goes to the scientist to buy the medicine. The janitor cannot afford it, but he offers to pay some now and the rest over the years. The scientist refuses. Later, the old man steals the medicine. He is caught and brought to trial. You are on the jury. Do you believe he is guilty? Why or why not?"

By the way, when a foreign student asked what a trial and a jury are, I realized I had committed the error of having assumed everyone knows what a jury trial is. As the after-school high school student had said, the best teachers do not assume (Figure 8.2).

The posttest required more critical thinking than the pretest and yet, even with this more difficult writing prompt, Khiet's writing shows he had become more knowledgeable of, and more fluent in, English.

Planning the Curriculum for the Grammar Course: Which Unit When

This is how I answered the curriculum planning questions posed in Figure 6.6A:

At the end of this course (Basic Writing: Sentence-Level Grammar)

- I want my students to know the grammar tools. (The grammar rules are called "tools" in this curriculum because "rules" can be forbidding and daunting whereas "tools" are handy and empowering.)
- I want my students to be able to

  1. Present their ideas in grammatically correct sentences

  2. Identify and correct any grammatical errors in their sentences according to the grammar tools

Using the planning guidelines (Figures 6.6A and 6.6B) to decide which units should be in this course and in which order, I asked myself what the students would need to know and be able to do to reach the final goal of knowing how to express themselves in correct sentences. Thinking long and hard, I realized they would first need to know what clauses are. They would need to know this because sentences are made up of clauses. If they could not recognize clauses, they would never be able to recognize whether they were writing sentences.

Then I asked myself, "But what do they first need to know before they can know what clauses are?"

The answer, I realized, was that they would need to know what subjects and verbs are because all clauses—and only clauses—contain a subject and verb. If they did not know what subjects and verbs are, they would never be able to know whether they were writing a clause. And only if they knew what a clause is would they be able to know what a sentence is.

The Grammar Course

I then started my developmental grammar classes with a unit on subjects and verbs. But it quickly became apparent that another grammatical structure, the prepositional phrase (under the house, in the bookcase, before eating, after running, etc.), kept causing problems. Students would misidentify words in the prepositional phrases as subjects or verbs (house, bookcase, eating, running). Then they would be in serious trouble. It was clear, then, that before they could step up to the higher level of learning subjects and verbs, they first had to construct a foundation of knowledge about prepositional phrases. After that, learning about subjects and verbs would be less confusing.

Consequently, the first five class sessions are about prepositional phrases. Some might think this is an inordinate amount of time to spend on identifying prepositional phrases. But this grammar curriculum front loads not only this first concept and skill, it also front loads how to learn about grammar: Be careful, use the tools, use your innate sense of logic, look for patterns, solve problems. The curriculum itself follows the brain's rules. For example, every new step is constructed from a relevant prerequisite foundation; the activities are stimulating because they ask the students to use their innate resources, and students are being active learners. Moreover, by using their brains' natural learning process, the students are attentive, motivated, and confident.

Here is the first learning activity in this prepositional phrase unit (Figure 9.5), which they do after the NHLP activity (Chapter 2) and after learning about the brain (Chapter 3).

All the learning activities in this course, and in all NHLP curricula, are on target instead of being off target (i.e., using workbooks or worksheets and then relying on transfer to occur). For example, in this grammar curriculum, students do their own writing, identifying parts of speech and structures and correcting errors in their own writing.

Then they learn tools (Figure 9.6), such as "a preposition is on the preposition list"; "it is not a preposition if it is on the never-a-preposition list"; "prepositions never have 'a,' 'an,' or 'the' in front of them" (Smilkstein, 1998, p. 345).

When students see these tools, they say, with relief and confidence, "I can do that!" Yes, they can because this is where they are, at this level. Then they can construct their new knowledge and skill, level by level

Figure 9.5   Prepositional Phrase Unit: First Learning Activity

Classwork 2-1: Prepositions, Objects of Prepositions, Prepositional Phrases (Tools 1–9)

"List of Prepositions" for you to fill in on pages 38 to 39
"List of Prepositions" on pages 44 to 45

Individual Activity: Look at the picture that follows and then, in the space provided under the picture, answer this question:

Where is this person?

Your answer: _____

In small groups, and then as a whole class, compare and talk about what you wrote.

from there, cumulatively adding new connections seamlessly, activity by activity, forming a richer and richer neural network for grammar. Also, as usual, students first do each activity individually. Then they check, discuss, and correct each other's work in small groups. Finally, as a whole group, volunteers write their work on the board; then the class discusses the work and the relevant tools. The teacher, using the formative assessment tool (1 – – – – 6), sees whether another activity (more practice) is needed to help the students gain more skill and understanding of a particular object of learning and, if so, figures out what that activity should be.

Figure 9.6   Prepositional Phrase Unit: The First Tools

Prepositional Phrases (Chapter 2)

Tools for Prepositions (P) and Objects of Prepositions (OP)

TOOL 1: A word is a preposition (P) if it is on the "Preposition List." A word is not a preposition (P) if it is on the "Never-a-Preposition List."

TOOL 2: Prepositions (P) can never have "a," "an," or "the" before them.

PART OF THE "NEVER-A-PREPOSITION LIST"							
a	this	those	you're	their		am	was
an	that	my	his	any number		is	were
the	these	our	her	action words		are	will
words that end in "ing" (except "during" and some words used in business correspondence like "according to," "including," and "relating to")							

TOOL 3: Ask the question "what?" or "whom?" after a preposition (P). If there is an answer, the answer is the object of the preposition (OP). Use your logic to decide what the answer is. If there is no answer (no object of the preposition [OP]), then there is no preposition in that sentence. The word that looks like a preposition (P) is not a preposition (P) in that particular sentence.

with <u>whom</u>?	behind <u>what</u>?	after <u>what</u>?	inside <u>what</u>?
P --OP--	P --OP--	P --OP--	No OP or P
With my friend	behind the desk	after 2:00	inside

around what?   This is the <u>whole answer,</u> the whole OP.

      P   ----------------OP--------------------

Jan swam around the ten-mile, freezing cold, rough lake.

Outside what?

      P

They worked outside all day.

There is no answer, so "outside" is not a preposition (P) in this sentence. "All day" answers "when?" and not "what?" and "when?" is not a preposition question. Be careful to ask the right question (*only* "what?" or "whom?").

Outside <u>what</u>? the house

      P --OP--

They worked (outside the house) all day.

"All day" answers "when?" so it is not part of the object of the preposition (OP).

SOURCE: Smilkstein (1998), p. 345.

After 1 week on prepositional phrases, we spend 5 to 6 weeks on subjects and verbs, which are vastly more complicated than prepositional phrases. Once students, however, are skillful at identifying their own prepositional phrases, they are better able to start learning the more various and complex tools about subjects and verbs. Then they become knowledgeable and skillful about writing subjects and verbs by doing a lot of their own writing and analyzing what they have written. When they are able to identify and correct subject and verb errors in their own writing, the next unit on clauses, which is usually difficult, goes quickly and easily.

Then, after a few weeks on clauses, they are ready for sentences, which they also learn relatively easily, even at this higher level of complex knowledge and skill. They can do this because of the cumulative growth of complex knowledge networks constructed over the preceding weeks.

One Student's Progress Through the Course

Here are samples of Eva Slaughter's work as she progressed through the course (Figures 9.7–9.13). It is not important here to pay attention to the letters and marks of her own analysis of her writing. Just look at the progress she makes in her ability to express herself. Remember, not one word is said in this course about spelling and vocabulary. But we can see her increasing her knowledge and skill on every front as she advances level by level.

A LEARNING COMMUNITY CURRICULUM FOR A WHOLE COURSE

The term "learning community" refers to two or more courses taught collaboratively by two or more teachers. The distinguishing features of a learning community, as specified by Jean MacGregor, a leader in the development of learning communities, are compatible with the elements of the brain's natural learning process, for example "more time-on-task, more time to build a sense of community, and more time for focused practice and reflection" (personal communication, June 3, 2002). A learning community course is, as well, an antidote to a problem from which many students, especially dendrite-disadvantaged students, suffer: "When students move from discrete class to discrete class, they constantly have to shift focus. This is especially tough for dendrite deprived students" (MacGregor).

Coordinated Studies

Learning communities are offered in different forms. The one that most fully incorporates elements of the NHLP is the coordinated studies

(text continues on p. 226)

Figure 9.7   Eva Slaughter: April 2

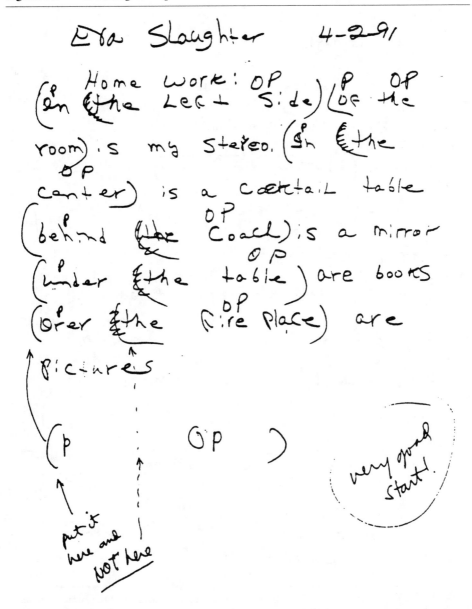

Note: The prompt was to "describe where things are in your home. Analyze your prepositional phrases." Notice that Eva did not have a complete concept of a prepositional phrase; I crossed out her incorrectly placed parenthesis and added parentheses at the start of the phrase.

Figure 9.8 Eva Slaughter: April 4

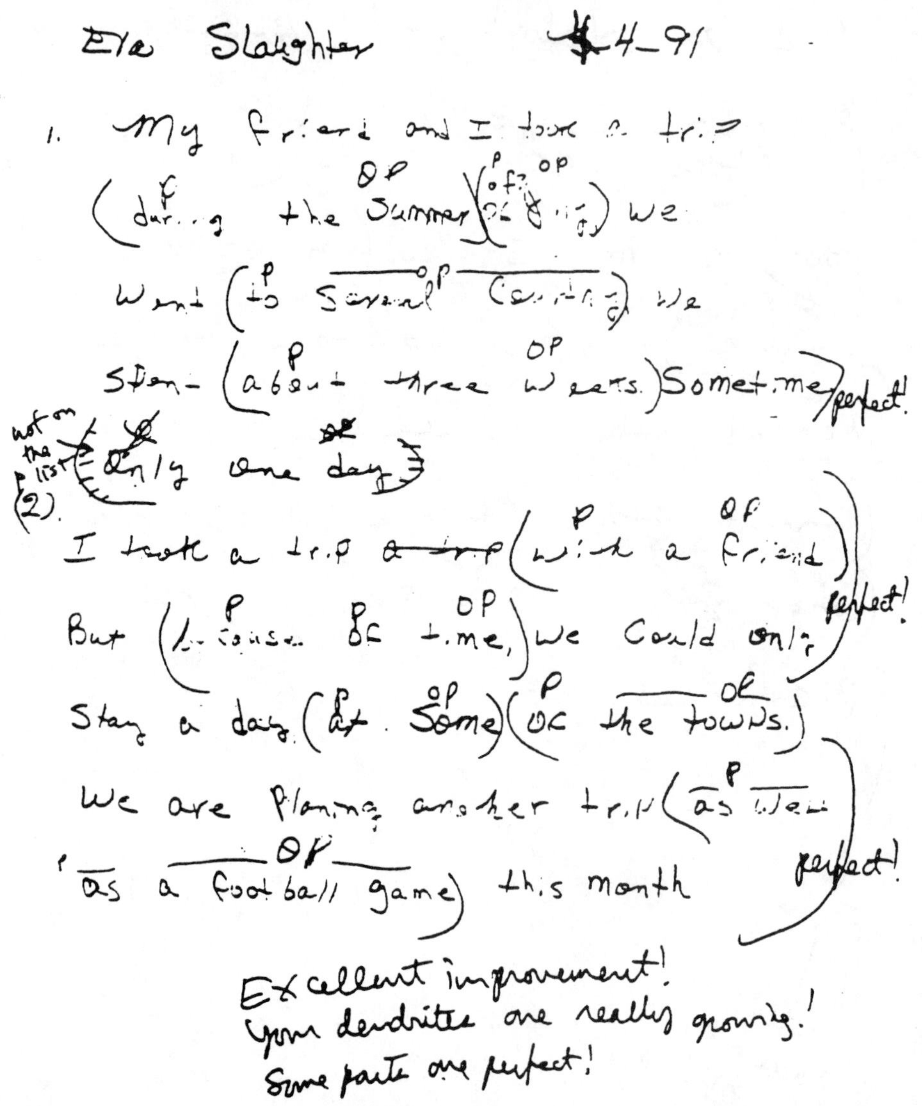
Eva Slaughter 4-4-91

1. My friend and I took a trip (during the summer (of trip)) we went (to several countries) we stay (about three weeks.) Sometime perfect!

not on the list (only one day.)

(2). I took a trip ~~a trip~~ (with a friend) But (because of time,) we could only stay a day (at some) (of the towns.) perfect!

We are planing another trip (as well as a football game) this month perfect!

Excellent improvement!
Your dendrites are really growing!
Some parts are perfect!

Note: The prompt was to "write two to three sentences about anything of interest; it could be about an experience or one of the homework assignments given in the textbook. Analyze your prepositional phrases." She now had a firm concept of this structure and made only one error ("only" is not a preposition). Every "perfect!" was a guideline and support to help her continue to shape her understanding and tool use.

Figure 9.9 Eva Slaughter: April 5

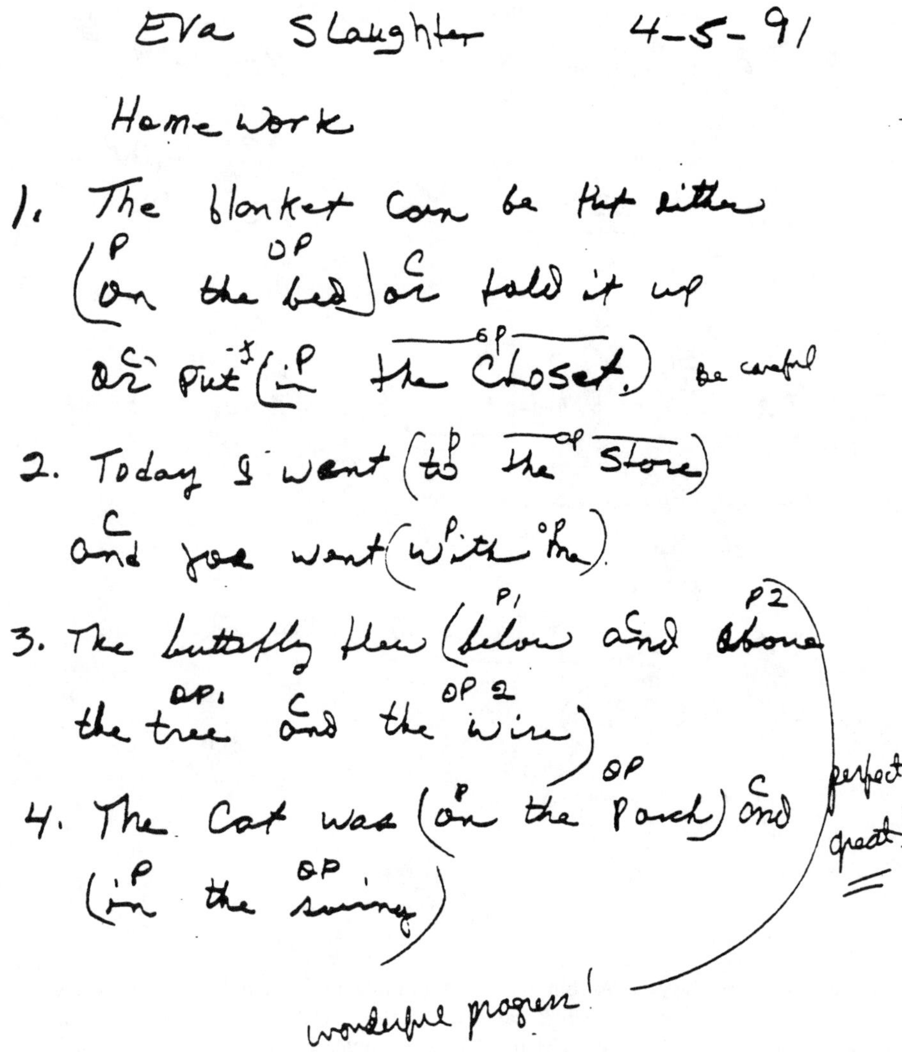
Eva Slaughter 4-5-91

Home work

1. The blanket can be put either (on the bed) or fold it up or put (in the closet.) Be careful

2. Today I went (to the store) and you went (with me).

3. The butterfly flew (below and above the tree and the wire)

4. The cat was (on the porch) and (in the swing)

perfect! great!

wonderful progress!

Note: The prompt was to "write three sentences using compounds. Analyze your prepositional phrases and compounds." Her error in the first sentence was not prematurely commented on at this point. Her grasp of compounds, however, was becoming quite refined and sophisticated.

Figure 9.10 Eva Slaughter: April 11

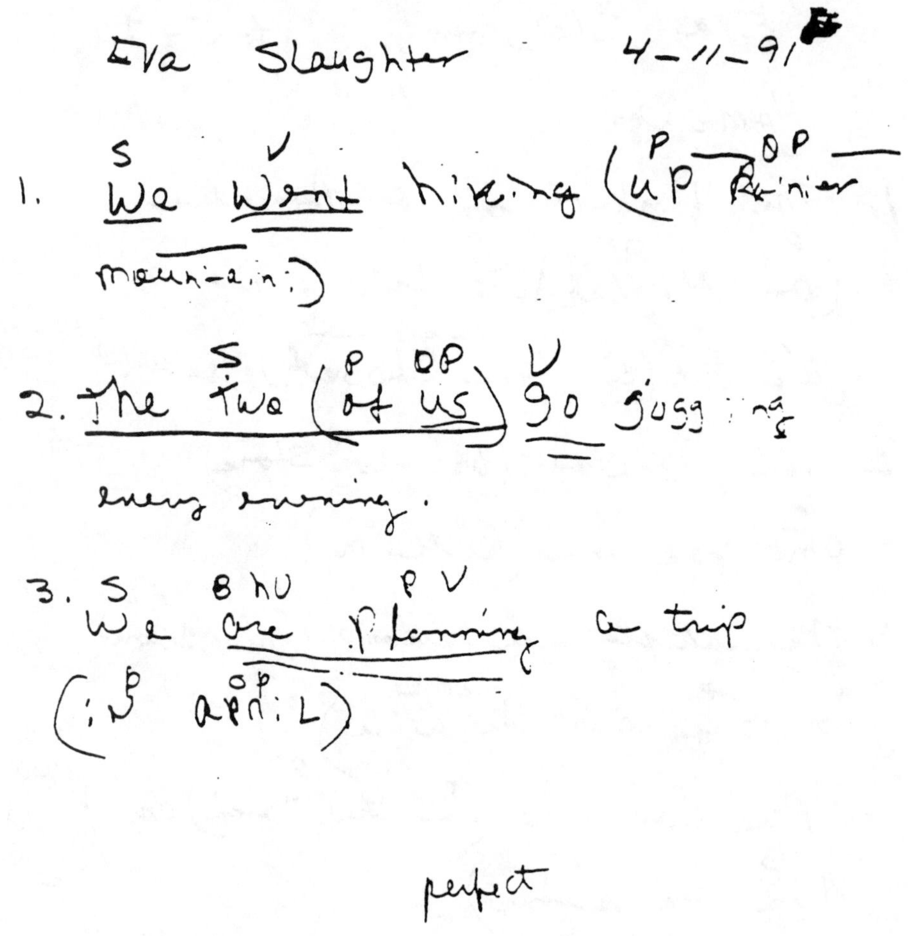

Eva Slaughter 4-11-91

1. We went hiking (up Rainier mountain)

2. The two (of us) go jogging every evening.

3. We are planning a trip (in April)

perfect

Note: The prompt was the same as that for April 4, but now included analyzing subjects, verbs, helper verbs, and continuous participles, called "continuing verbs (CV) in this curriculum. Eva now had clear concepts of all of these elements. For example, she knew that "hiking" and "jogging" could not be the continuing verbs because "went" and "go" are not "be helper" verbs (BH). Later in the course she would be able to identify "hiking" and "jogging" as verbals.

Figure 9.11   Eva Slaughter: April 22

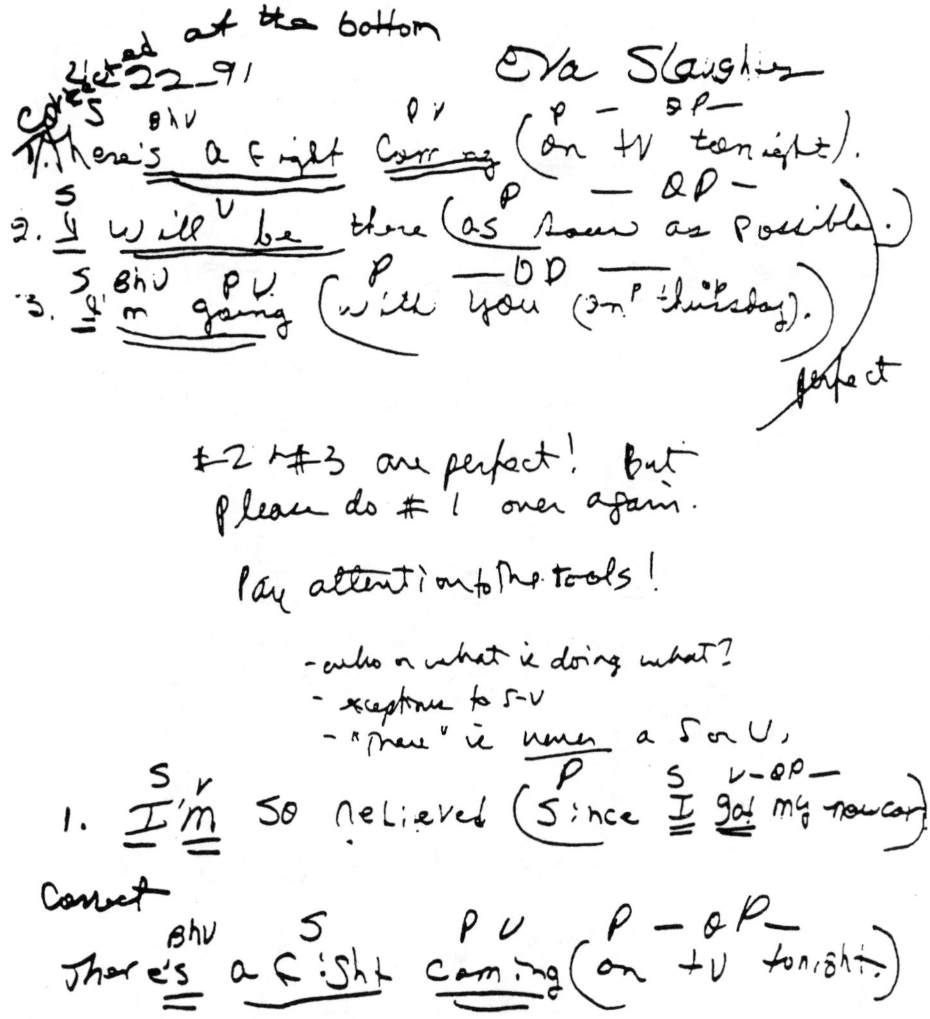

Note: The prompt was the same as that for April 11. Notice that Eva corrected her first sentence at the bottom of the page, shaping and constructing a more refined neural network for subjects and verbs: CV = Continuing Verb (later she will learn to distinguish between the two different kinds of participles). Also notice that she had one prepositional phrase inside another one: (with you (on Thursday)). Finally, she is analyzing a dependent clause as a prepositional phrase, which is correct at this point because the concept of clauses has not yet been introduced.

Figure 9.12 Eva Slaughter: May 10

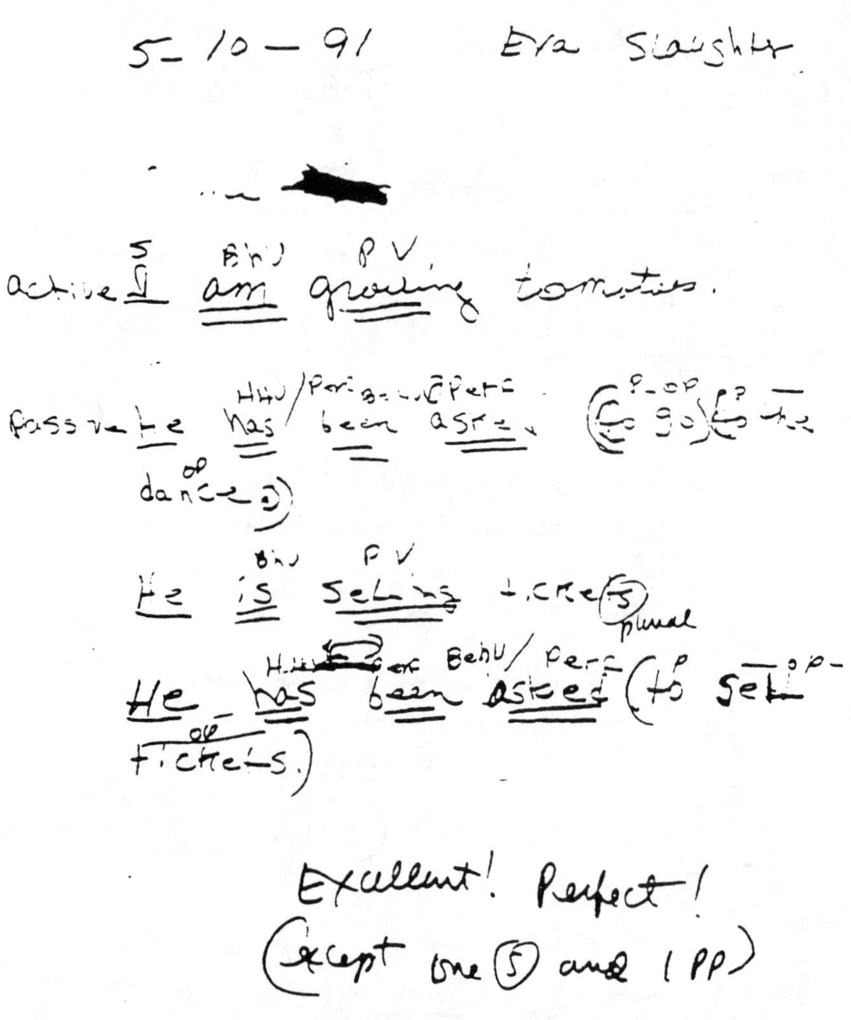

Note: The prompt was to "write two active and passive verbs. Analyze all elements."
Notice that in her passive verbs Eva analyzed the three parts of the verb.

Figure 9.13   Eva Slaughter: May 17

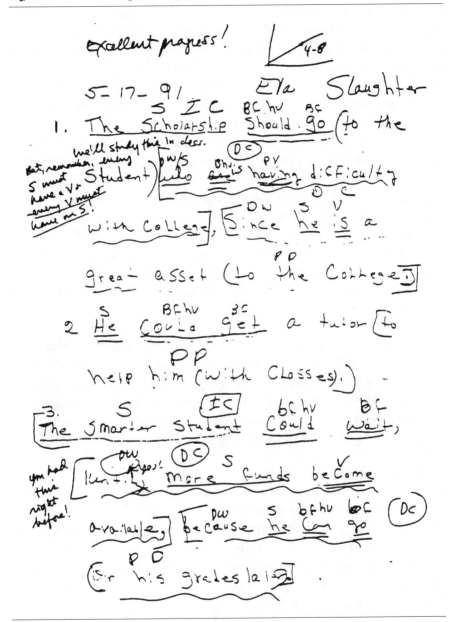

Note: The prompt was a moral dilemma. The directions were to "write what you truly feel and think about the topic" and then analyze each sentence, correcting it if necessary. Notice that Eva was now identifying independent clauses (IC) and dependent clauses (DC with wavy underlining), showing her clear and more refined network for these.

(CS) course. In a CS course, two or more teachers from two or more disciplines choose a theme to study through the perspectives of their different disciplines. As a team, they teach two or more courses as one integrated course. For example, in our community college, four teachers from different disciplines—philosophy, history, composition, and literature—taught a CS course on the theme of American values. The separate courses were taught as one integrated course in extended blocks of time rather than in separate 50-minute periods.

The team plans "one syllabus of integrated study, although the transcripts reflect the [discrete] classes that are embedded in the learning community" (MacGregor, personal communication, June 3, 2002). The syllabus of "American Values" and other coordinated studies courses can be found on the Born to Learn Web site (www.borntolearn.net).

Faculty who will be teaching a CS course meet regularly the term before the course is offered to plan it—the theme, the goals, the material (focusing on primary sources rather than textbooks); the format; and what will be taught when, how, and by whom. As is typical of a coordinated studies program,

> these programs generally offer students a more complex intellectual environment. They expose students to topics from the perspectives of different disciplines, teachers and peers, and ask them to build larger connections and meanings. Most learning communities demand a level of student participation and responsibility not typically found in general education offerings. (MacGregor, 1991, p. 6).

Thus, students in a CS learning community are given the opportunity to learn by their brains' natural learning process, for example to do their own thinking, to be active learners, to use their brain's innate resources, which they love to do. This, perhaps, is why a study of CS courses in colleges and universities in Washington state reported that "retention was higher in learning community programs; students in learning communities stayed enrolled for longer periods of time and more often completed degrees at the college" (MacGregor, 1991, p. 5).

James Harnish's evaluation (2002) of CS courses at North Seattle Community College (NSCC), looking at data from 1997–98 through 2000–01, shows the same positive results, including the following:

- Successful completion rate (retention) within a typical term is more than 83%.
- Persistence rates comparing CS students and all academic transfer intent students in 1997–98 show that 87% of the CS students

enrolled the following term, whereas only 55% of the other students enrolled the next term.

- Of the CS students, 55% completed associate's degrees in 1998–99 whereas the college average for students with academic transfer intent in the same period was only 13%.
- On average, 76% of the CS students receive a grade of A or B.

Linked Courses

In a linked learning community, also called a paired or clustered learning community, two or more courses are taught separately as stand-alone courses; however, students enroll in the linked courses as a cohort and the faculty collaborate on some or all of the materials, assignments, and exams.

Eric Mould and Judy Moore, biology teachers at Yakima Community College (YCC) in Washington, compared the retention and performance of 650 students over several years in a biology course taught as a stand-alone course and also as a course linked with writing and speech in a learning community. They found that both retention and grades were higher for students in the linked course. For example, 56.8% of the students in the linked course earned A's and B's, whereas only 37.2% did so in the stand-alone course. When questioned about the validity of using grades to evaluate the difference between the courses, Mould and Moore replied that they "are finding that these increases in performance are occurring with more rigorous exams requiring higher level thinking and communicating skills" (in MacGregor, 1991, p. 5).

Linked Courses for Developmental Students

At Tennessee State University (TSU), their Emerging Scholars Program (ESP)—for students testing below the designated skill levels for entering students—offers a variety of linked learning communities. Some communities link as many as four developmental courses (writing, reading, math, study skills). Students, as a cohort, take all the linked courses, meet periodically for group discussions, have study groups, and are, in short, part of a community of teachers and learners.

The teachers collaborate on developing curricula that give students the opportunity to use the skills and concepts of one course to enrich their learning in the other courses. For example, math teachers might have students write paragraphs about mathematical concepts or journals about their experiences learning math. Also, a cohort of students in a learning community might be assigned to read the same novel; then each teacher uses the novel in one way or another in his or her separate course. Sample curricula from the TSU Emerging Scholars Program are posted on the Born to Learn Web site.

Positive Results

Vincent Tinto and his colleagues have done the most comprehensive study of learning community results, but numbers of other studies of learning community programs around the country also reveal promising results, including increased rates of course completion and persistence, greater engagement in learning, and increased academic confidence. In the most carefully designed programs, a pattern of increased grades and intellectual development are also seen (MacGregor, personal communication, June 3, 2002).

For example, Tinto's (1997) findings that students in these learner-centered, natural-learning coordinated and linked courses had higher grades and retention rates than students in stand-alone courses are corroborated by the findings of Harnish at NSCC, of Mould and Moore at YCC, and from the Emerging Scholars Program at TSU (Coordinator N. Bullock, personal communication, June 18, 2002).

As a result of such studies and our own students' higher grades, better retention, and more positive attitude, graduation requirements at North Seattle Community College now include enrollment in at least one learning community.

Resources

For more information about learning communities, see "Learning Communities" in the bibliography, which also includes a Web site for The National Learning Communities Project, headed by Barbara Leigh Smith and Jean MacGregor.

A DEVELOPMENTAL ENGLISH CURRICULUM: COURSES IN A PROGRAM

Colleges have many sequential programs. They typically start with an introductory course and then progress through one or more subsequent, higher-level courses. These program courses might be numbered Physics 100, Physics 200, Physics 300. Our college-level English composition program consists of two courses, English 101 and English 102.

Planning a Developmental English Program

Our English department also has a number of precollege or developmental English courses to help underprepared or at-risk students develop the skills and knowledge they need to succeed at the college level. New students at our college take an English placement test. If they read at the fourth- to sixth-grade level and cannot write correct sentences, they are placed in the first of these sequential courses. Because our college is an open-door institution, we do not turn any students away. If students are unprepared for college-level work, the college provides them with the opportunity to overcome their dendrite disadvantage.

Our department has spent many hours—days, weeks, months, years—figuring out how many courses we need to bring students from that beginning level to the English 101 level, which courses, and in which order. Our curriculum-planning question was, as described earlier, "What do they need to know and be able to do before they can understand and are able to do the work in the next higher course?" In other words, we needed the answer to the key curriculum development question: "Will they be able to know and do *that* if they do not first know and can do *this?*"

Years ago we began by putting one precollege reading-writing course, English 099, below English 101. But many students still did not do well in 101, and there were larger than anticipated dropout and failure rates. Then we put another course, 098, below that to prepare students for 099. When that did not solve the problem, we put another course below 098. Eventually, because we were still losing students, we made a major change in the sequential curriculum for this program. We decided the students needed more than one course at each level in order to develop both their reading and writing skills.

As a result, we instituted a sequence of modified learning communities: two courses taught by one teacher in 100-minute blocks. The introductory courses are 093 (reading and study skills) and 094 (basic sentence grammar). The first writing course focuses on sentence grammar because if the students cannot control their sentences, there is little chance they will succeed in any of the higher-level writing courses. The first reading course focuses on study skills, along with reading, as a way to further prepare the students for both the precollege courses as well as, later, college-level courses.

The second-level courses are 095 (reading) and 096 (writing short essays). Then students proceed to the third level: 097 (reading) and 098 (pre-101 writing). If any students still need more preparation, they go on to 099. For students who test below the 094 level, there are two stand-alone grammar courses, 086 and 088, to prepare them for the first-level courses (Figure 9.14).

Figure 9.14   Developmental English Curriculum: Sequence of Courses

English 101 Composition	
English 099 College Prep Writing V	
English 097 College Prep Reading IV	English 098 College Prep Writing IV
English 095 College Prep Reading & Study Skills III	English 096 College Prep Writing III
English 093 Reading and Study Skills II	English 094 Writing Improvement II
	English 088 Grammar & Punctuation Ib
	English 086 Grammar & Punctuation Ia

On the basis of their initial English placement test, students begin the program at their skill level. Some students need only 099 whereas others need to start at the first, second, or third level. In this way, students have the time and opportunity they need to grow the knowledge structures that will prepare them for college-level reading and writing.

It also happens sometimes that a student can skip a level, perhaps jumping from the second level to 099, if that student's work shows the student has been able to acquire the knowledge and skill needed to succeed in the higher-level course. As commonly happens, that student once had well-grown knowledge (neural) structures but had been out of school for so many years that some of those structures had been pruned. With a refresher course, the complex structures still present are able to begin growing again.

In this way, after much trial and error, much thinking and rethinking, much work and talk, much sharing and brain cudgeling at meeting after meeting, we colleagues finally constructed a sequential curriculum in our precollege English program that helps students get ready for—and succeed at—each higher level of challenge and learning.

FINAL WORDS

What This Book Is About

Imagine what our world would be like if all people could fulfill their potential to be the learners, thinkers, problem solvers, and creators they were born to be. We can help make that happen. This book is about a brain-based natural-learning process that leads to a theory and method for developing and delivering curricula that invite and empower the innate critical and creative thinking abilities of every student.

This book is about students—actually everyone—wanting to learn and loving to learn, to think and discover and work hard to solve problems, to be independent thinkers, to be empowered. It is about providing an environment in which learning can happen. It is about creating and delivering curricula that make it possible for students to be the eager, motivated, successful learners they were born to be.

I hope this book helps to sustain, and perhaps even to nourish, you in your teaching, your creativity, your love for the subjects you teach, and in your love for seeing your students fulfill their potential as learners.

Sharing

If you have questions, comments, or any NHLP syllabi or curricula that you would like posted on the Born to Learn Web site to share with others, please let me know (contact me through the Web site).

"The sharing is significant since it relates to the power of the sun to foster life and illuminate all things with its light" (Blum, 1982, p. 95).

References

Allen, R. (2002, Winter). Honing the tools of instruction: How research can improve teaching for the 21st century. *Curriculum update*. Alexandria, VA: Association for Supervision and Curriculum Development.

Allman, W. F. (1989). *Apprentices of wonder: Inside the neural network revolution.* New York: Bantam Books.

Anderson, J. (1988). Cognitive styles and multicultural populations. *Journal of Teacher Education, 39*, 2–9.

Anderson, J. (1992). Acknowledging the learning styles of diverse populations: Implications for instructional design. *Teaching for diversity*. San Francisco: Jossey-Bass.

Barr, R. B., & Tagg, J. (1995). From teaching to learning: A new paradigm for undergraduate education. *Change, 26*(6), 13–25.

Barrows, H. S., & Kelson, A. M. (1996). Problem-based learning: A total approach to education. Springfield: Southern Illinois University School of Medicine.

Bartoszeck, A. B. (1996). Enhancing active learning of neurophysiology through the use of concept mapping. *The Basic Science Teacher, 2*, 2–5.

Bjorklund, D. F. (2000). *Children's thinking: Developmental function and individual differences* (3rd ed). Belmont, CA: Wadsworth/Thomson.

Blum, R. (1982). *The book of runes.* New York: St. Martin's Press.

Bower, B. (2002, May 25). Verbal brains: Neural paths take a mature turn. *Science News, 161*, 326.

Boylan, H. R. (2002). *What works: Research-based best practices in developmental education.* Boone, NC: Continuous Quality Improvement Network and National Center for Developmental Education, Appalachian State University.

Boylan, H. R., & Bonham, B. S. (1992). The impact of developmental education programs. *Review of Research in Developmental Education, 9*, 1–3.

Bransford, J. D., Brown, A. L., & Cocking, R. R. (Eds.). (1999). *How people learn: Brain, mind, experience, and school.* Washington, DC: National Academy Press.

Caine, G., & Caine, R. N. (1991). *Making connections: Teaching and the human brain.* Alexandria, VA: Association for Supervision and Curriculum Development.

Caine, G., & Caine, R. N. (1997). *Unleashing the power of perceptual change: The potential of brain-based teaching.* (To order, write to The Brain Store, 4202 Sorrento Valley Blvd., Suite B., San Diego, CA 92121).

Calvin, W. H., & Ojemann, G. A. (1994). *Conversations with Neil's brain: The neural nature of thought and language.* Reading, MA: Addison-Wesley.

Carper, J. (2000). *Your miracle brain.* New York: HarperCollins.

Carroll, J. (1963). A model of school learning. *Teachers College Record, 64,* 723–733.

Caverly, D. C., & Orlando, V. P. (1991). Textbook study strategies. In R. F. Flippo & D. C. Caverly (Eds.), *Teaching reading and study strategies at the college level* (pp. 86–165). Newark, DE: International Reading Association.

Checkley, K. (1999, Spring). Math in the early grades: Laying a foundation for later learning. *Curriculum update.* Alexandria, VA: Association for Supervision and Curriculum Development.

Cole, M., & Schribner, S. (1974). Culture and thought: A psychological introduction. New York: John Wiley & Sons.

Continuous Quality Improvement Network/American Productivity and Quality Center. (2000). *Benchmarking best practices in developmental education.* Houston, TX: American Productivity and Quality Center.

Damasio, A. (1999). *Feeling of what happens: Body and emotion in the making of consciousness.* Orlando, FL: Harcourt Brace.

Delpit, L. (1988). The silenced dialogue: Power and pedagogy in educating other people's children. *Harvard Educational Review, 58,* 280–297.

Diamond, M. (1967). Extensive cortical depth measurements and neuron size increases in the cortex of environmentally enriched rats. *Journal of Comparative Neurology, 131,* 357–364.

Diamond, M. (1988). *Enriching heredity.* New York: Free Press.

Dumbauld, E. (Ed.). (1955). *The political writings of Thomas Jefferson: Representative selections.* Indianapolis, IN: Bobbs-Merrill.

Eccles, J., & Robinson, D. N. (1984). *The wonder of being human: Our brain and our mind.* New York: Free Press.

Edelman, G. M. (1992). *Bright air, brilliant fire: On the matter of the mind.* New York: Basic Books.

Forrester, K. (1983). Why nothing works. *Teaching English in the two-year college, 5,* 16–22.

Freedman, J. (2000). *Wall of fame.* San Diego, CA: AVID Academic Press (in collaboration with San Diego University).

Freeman, W. (1995). *Societies of brains.* Hillsdale, NJ: Erlbaum.

Friere, P. (1970). *The pedagogy of the oppressed.* New York: Continuum.

Gallwey, T. (1974). *The inner game of tennis.* New York: Random House.

Gardner, H. (1993). Multiple intelligences. New York: Basic Books.

Glasser, W. (1992). *The quality school.* Scranton, PA: HarperCollins.

Goldblum, N. (2001). *The brain-shaped mind: What the brain can tell us about the mind.* Cambridge, UK: Cambridge University Press.

Golinkoff, R. M., & Hirsh-Pasek, K. (1999). How babies talk: The magic and mystery of language in the first three years of life. New York: Dutton.

Golinkoff, R. C., Mervis, C. B., & Hirsh-Pasek, K. (1994). Early object labels: the case for a developmental lexical principles framework. *Journal of Child Language, 21,* 125-155.

Gopnik, A., Meltzoff, A. N., & Kuhl, P. K. (1999). *The scientist in the crib: Minds, brains, and how children learn.* New York: William Morrow.

Greenfield, S. A. (1997). *The human brain: A guided tour.* New York: Basic Books.

Greenough, W. T., Black, J. E., & Wallace, C. S. (1987). Experience and brain development. *Child Development, 58,* 547.

Gregory, R. L. (Ed.). (1987). *The Oxford companion to the mind.* Oxford, UK: Oxford University Press.

Hart, L. (1999). *Human brain and human learning* (5th ed.). Kent, WA: Books for Educators.

Healy, J. M. (1994). *Your child's growing mind: A practical guide to brain development and learning from birth to adolescence.* New York: Doubleday.

Heath, S. B. (1982). Questioning at home and at school: A comparative study. In G. Spindler (Ed.), *Doing the ethnography of schooling: Educational anthropology in action.* Prospect Heights, IL: Waveland Press.

Heath, S. B. (1983*). Ways with words: Language, life, and work in communities and classrooms.* New York: Cambridge University Press.

Hull, G., Rose, M., Fraser, K. C., & Castellano, M. (1991). Remediation as social construct: Perspectives from an analysis of classroom discourse. *College Composition and Communication, 42,* 299–329.

Hunt, M. (1982). *The universe within: A new science explores the human mind.* New York: Simon & Schuster.

Jacobs, B., Schall, M., & Scheibel, A. B. (1993). A quantitative dendritic analysis of Wernieke's area in humans. II. Gender, hemispheric, and environmental factors. *Journal of Comparative Neurology, 327,* 97–111.

Jensen, E. (1998). *Teaching with the brain in mind.* Alexandria, VA: Association for Supervision and Curriculum Development.

Johnson, K. A. (2002). The downside to small class policies. *Educational Leadership, 59*(5), 27–29.

Johnson, R. C., & Brown, C. (1988). *Cognizers: Neural networks and machines that think.* New York: Wiley Science Editions.

Khalsa, D. S., & Stauth, C. (1997). *Brain longevity.* New York: Warner Books.

Kohlberg, L. (1981). *Essays on moral development. Volume 1: The philosophy of moral development.* San Francisco: Harper & Row.

Kohn, A. (2000). *The case against standardized testing: Raising the scores, ruining the schools.* Portsmouth, NH: Heinemann.

Kovalik, S. J., & Olsen, K. D. (2001). *Exceeding expectations: A user's guide to implementing brain research in the classroom.* Covington, WA: Susan Kovalik & Associates.

Krathwohl, D. R., & Bloom, B. S. (Eds.). (1989). *Taxonomy of educational objectives, Book 1: Cognitive domain.* Reading, MA: Longman.

Krathwohl, D. R., & Bloom, B. S. (Eds.). (1999). *Taxonomy of educational objectives, Book 2: Affective domain.* Reading, MA: Longman.

Ladson-Billings, G. (1995). Toward a theory of culturally relevant pedagogy. *American Educational Research Journal, 32,* 465–491.

LeDoux, J. (2002). *Our synaptic self: How our brain becomes who we are.* New York: Viking.

Levine, M. (2002). *A mind at a time.* New York: Simon & Schuster.

MacDonald, A. (2002, March–April). Sophisticated listeners: Infants comprehend words at surprisingly young age. *BrainWork: The neuroscience newsletter, 12*(2), 6.

MacGregor, J. T. (1991). What differences do learning communities make? *Washington Center News* 6(1) 4–9.

Martinez, J. G. R., & Martinez, N. C. (1987). Are basic writers cognitively deficient? *Journal of College Reading and Learning, 20,* 16–23.

Marzano, R. J., Pickering, D. J., & Pollock, J. E. (2001). *Classroom instruction that works: Research-based strategies for increasing student achievement.* Alexandria, VA: Association for Supervision and Curriculum Development.

McPhail, I. P. (1979). A study of response to literature across three social interaction patterns: A directional effort. *Reading Improvement, 16,* 55–61.

McPhail, I. P. (1982). Toward an agenda for urban literacy: The study of schools where low-income minority children read at grade level. *Reading World, 22,* 132–149.

McPhail, I. P. (1983). A critical evaluation of George Weber's classic study of schools where low-income minority children read at grade level. In L. M. Gentile, M. Kamil, & J. Blanchard (Eds.), *Reading research revisited* (pp. 549–558). Columbus, OH: Charles E. Merrill.

McPhail, I. P., & McPhail, C. J. (1999). Transforming classroom practice for African American learners: Implications for the learning paradigm. *Removing Vestiges: Research-Based Strategies to Promote Inclusion, 2,* 25-35.

McPhail, I. P., & Morris, P. L. (1986). A new look at reading/communication arts in the inner-city junior high school. *Reading Improvement, 23,* 49–60.

McQueen, M. (1998, June 24). Cedric's journey. *ABC's Nightline.* ABC transcript #4457.

Mestel, R. (2001, December 3). This is your brain at work. *Los Angeles Times,* p. 2.

Morowitz, H. J., & Singer, J. L. (Eds.). (1995). *The mind, the brain, and complex adaptive systems.* Proceedings Vol. XXII, Santa Fe Institute Studies in the Sciences of Complexity. Reading, MA: Addison-Wesley.

Nist, S. L., & Mealey, D. L. (1991). Teacher-directed comprehension strategies. In R. F. Flippo & D. C. Caverly (Eds.), *Teaching reading & study strategies at the college level* (pp. 42–85). Neward, DE: International Reading Association.

Ornstein, R. (1991). *The evolution of consciousness: Of Darwin, Freud, and cranial fire—the origins of the way we think.* New York: Prentice Hall.

Ornstein, R., & Thompson, R. F. (1984). *The amazing brain.* Boston: Houghton Mifflin.

Piaget, J. (1970). *Genetic epistemology.* New York: Norton.

Piaget, J. (1973). *The child and reality.* New York. Grossman.

Piaget, J., & Inhelder, B. (1969). *The psychology of the child.* New York: Basic Books. (Original work published 1966)

Plomin, R., & Kosslyn, S. M. (2001). Genes, brain and cognition. *Nature Neuroscience, 4*(12), 1153–1155.

Ratey, J. J. (2001). *A user's guide to the brain: Perception, attention, and the four theaters of the brain.* New York: Pantheon.

Renner, M., & Rosenzweig, M. (1987). *Enriched and impoverished environments: Effects on brain and behavior.* New York: Springer Verlag.

Restak, R. M. (1994). *Receptors.* New York: Bantam Books.

Restak, R. M. (2001). *The secret life of the brain.* New York: The Dana Press and Joseph Henry Press.

Reynolds, R. C. (1986, October 15). The long walk to room 114: The realities of teaching remedial English in college. *Chronicle of Higher Education, XXXIII,* 104.

Rose, M. (1988). Narrowing the mind and page: Remedial writers and cognitive reductionism. *College Composition and Communication, 39*, 267–302.

Rose, M. (1995). *Possible lives: The promise of public education in America.* New York: Houghton Mifflin.

Rose, S. (1992). *The making of memory: From molecules to mind.* New York: Doubleday.

Russell, P. (1979). *The brain book.* New York: Penguin.

Schwartz, D., & Bransford, J. D. (2000). A time for feeling. *Cognition and Instruction, 16, 475–522.*

Schwarz, J. (1988). School for neurons. *The Omni: Whole Mind, 1*(5), 5.

Skinner, B. F. (1957). Verbal behavior. New York: Appleton-Century-Crofts.

Smilkstein, R. (1983). *The successful student's handbook.* Seattle: University of Washington Press.

Smilkstein, R. (1993). The natural human learning process. *Journal of Developmental Education, 17*(2), 2–10.

Smilkstein, R. (1998). *Tools for writing: Using the natural human learning process.* Fort Worth, TX: Harcourt Brace. (Out of print but available through Barnes & Noble).

Smith, B. C. (2001). The challenge of learning communities. *Peer Review, 3/4*(4/1), 4–8.

Smith, F. (1986). *Insult to intelligence: The bureaucratic invasion of our classrooms.* New York: Arbor House.

Snowdon, D. (2001). *Aging with grace: What the nun study teaches us about leading longer, healthier, and more meaningful lives.* New York: Bantam Books.

Sousa, D. (2001). *How the special needs brain learns.* Thousand Oaks, CA: Corwin Press.

Spindler, G., & Spindler, L. (1982). Roger Harker and Schönhausen: From the familiar to the strange and back again. In G. Spindler (Ed.), *Doing the ethnography of schooling: Educational anthropology in action* (pp. 20–46). Prospect Heights, IL: Waveland Press.

Sprenger, M. (1999). *Learning and memory: The brain in action.* Alexandria, VA: Association for Supervision and Curriculum Development.

Sternberg, R. J., & Williams, W. M. (2002). *Educational psychology.* Boston: Allyn & Bacon.

Sylwester, R. (1995). *Celebration of neurons: An educator's guide to the human brain.* Alexandria, VA: Association for Supervision and Curriculum Development.

Thompson, R. F. (1985). *The brain: An introduction to neuroscience.* New York: W. W. Freeman.

Tinto, V. (1997). Classrooms as communities: Exploring the educational character of student persistence. *Journal of Higher Education, 68*, 599–623.

Treisman, U. (1992). Studying students studying calculus: A look at the lives of minority mathematics students in college. *College Mathematics Journal, 23*, 362–372.

Vedantum, S. (2002, May 20). Descartes notwithstanding, some neuroscientists find the answer in chemistry, not philosophy. *Washington Post*, p. A9.

Waller, G., McCormick, K., & Fowler, L. J. (1987). The Lexington introduction to literature. Lexington, MA: D. C. Heath.

Waycaster, P. (2002). Factors impacting success in developmental and subsequent mathematics courses. *Research in Developmental Education, 17*(1), 1–6.

Wesson, K. (2000, November). The Volvo Effect. *Education Week*. Retrieved May 14, 2002, from http://www.edweek.org/ew/ewstory.cfm?slug=12wesson.h20

Wesson, K. (2002). Emotions, the brain and human learning. *Proceedings of Learning Brain Expo 2002*. San Diego, CA: The Brain Store.

Wynn, K. (1992). Addition and subtraction by human infants. *Nature, 356,* 749–750.

General Bibliography

Barinaga, M. (1995, April). Dendrites shed their dull image. *Science, 268* (April), 200–201.

The Brain in the News. To subscribe: 1001 G. St., NW, Suite 1025, Washington, DC 2001.

Cross, P. K., & Angelo, T. A. (1993). *Classroom assessment techniques: A handbook for colleges teachers.* San Francisco: Jossey-Bass.

Finkel, D. L. (2000). *Teaching with your mouth shut.* Portsmouth, NH: Heinemann Boynton Cook.

Fischbach, G. D. (1992). Mind and brain. *Scientific American, 267*(3), 48-57.

Flippo, R. F., & Caverly, D. C. (Eds.). (1991). *Teaching reading and study strategies at the college level.* Newark, DE: International Reading Association.

Kandel, E. R., & Hawkins, R. D. (1992). The biological basis of learning and individuality. *Scientific American, 267*, 78–86.

Kotulak, R. (2001, November 25). Brain cells: The mind's decline is no longer a given. *Chicago Tribune*, p. C1.

Milgram, N. W., MacLeod, C. M., & Petit. T. L. (Eds.). (1987). *Neuroplasticity, learning, and memory.* New York: Alan R. Liss.

Petit, T. L., & Markus, E. J. (1987). The cellular basis of learning and memory: The anatomical sequel to neuronal use. In H. W. Milgram, C. M. Macleod, & T. L. Petit (Eds.), *Neuroplasticity, learning, and memory* (pp. 87–124). New York: Alan R. Liss.

Rose, S. (1976). *The conscious brain.* New York: Vintage.

Sylwester, R. (1993–1994). What the biology of the brain tells us about learning. *Educational Leadership, 51*(4), 46–51.

Washington Center for Improving the Quality of Undergraduate Education (1998). *Seminars: A collection of materials on seminar approaches and evaluation strategies.* Olympia, WA: The Evergreen State College. (To order, call 360-867-5611.)

Zinn, H. (1980). *A people's history of the United States.* New York: HarperCollins.

Bibliography About Learning Communities

Brookfield, S. D., & Preskill, S. (1999). *Discussion as a way of teaching: Tools and techniques for democratic classrooms.* San Francisco: Jossey-Bass.

Cross, K. P. (1998, July–August). Why learning communities? Why now? *About Campus, 3*(3), 4–11.

Davis, J. R. (1995). *Interdisciplinary courses and team teaching: New arrangements for learning.* Phoenix, AZ: American Council on Education and Oryx Press.

Gabelnick, F., MacGregor, J. L., Matthews, L. R., & Smith, B. L. (1990). Learning communities: Creating connections among students, faculty and disciplines. *New Directions for Teaching and Learning, 41.* San Francisco: Jossey-Bass.

Goodsell, A., & Tinto, V. (1994). Freshman interest groups and the first year experience: Constructing student communities in a large university. *Journal of the Freshman Year Experience, 6*(1), 7–28.

MacGregor, J. L. (1991). What differences do learning communities make? *Washington Center News 6*(1).

MacGregor, J. L. (Ed.). (1993). Student self-evaluation: Fostering reflective learning. *New Directions in Teaching and Learning, 56.* San Francisco: Jossey-Bass.

MacGregor, J. L., Cooper, J. L., Smith, K. A., & Robinson, P. (2000). Strategies for energizing large classes: From small groups to learning communities. *New Directions in Teaching and Learning, 81.* San Francisco: Jossey-Bass.

Millis, B, J., & Cottell, P. G. Jr. (1998). *Cooperative learning for higher education faculty* (American Council on Education Series on Higher Education). Phoenix, AZ: Oryx Press.

Palmer, P. (1988). *The courage to teach: Exploring the inner landscape of a teacher's life.* San Francisco: Jossey-Bass.

Shapiro, N. S., & J. H. Levine (1999). *Creating learning communities: A practical guide to winning support, organizing for change, and implementing programs.* San Francisco: Jossey-Bass.

Smith, B. L. (1994). Team teaching. In K. Prichard & B. M. Sawyer (Eds.), *Handbook of college teaching.* Westport, CT: Greenwood Press.

Smith, B. L. (2001, Summer–Fall). The challenge of learning communities as a growing national movement. *Peer Review, 3/4*(4/1). Washington, DC: American Association of Colleges and Universities.

Smith, B. L., & MacGregor, J. T. (1992). What is collaborative learning? In A. S. Goodsell, M. R. Maher, & V. Tinto (Eds.), *Collaborative learning: A sourcebook for higher education* (National Center on Postsecondary Teaching, Learning, and Assessment). University Park, PA: Syracuse University.

Smith, B. L., & McCann, J. (2001). *Reinventing ourselves: Interdisciplinary education, collaborative learning, and experimentation in higher education.* Bolton, MA: Anker.

Web Site

The National Learning Communities Project Website: http//learningcommons. evergreen.edu

Index

**CORWIN
PRESS**

The Corwin Press logo—a raven striding across an open book—represents the happy union of courage and learning. We are a professional-level publisher of books and journals for K-12 educators, and we are committed to creating and providing resources that embody these qualities. Corwin's motto is "Success for All Learners."